EXPORTING ESSENTIALS

SELLING PRODUCTS AND SERVICES TO THE WORLD SUCCESSFULLY

Laurel J. Delaney

Apress®

Exporting Essentials: Selling Products and Services to the World Successfully

Copyright © 2014 by Laurel J. Delaney

This work is subject to copyright. All rights are reserved by the Publisher, whether the whole or part of the material is concerned, specifically the rights of translation, reprinting, reuse of illustrations, recitation, broadcasting, reproduction on microfilms or in any other physical way, and transmission or information storage and retrieval, electronic adaptation, computer software, or by similar or dissimilar methodology now known or hereafter developed. Exempted from this legal reservation are brief excerpts in connection with reviews or scholarly analysis or material supplied specifically for the purpose of being entered and executed on a computer system, for exclusive use by the purchaser of the work. Duplication of this publication or parts thereof is permitted only under the provisions of the Copyright Law of the Publisher's location, in its current version, and permission for use must always be obtained from Springer. Permissions for use may be obtained through RightsLink at the Copyright Clearance Center. Violations are liable to prosecution under the respective Copyright Law.

ISBN-13 (pbk): 978-1-4842-0836-6

ISBN-13 (electronic): 978-1-4842-0835-9

Trademarked names, logos, and images may appear in this book. Rather than use a trademark symbol with every occurrence of a trademarked name, logo, or image we use the names, logos, and images only in an editorial fashion and to the benefit of the trademark owner, with no intention of infringement of the trademark.

The use in this publication of trade names, trademarks, service marks, and similar terms, even if they are not identified as such, is not to be taken as an expression of opinion as to whether or not they are subject to proprietary rights.

While the advice and information in this book are believed to be true and accurate at the date of publication, neither the authors nor the editors nor the publisher can accept any legal responsibility for any errors or omissions that may be made. The publisher makes no warranty, express or implied, with respect to the material contained herein.

> Managing Director: Welmoed Spahr
> Acquisitions Editor: Jeff Olson
> Editorial Board: Steve Anglin, Mark Beckner, Gary Cornell, Louise Corrigan, James DeWolf, Jonathan Gennick, Robert Hutchinson, Michelle Lowman, James Markham, Matthew Moodie, Jeff Olson, Jeffrey Pepper, Douglas Pundick, Ben Renow-Clarke, Gwenan Spearing, Matt Wade, Steve Weiss
> Coordinating Editor: Rita Fernando
> Copy Editor: Jana Weinstein
> Compositor: SPi Global
> Indexer: SPi Global
> Cover Designer: Anna Ishchenko

Distributed to the book trade worldwide by Springer Science+Business Media New York, 233 Spring Street, 6th Floor, New York, NY 10013. Phone 1-800-SPRINGER, fax (201) 348-4505, e-mail orders-ny@springer-sbm.com, or visit www.springeronline.com. Apress Media, LLC is a California LLC and the sole member (owner) is Springer Science + Business Media Finance Inc (SSBM Finance Inc). SSBM Finance Inc is a Delaware corporation.

For information on translations, please e-mail rights@apress.com, or visit www.apress.com.

Apress and friends of ED books may be purchased in bulk for academic, corporate, or promotional use. eBook versions and licenses are also available for most titles. For more information, reference our Special Bulk Sales–eBook Licensing web page at www.apress.com/bulk-sales.

Any source code or other supplementary materials referenced by the author in this text is available to readers at www.apress.com. For detailed information about how to locate your book's source code, go to www.apress.com/source-code/.

Apress Business: The Unbiased Source of Business Information

Apress business books provide essential information and practical advice, each written for practitioners by recognized experts. Busy managers and professionals in all areas of the business world—and at all levels of technical sophistication—look to our books for the actionable ideas and tools they need to solve problems, update and enhance their professional skills, make their work lives easier, and capitalize on opportunity.

Whatever the topic on the business spectrum—entrepreneurship, finance, sales, marketing, management, regulation, information technology, among others—Apress has been praised for providing the objective information and unbiased advice you need to excel in your daily work life. Our authors have no axes to grind; they understand they have one job only—to deliver up-to-date, accurate information simply, concisely, and with deep insight that addresses the real needs of our readers.

It is increasingly hard to find information—whether in the news media, on the Internet, and now all too often in books—that is even-handed and has your best interests at heart. We therefore hope that you enjoy this book, which has been carefully crafted to meet our standards of quality and unbiased coverage.

We are always interested in your feedback or ideas for new titles. Perhaps you'd even like to write a book yourself. Whatever the case, reach out to us at editorial@apress.com and an editor will respond swiftly. Incidentally, at the back of this book, you will find a list of useful related titles. Please visit us at www.apress.com to sign up for newsletters and discounts on future purchases.

The Apress Business Team

This book is dedicated to my husband Bob Marovich. And to the millions of entrepreneurs and small business owners who desire to export—you motivate me! Next, to my friends and family for their support in helping me make my work in exporting a dream come true. Finally, to booksellers, with gratitude.

Contents

Author Note ix
About the Author. xi
Acknowledgments xiii
Introduction xv

Chapter 1: Are You Ready to Export? 1
Chapter 2: Writing an Export Business Plan 13
Chapter 3: Prepping For Exports 27
Chapter 4: Exploring Your Territory 39
Chapter 5: Preparing and Adapting Your Product for the Export Marketplace 59
Chapter 6: Preparing Your Service for Export. 69
Chapter 7: Finding Cross-Border Customers 83
Chapter 8: Methods of Exporting 101
Chapter 9: Transport, Logistics, and Fulfillment Options 125
Chapter 10: Pricing and Preparing Quotations 143
Chapter 11: Getting Paid 163
Chapter 12: Booking, Marking, Labeling, and Insuring 195
Chapter 13: Documentation, Export Licensing, and Other Procedures 207

Index 225

Author Note

Dear Reader,

More businesses are exporting today because it leads to growth and innovation, revitalizes our economy, and helps create jobs.

If you are a first-time reader of my work, *Exporting Essentials* provides the nuts and bolts to get started fast in exporting and succeed in the export marketplace.

As you delve into this hard-hitting book, use each chapter as a springboard to grow your business. For a more in depth look at exporting, including how to leverage the Internet to export, read *Exporting: The Definitive Guide to Selling Abroad Profitably*, which takes a more comprehensive look at exporting.

Success in exporting is essential for a vibrant creative economy. America's exporters, especially small businesses, are among the country's most dynamic and strongest enterprises. Those strengths are what allow companies to enter and succeed in the export marketplace.

You may be small today, but through exports you can grow to be large tomorrow.

May this book inspire you to reach outside your comfort zone and take on the exciting world of exporting. Strive to be creative. Be fearless. And have fun.

Now go take on the world!

Laurel Delaney

About the Author

Laurel J. Delaney is founder and president of Chicago-based GlobeTrade.com, a management consulting company that helps entrepreneurs and small businesses go global. The United States Small Business Administration has recognized Ms. Delaney as a world-renowned global small business expert by naming her the Illinois Exporter of the Year. She is the author of *Start and Run a Profitable Exporting Business and Exporting: The Definitive Guide to Selling Abroad Profitably*, as well as numerous articles that have appeared in international and scholarly publications such as *The Wall Street Journal* and *The Conference Board*. She is the creator of The Global Small Business Blog (http://www.globalsmallbusinessblog.com), which is ranked No. 1 in the world for entrepreneurs and small businesses interested in going global, Women Entrepreneurs GROW Global (www.WomenEntrepreneursGROWGlobal.org) and Exporting Guide (http://www.ExportingGuide.com). She serves as the About.com Import & Export expert (http://importexport.about.com/), is a charter member and a board member by appointment of the World Entrepreneurship Forum, and a member of the International Council for Small Business. She also serves as the Chicago Chapter Chair for the Women Presidents' Organization. Ms. Delaney's passion for going global goes back to 1985, when she first started her business. Since then, she has devoted more than 60,000 hours of work in the area—from consulting to writing to teaching.

Ms. Delaney holds a Bachelor of Arts degree in Advertising from Columbia College Chicago and a Master in Business Administration from Lake Forest Graduate School of Management.

Acknowledgments

There are several people whose contributions I'd like to acknowledge, starting with the Apress team: Jeff Olson, executive business editor extraordinaire, who once again expertly guided me through the arduous task of putting together another book, and Rita Fernando, coordinating editor wizard, and Jana Weinstein, copyedit super pro. What a crew! This book would not have been possible without Jeff, who is a remarkable person doing extraordinary things for me and other authors at Apress.

And speaking of remarkable people . . . everything I do is inspired by the love and support I get from Bob. I am the luckiest gal in the world to have a husband like him—talented, fun, and energetic!

Finally, to you, dear reader: I am grateful for your interest in exporting. You inspire me to keep on keeping on.

I thank all of you.

Introduction

> *The economy of the future requires that American businesses compete and win in the global marketplace.*
>
> —Francisco Sánchez,
> Undersecretary of Commerce for International Trade,
> U.S. Department of Commerce,
> International Trade Administration (2012)

There are more than seven billion potential customers in the world. How many of those customers is your company reaching? Exporting—or sending goods and services out of a country—increases a company's sales and profits, enhances its prestige, creates jobs, and offers a valuable way to level seasonal fluctuations. Exporting is also a powerful force that contributes to economic growth, development, and prosperity in our world.

The explosion of US entrepreneurs and small businesses—more than twenty-eight million combined—engaging in the world economy in the last few years is largely attributable to the Internet. This transition has taken place as businesses have sought new ways to grow and tap into the more than 96 percent of the world's consumers and 73 percent of the world's purchasing power that lie outside the United States. Surprisingly, though, less than 1 percent of these businesses and individuals operate in the US export marketplace, even though the amount of exporters has grown faster than the amount of nonexporters in terms of both goods sold and employment. Converting nonexporters to exporters is what this book is all about.

Tip Start planning to sell abroad. The businesses of exporters grow faster, and they employ more people than the businesses of nonexporters.

What This Book Can Do for You

Exporting Essentials, a derivation of *Exporting: The Definitive Guide to Selling Abroad Profitably,* equips you with the basics to export successfully.

Whereas *Exporting: The Definitive Guide to Selling Abroad Profitably* covers everything from Internet marketing to e-commerce, web globalization to cross-cultural learning, *Exporting Essentials* supplies the nuts and bolts to export in a fast, hard-hitting manner.

There are many benefits to exporting, including:

- Improving your return on investments
- Creating jobs
- Overcoming low growth in your home market
- Outmaneuvering competitors
- Becoming more productive
- Generating economies of scale in production
- Exploring previously untapped markets
- Making productive use of excess domestic capacity
- Diversifying sources of revenue
- Extending the product life cycle
- Insulating your seasonal domestic sales by allowing you to find new foreign markets
- Broadening your personal intellectual horizons
- Enriching your country
- Traveling to new countries

The Current State of Exporting

Export-driven entrepreneurs and small businesses play a significant role in the overall economic growth and prosperity of the United States and the world at large. They have the potential to improve productivity, achieve greater efficiencies, enhance world-class competitiveness, and create jobs. This is possible because:

- *Exporting lends itself to small business.* The number of firms exporting increased by more than 28,000 between the years 2009 and 2012 (the latest available data), reaching a record high of almost 305,000 exporting firms.[1] Small companies also account for about one third of the total value of US merchandise exports in 2012.

---

[1] The Role of Exports in the United States Economy, an economic report by the U.S. Department of Commerce, May 13, 2014: http://trade.gov/neinext/role-of-exports-in-us-economy.pdf.

- *Exports generate revenue.* The known export revenue of small- and medium-sized enterprises in the United States rose to $383.4 billion in 2010 (latest available data), up 24.1 percent from 2009. SMEs were responsible for 33.7 percent of goods exports in 2010.[2]

- *Exports are growing.* Total US exports for 2013 reached $2.3 trillion. Goods totaled $1.58 trillion with records in a number of important sectors, including industrial supplies, consumer goods, and capital goods. Service exports hit an all-time high of $682 billion, with records in several major service sectors, including travel and tourism, as international visitors contributed $139.6 billion to the American economy.[3]

- *Exporting helps you find new customers and develop new markets.* The International Monetary Fund (www.imf.org) forecasts that nearly 87 percent of the world economic growth during the next five years will take place outside of the United States.

- *Exporting supports jobs.* Jobs supported by total exports were 11.3 million in 2013, up 1.6 million since 2009.[4]

- *Exporting using the Internet offers a new sales channel.* Thanks to the Web, entrepreneurs and small business owners have a potent new way of doing business, one that leverages social media and networking to find new business—no matter from where it comes. The Internet has become the ultimate platform by which businesses can innovate through personalization and export around the world.

- *Exporting is imperative.* An export-or-die mentality is required by those individuals and business owners who don't want to be beaten by their competitors—both local and global—in the world marketplace. More so, those who don't export will become obsolete in a world where global connectivity is increasingly prevalent and easy.

---

[2]International Trade Administration, http://www.trade.gov/mas/ian/smeoutlook/tg_ian_001925.asp#P27_2705.
[3]Tradeology, the ITA Blog, http://blog.trade.gov/2014/02/06/another-year-another-export-record/.
[4]Ibid.

The Future of Exporting

Exporting Essentials intends to help US companies become more competitive internationally through exporting and to bring thousands of new businesses into the world marketplace. Small- and medium-sized companies account for almost 97 percent of US exporters, but they represent only about 30 percent of the total export value of US goods. With 80 percent of global demand now outside of the United States, it is expected there will be $40 to $50 billion worth of export opportunity for the United States within five years. In FY 2013, the Export-Import Bank approved more than $27 billion in total authorizations to support an estimated $37.4 billion in U.S. export sales and approximately 205,000 American jobs in communities across the country. For the year, the bank approved a record 3,413 transactions, or 89 percent for small-businesses. Exporting is not just an option; it's an absolute must for building and sustaining a successful future.

What will your business look like in a decade? Our world is in constant motion and growth. Whether researching, buying, or selling, can you imagine operating *anything* these days without crossing borders? Don't be scared if your answer is "Yes." By the time you finish this book, you will have mastered the mechanics to exporting and be ready to export successfully. Until then, don't let fear immobilize you. Keep reading.

Remember Exporting isn't rocket science. You can do it. And your bottom line will soon show the results of your efforts.

Who This Book Is For

Exporting Essentials is for entrepreneurs and small business owners who are new to the practice, are interested in mastering the mechanics to exporting in a quick read, and are ready to take their business to the next level of growth. It is also for entrepreneurs and small business owners who currently export but are looking for a refresher on the fundamentals.

Exporting Essentials will help you:

- Develop a clear strategy on how to export
- Export your product or service efficiently and profitably
- Find customers, enter new markets, get paid, and ship

- Discover your best territory through statistics and market research
- Develop pricing and prepare documentation

How to Use This Book

Exporting Essentials has been created and structured in a way to make it as easy and fast as possible to learn the mechanics of exporting. The book's thirteen chapters work together to achieve that goal by providing the following descriptions of the process:

Chapters 1–3 look at whether you are ready to export, how to write an export business plan, and how to prepare for exporting by describing the legal and financial considerations.

Chapters 4–6 examine how to research an export market, adapt a product for export, and prepare a service for export.

Chapters 7–8 offer ways to find cross-border customers and several different methods of exporting.

Chapters 9–13 explore transport options, pricing considerations, payment methods, cargo details, and documentation.

First things first: You need to be *ready* to export, because the world wants what America makes. As you turn the page to Chapter 1, you are opening the gateway to selling globally. *Let's export!*

CHAPTER 1

Are You Ready to Export?

> *Over the next five years, we will double our exports of goods and services around the world—an increase that will boost economic growth and support millions of American jobs in a manner that is deficit-friendly.*
>
> —President Barack Obama (2012)

Anyone who wants to export, can. The world awaits. The essential element needed to be successful exporting is readiness. The rest is mechanics and know-how. Whether you're a first-time exporter or entering a new market, selling goods and services across borders is easy and just a mouse click away. I'm here to show you how. But before I get to that, let me take you back to a little more than twenty-five years ago.

It was 1985. Even back then, I challenged conventional assumptions about how to compete and started to view markets outside the United States as the future of the business I had started: Global TradeSource, Ltd. I even put "global," "trade," and "source" in the company name, thereby shifting the buyer's possibilities from being local to those of the world and drawing upon the distinctive strengths of alternative, growing overseas markets as those that would offer the company's products and services.

That kind of vision, along with a more recent facilitator called the Internet, has broken down every imaginable barrier to growth and prosperity and has transformed not just how we conduct business but the world at large. The moment you create a Web site, blog, or Facebook account, your point of contact with consumers becomes global. The Internet is the great global leveler and gives everyone a chance to make spectacular strides in exporting—by finding, acquiring, and servicing customers the world over faster than ever—which in turn drives profits and growth for businesses. The blueprint for prosperity in exports is right at your fingertips. Never has there been such attention to the Internet, interconnectedness, and exporting than now.

> **Note** The Internet has broken down all barriers to world commerce. It is your most potent weapon in the battle to capture more international sales.

The use of technology, especially social networks such as Facebook, LinkedIn, and Twitter, along with the advent of smart phones and tablets, makes finding and exporting opportunities in the world marketplace a breeze for small business owners and executives. And as a result of these incredible advancements in technology, these same empowered individuals can create opportunities on the web—not just browse for themselves—and even launch whole new enterprises in a heartbeat based on unmet needs and interests expressed by consumers.

Because social networks enable us to extend our worldwide connections rapidly, increasing our ability to identify opportunities on a more open, transparent basis, none of us operates in a vacuum as a solo entrepreneur any longer.

What does this have to do with exporting and your readiness to do so? Plenty. It defines how an export business is born and can grow, if nurtured correctly, into something absolutely amazing.

Next, let's take a look at a three examples of real-world situations that could arise that will shape how you view the potential of exporting and how it gets done. After that, we'll move on to what it takes to succeed in exporting. Last, we'll make a distinction between exporting services and products—which will allow you to decide what you are going into the international market with.

You'll note that at this point I do not talk about the financial considerations of exporting. They are obviously an important aspect that you must consider before you export in order to be properly capitalized. However, I am intentionally leaving the discussion out of this section because it will be covered later, beginning with Chapter 3.

How an Export Product Business Is Born

Imagine someone named Abel Anderson who is working in the automotive industry while running a food-export business. In the evenings and weekends, he goes to food fairs. Although he works full time in the automotive industry, his real passion is food. He's always seeking novel food items to try.

At one local trade show that Abel attends in Chicago, he falls in love with a specialty item that tastes like cheesecake, caramel, chocolate, and butter crumbs all rolled into one scrumptious cookie the size of a hockey puck. He chats with the person at the booth named Samantha and asks her if she exports the product. She tells him she does not. Abel expresses interest in working with her baking company in his spare time as an independent contractor to export its products to a select few countries. Lo and behold, she agrees.

After spending a few days with Samantha making sure the ingredients in the cookie can hold up in overseas transit and pass regulatory laws, Abel draws up a contract. He then contacts the International Trade Administration via the Internet to conduct a partner search for agents located in Dubai, Saudi Arabia, and Oman—areas of the world where he thinks there is significant demand and enough wealth to purchase gourmet food products. Within three months and with the help of ITA, he lines up importing distributors in two countries— all just by using e-mail and Skype. He sends a test shipment of cookies to each location and discovers in the process that everyone who samples the cookies loves them. He receives his first order from the Dubai agent for ten thousand packages of cookies.

Abel is now in the export product business. It won't be long before he gives up his full-time job in the automotive industry.

His story is an example of how the journey to exporting or launching an export business begins. Abel started first with his own good idea of exporting a product, and then, with the help of technology that most of us use every day, he was able to turn his idea into a new business venture. Here, then, we have a new paradigm for world competitiveness built on information and technology. So while nothing beats a good face-to-face encounter to help deepen your knowledge of a country and the customer, making the most of technology should also be a priority.

In the future, the economic transformation of countries will require businesses to rely less on selling to locals and more on selling abroad. This gets back to how exporting boosts economic productivity and also suggests its capacity to solve the problems caused by a growing world population, rapid urbanization, and even climate change.

Everything we do today is potentially relevant to consumers anywhere in the world, provided they understand what we are doing. Consider, for example, running a public relations firm. Think it has international legs? Let's find out.

Tip Any product or service you sell no doubt has potential customers abroad. And guess what, you will need them all in order to stay relevant as the twenty-first century progresses.

How an Export Service Business Is Born

Envision offering your local marketing service, which is booming in North America, to someone in the United Kingdom. Let's imagine that someone named Katie Schroeder does just that. She runs a successful Chicago-based public relations company called Take It Viral, or TIV, representing some of the most popular big-name consumer brands in the United States. TIV has received numerous accolades for its creative social media campaigns using Twitter, Facebook, Instagram, and Google+.

As a result of media fanfare, a business owner in the United Kingdom—we'll call him Joe—has tracked Katie's work and e-mails her with a request for her company to conduct a social-media PR campaign in the United Kingdom. Joe makes luxury ties and wants to broaden his brand recognition in the United Kingdom and expand his business into the United States. Although Katie has reservations about delivering that type of specific service outside her normal selling channels, she contemplates how to go about it. All she really needs is a plan, technology, a couple of additional support people, and a few good local UK connections to make it happen.

So Katie decides to take the project. Her first step is to develop a road map. Her next step is to execute it. She deploys her existing employees to launch the program, and as the UK business grows, Katie outsources work through the online freelance employment databases Guru.com, Elance.com, and Odesk.com, specifically seeking people in the UK market who are capable of managing social media campaigns.

At the same time, Katie consults her international accountant on how best to handle the tax impact on her business for the newly generated overseas revenue stream and payments made to independent contractors located in the United Kingdom. Further, she explores all payments options—for both money received from clients and money paid to workers—with her trusted international banker. Last, she goes over the potential pitfalls on the legal front with her international attorney.

Through the advice of her banker, Katie sets up a PayPal account to pay off-site workers and receives her first UK client payment via a wire transfer to her bank account. Voila! She has gone global and achieved her first service export! She is already considering opportunities in France, Ireland, and Germany. Her new goal is to become less dependent on the ebb and flow of the North American market, build up a profitable alternative revenue stream (e.g., in the United Kingdom), and expand into additional international markets so that the world will eventually become her revenue stream.

> **Note** Exporting requires a team of experts—accountants, lawyers, and others—who understand the markets you are selling into. Get them involved early to help you avoid missteps.

How a Business Expands into New Foreign Markets

Ever dream about branching out into new overseas markets? Meet someone we will call Alfild Nelsen. Alfild is currently running a successful specialty chemical-cleaning-product business with revenues of more than $10 million. Thanks to NAFTA, she currently exports to Canada and Mexico, but to further offset the anticipation of slowing local growth, she wants to branch out into other international markets. While thinking about that, she ventures off to Australia with her husband for a vacation. She visits a huge do-it-yourself store in Melbourne and spots a wide array of high-end cleaning products not unlike the ones she makes in her own business. She buys a couple of the products and thinks about how she could find a qualified representative for her own line of cleaning supplies to be sold in the same store. Nothing beats healthy competition!

When she returns home to the United States, Alfild places the cleaning products she bought underneath her kitchen sink and forgets about the idea of exporting to Australia. Besides, she's too busy with her efforts that go into expanding her business into the Mexican and Canadian markets! Several months go by and when she has some spare time, she suddenly revisits the idea of exporting her specialty chemical cleaning products to Australia. She pulls out her laptop, remembers a service a colleague uses for exporting to New Zealand called Gold Key Service, and finds the Web site. She e-mails the organization and within thirty days has a customized market research report, an appointment with a prospective trade partner in the chemical cleaning industry, and a trip scheduled to meet face-to-face with the partner in Australia. Alfild has made the first step in branching out into new international markets. These examples show that you can escape constraints on growth at home by way of exports and entering new markets. The potential is as vast as your imagination. Whether you are an export newbie like Abel or Katie or an experienced exporter like Alfild, at some point you must decide whether to export a product or a service, or both. As I just highlighted, most people begin with a single idea that they are comfortable with, know like the back of their hand, and have rich experience with and therefore feel that they have a competitive advantage in the global marketplace. Understanding the difference between exporting a product or a service is critical to making the right choice for your business and your personal fulfillment.

The Difference Between Product and Service Exports

Exporting a product involves transporting something you can see, hold, easily assign a monetary value to, and physically move from point A to point B. Exporting a service, such as one that is business oriented, professional, technical, financial, or based on franchising or insurance, requires a somewhat-different approach. Here's a quick rundown of the differences between a product and a service as they affect the export process:

Product	Service
Tangible	Intangible
Visible	Invisible
Measurable	Immeasurable
High perceived value	Low perceived value
High freight costs	Negligible freight costs
Negligible human interaction	High human interaction
Low maintenance	High maintenance
High standardization	Negligible standardization

You cannot see or touch a service—and you often cannot assess its true value until after you have used it and discovered all the resulting benefits.

Services are in many ways a tougher sell than a product, either at home or abroad, yet once sold, they move faster thanks to technology. Each of the listed differences creates a marketing challenge for the service exporter; perhaps the most crucial being the need to convince a distant customer to buy your service sight unseen and without any real idea of how they will benefit. This is why a service business depends first and foremost on people. Of course, when you export a product, you are also relying on a whole string of people to do their jobs—banks to help you get paid, freight forwarders to move your goods, local distributors to get your product on store shelves—but exporting a service demands a special emphasis on human interaction, both at home and abroad.

The United States is the largest exporter of services in the world. The most competitive advantage of service exports, especially during any recession, is that they perform better than goods exports. Service exports typically don't face tariffs, as goods sold overseas often do, but some barriers still persist.

People Power Drives Your Service Exports

Selling a service requires even-more people power than product sales to be successful. When you export a product, you offer it, clinch your sale, follow through, and troubleshoot as needed. Then, once the product is in your customers' hands, they oversee sales in their geographic territory and contact you to order more products when they sell out. There is little need for communication between buyer and seller once the product is in the distribution pipeline and moving—being bought, sold, and enjoyed.

By contrast, a service export requires direct interaction with your customer, not just initially but for the duration of the service contract. For some services, of course, the quality of the interaction with your customer is exactly what they're paying for. This is why people with superior communication skills, diplomacy, and—this can't be emphasized enough—acute cultural awareness are the greatest assets for delivering a quality service export.

An example of a service export is an architectural firm that designs buildings in the United States and reaches out overseas to perform its work, or it can involve providing royalties and licensing fees, including the money people pay to use American software.

I will go into greater detail on service exports in Chapter 6, but for now I reference the distinction between a product and service export because the differences have implications for the marketing and management of the export. It is important to decide at the outset what you wish to accomplish: exporting a product, service, or both. Although the process is transferable from goods to services, each type of export requires its own distinct strategic approach.

What It Takes to Export

So where do you start? As with any new business venture, you need to first take stock of both yourself and your business to see if you have the personality, mindset, and business that can benefit from exporting. Let's begin with an assessment of *you* and then we'll cover the business.

Assessment of You: The Global Mindset

What unique qualities and characteristics does it take to become a successful exporter? To crack open a new overseas market? To become a top-notch international executive at a global conglomerate? The answer is that it takes the same qualities to do any of these things. Successful exporters, international expansion artists, and global executives may vary in their temperament, personality, and experience, but in the ways that really count, they are more alike than different. What counts is their ability to venture out in the world and adapt as they go. I call it a global mindset.

Note Successful exporters have, or develop, a global mindset—the ability and courage to operate their business in an unknown environment.

I somewhat liken exporting to riding a roller coaster at an amusement park. You eagerly jump into the coaster car, fasten your seatbelt, and get ready for the exhilarating ride of your life. Exporting offers a similar experience. It's an adventure that challenges every way you run a business. So the first question I ask individuals who express interest in exporting is: Do you have the mindset and guts to ride it out? After we clarify what that means—dealing with the highs and lows of attempting to do business in far-off places that are hard to access quickly and impossible to understand culturally—we discuss what is really involved in preparing to export. It's called doing your homework.

Homework can be done on your temperament and abilities, on how to export, on researching the market, on financial considerations, and on determining whether your product or service is in demand anywhere in the world. The more preparation you undertake, the greater your chance of reducing mistakes. But before you can advance from Point A, thinking about an export idea, to Point B, launching the export idea, you must first take stock of yourself and decide if you are ready and willing to develop the dynamic outlook that will enable you to export. It starts with a determined global mindset: a mix of intellectual and behavioral qualities that enable individuals to understand and operate a business in environments unlike their own.

Examining the State of You: The Global Mindset

A global mindset starts with self-awareness, reflects an authentic openness to and engagement with the world, and employs a heightened awareness to the sensitivity of cross-cultural differences. Toss in that adventuresome spirit I mentioned early on, adaptability, a solid educational background, core business competencies, and life experiences that preferably involve international travel, and you have a recipe for the ideal global thought leader. Capitalizing on these attributes is a powerful factor for developing a global mindset and achieving success in the export world.

Here's my shortlist of twelve characteristics that I find work in the export marketplace. They are based on my own hands-on experiences and the observations of others who have achieved success crossing boundaries in the business world:

1. The ability to venture out in the world and adapt quickly
2. Being comfortable and confident in your own skin, along with having a heightened sensitivity to others
3. Carrying a high level of intelligence, including cultural and emotional
4. Enjoying living in different parts of the world and relishing learning a foreign language
5. Knowing how to bring out the best in people no matter where they are from
6. Getting things done with people who come from diverse backgrounds in any part of the world
7. Being curious, having a love of learning, and immersing oneself in foreign cultures
8. Being objective and open to people and the environment
9. Having enough flexibility to focus on serving and helping others
10. Possessing the ability to take something complex and simplify it
11. Confronting obstacles with optimism and a willingness to continue learning new ways of doing things
12. Being resilient—or having the ability to bounce back from even the most challenging of circumstances

You may not have all of these characteristics, and I am sure there are some I have overlooked, but if you have most of them, you will be comfortable operating anywhere in the world and well on your way to success in exporting.

Assessing Your Business: The Local Business Model

You have a successful local business; now what? You've saturated your domestic market and there's no room to grow geographically unless you look outside your own borders.

Export.gov offers a questionnaire that highlights the "state of a business" characteristics common to successful exporters (http://export.gov/begin/assessment.asp).

The following are the questions you should answer:

1. Does your company have a product or service that has been successfully sold in the domestic market?

    Yes   No

2. Does your company have or is your company preparing an international marketing plan with defined goals and strategies?

    Yes   No

3. Does your company have sufficient production capacity that can be committed to the export market?

    Yes   No

4. Does your company have the financial resources to actively support the marketing of your products in the targeted overseas markets?

    Yes   No

5. Is your company's management committed to developing export markets and willing and able to dedicate staff, time, and resources to the process?

    Yes   No

6. Is your company committed to providing the same level of service to export markets that is given to your domestic customers?

    Yes   No

7. Does your company have adequate knowledge in modifying product packaging and ingredients to meet foreign import regulations and cultural preferences?

    Yes   No

8. Does your company have adequate knowledge in shipping its product overseas, such as the ability to identify and select international freight forwarders and freight costing?

   Yes   No

9. Does your company have adequate knowledge of export payment mechanisms, such as developing and negotiating letters of credit?

   Yes   No

Once you complete the questionnaire, you will immediately receive an online score, which will help you assess your export readiness as well as identify areas that your business needs to strengthen in order to improve its export activities. Don't be daunted by the fact that you may not be able to provide an affirmative answer to all the questions. After all, that is why I am writing this book—to help you easily export in the digital age. If you don't pass the assessment, it doesn't mean you can't export, it only means you have more homework to do in preparation for the end goal: export success.

One last related question that begs to be answered: Can you use your home base—your domestic operation—as a template for exporting? The answer is: it depends. That's a tall order. You naturally want exporting to become a profitable extension of your domestic operation, but there are no guarantees. I encourage you not to count on it. A lot will depend on your firm's orientation. For example, you might believe that because your goods and services sell well in the United States, they will sell anywhere in the world, but success will depend on your marketing approach to modifying those goods and services, if needed, to fit your selected export market. Each market is different and should be treated as such by adapting to a local country's culture.

Tip Focus on similarities in exporting across markets whenever possible to standardize your business model worldwide and to achieve economies of scale in production.

Assessing an Export Start-Up: The "Born Global" Firm

There is a new class of entrepreneurs who have changed the export paradigm and show that it is possible to do business and succeed in world markets without having an established domestic base. The concept is referred to as "born global." Born-global companies are run by individuals of a generation that only knows of communicating and transacting business via the Internet.

Virtually from inception, their companies compete on a global scale against large, established players in the world arena. They are global by technology, not by strategy, and the individuals who start and run these firms tend to bypass rules and regulations to get things done.

Contrary to conventional methods, born-global individuals don't build export businesses through gradual expansion into foreign markets. Rather, they leap into the foreign market and figure things out as they go. For example, a born-global entrepreneur will review the earlier assessment questionnaire, complete it on a lark, and even if their answers are all "No," will still proceed in exporting. What they are banking on is their own tech know-how and the suitability of their product or service for the international market coupled with their own chutzpah to get them over speed bumps.

I can relate to that disruptive, adventuresome spirit. But I caution you: Rather than making progress at every step of the way during the process of exporting, there will be a lot of scary tunnels, twists, and sharp turns involved in figuring it out. That is because the leaders of born-global companies have no prior knowledge or experience in exporting—only in leveraging technology. This runs counter to the notion of using your domestic operation, one that has a history of proven success, as a template for exporting. In other words, and as mentioned earlier, don't assume what works at home will work abroad. Big mistake. There will always be adjustments that have to be made to the changing condition of the company, the environment, and the marketplace, rather than a deliberate strategy.

If you are a start-up or are of the born-global generation, there is nothing stopping you from plunging into exporting. So skip the assessments and just *go for it.* Sometimes the only way to learn is by doing. If that is the case, use your passion as fuel to create new market opportunities and use this book as a guide to help you master the export process.

Summary

Remember how the chapter opened? I asked boldly: Are you ready to export? Then I provided three different exporting scenarios to help you understand how export initiatives are born. Next, I defined the difference between a product and a service export. Last, I offered a simple process to assess yourself as well as your existing business or start-up as to whether you have what it takes to export.

Now it's up to you. You can choose to deal with a stagnant climate and growth constraints at home or experience the thrill of exporting to fast-growing overseas markets. It's your decision. If you have the courage and mindset to export, and you are ready, turn the page. I want you wholeheartedly on this adventure with me!

CHAPTER 2

Writing an Export Business Plan

A Guide During the Life of Your Export Business

> "The plan is useless. But planning is essential." Former President Dwight Eisenhower said that. Planning is a process, setting concrete milestones and tracking progress, with frequent review and revisions. But you can't do planning without starting with a plan.
>
> —Tim Berry, founder, Bplans.com

Congratulations! You have determined you are export ready. You have what it takes to export and have decided on the type of export you wish to launch: a product, a service, or both. Now it's time to map out what you intend to accomplish during the life of your export business. It's time to think about your export prosperity in a new and dynamic way. This starts with the global mindset we covered earlier and moves to crafting what's ahead for your business on the international front. The process, which many dread because it requires a deep dive into strategic thinking, becomes an operational plan for controlling the export business and serves as a guide for growth and export success. The export business plan will become a part of your overall business plan—you'll see how and why later on.

■ **Note** The Internet plays a huge part in the exporting world, and that is reflected in this book. There are a lot of online tools and resources referenced throughout the book, so it will be handy to have a computer or tablet nearby.

Purpose of an Export Business Plan

There are four main purposes for the export business plan that you will write. The first is that it will serve as a guide during the initial stages of your export growth. The second is that it will give you a chance to describe your product or service offering, detail a realistic sales-and-marketing strategy (e.g., how you will reach your customers), provide a range of viable return-on-investment figures, and explain what variables will affect those numbers positively or negatively. The third purpose is that if you plan to seek out loans, whether export related or not, a business plan that includes an international expansion component is required by potential partners, lenders, and investors in order to understand your business strategy. And last, if you are looking for direction, creating a great export business plan will get you there quicker.

Putting a plan in place doesn't mean you look at it once and file it in a cabinet. It's a powerful, living document reflecting your ideas, team, and efforts. It's meant to be edited, referred to, and shared constantly throughout the growth of the business. A plan can be as simple as ideas jotted down on the back of a napkin or as thorough as a twenty-five-page report. Whether short or long, the plan should focus on what is important to you, what energizes and motivates you, and what gives you a sense of purpose and meaning—doing something bigger and beyond yourself. Start with the basics:

1. What do you like to do?
2. What are you planning to do?

Then ask yourself whether the two answers you came up with are in alignment. For example, my answers might be:

1. What do I like to do? I love to eat Italian food.
2. What am I planning to do? I plan to export hammers because I have a good supply source.

OK, you get it. I'm out of alignment on my vision for what I love to do versus what I intend to do to make that vision a reality. Let's try again:

1. What do I like to do? I love to eat pizza.
2. What am I planning to do? I plan to export frozen pizzas.

There you have it! My passion for something I love to do is in line with what I plan to do for a business—the ideal scenario for starting a business. That means my love of the product will sustain me during the sharp turns and bumps on the road to achieving exporting success. Experiment until you find your passion. Sometimes it can take several attempts before you realize what turns you on—whether it's selling pizzas, hammers, or making money!

Being purposeful is not something that just happens. You must be proactive and intentional. Did I personally start my business with an export business plan? Yes, for myself and the benefit of my team. Did we follow it? Not exactly. Our primary focus was to secure an initial overseas customer who would translate into an export sale and then push the transaction through to make a profit. We then reviewed the plan to see how we fared relative to what we were trying to accomplish, and we compared results to the realities of the market. We then decided to forge ahead on similar type deals in other countries.

In getting a business or an initiative like an export transaction off the ground, customers matter the most, but you need to go further. A great plan outlines and supports the assumptions you have going into the business and serves as a guide for where you're headed.

Pitfalls of *Not* Having an Export Business Plan

Not interested in developing a plan? That's an option and it is your choice. You must be short on time and eager to get to market. Bypassing strategic thinking for short-term gain can be risky (think along the lines of driving a car to a new, distant destination without a map or GPS). Yet it can be tempting because it is a quick way to test whether a product or service will sell in the export marketplace.

In my experience working with hundreds of start-ups and business owners, those who fail to develop a plan make several mistakes along the way. Here are some of the common pitfalls. Believe me, these aren't all of them.

1. They move too soon and fast—having a knee-jerk reaction as opposed to executing on a well-thought-out and -crafted strategy.
2. They fail to take a pulse on where their business stands currently.

3. They divert attention to the overseas market to the detriment of their local business.
4. They employ too-little staff to take on the overseas market.
5. They proceed to export in a complex market (e.g., where there is a lot of red tape or the natives speak a different language) or open up negotiations with the wrong party (e.g., someone who is untrustworthy or a bad fit).
6. They are too quick to execute on a sale and fail to secure a guaranteed payment.
7. They act in a too fast and aggressive manner in providing online banking information to get paid or to pay a supplier, only to find later on that they have been cyberattacked.
8. They don't state clearly on their Web site, blog, or Facebook page whether they accept international sales orders. If they don't, they should say so. If they do, then they should state specifically which countries they serve and follow through when inquiries roll in.
9. They put all their eggs in one basket and don't diversify enough to offset the ebbs and flows of the marketplace. They put too much emphasis on one product and one market that aren't working.
10. They never fully understand that they might have vulnerabilities that could impede their ability to get things done.

These so-called export sins are just the tip of the iceberg on what can potentially go wrong if you don't plan accordingly. If you are still dead set on moving ahead without a plan, do so at your own risk. I urge you, however, to at some point consider formalizing a plan so that you can fully capitalize on your idea and leverage it for luring potential partners, lenders, and investors.

Pointers for Developing an Export Business Plan

You should always measure your plan's progress against the market reality, which can be highly unpredictable. You can't go wrong with that approach. For example, you might sell designer diapers via your e-commerce site, emphasizing distribution to English-speaking countries such as Australia and New

Zealand, only to find out quickly that the bulk of your inquiries are in French, the native language of the majority of your prospective customers.

Whatever plan you select, have backup Plans B, C, and D in place. For example, let's say you select Ireland to export catfish to and find out two months later that the Irish don't like catfish. Plan B might be to sell your catfish to another market, say the United Kingdom, or to sell another fish that the Irish like. Be smart and apply the global mindset we talked about in Chapter 1, which is to stay flexible and adaptable. Just because you revert to Plan B or C doesn't mean you failed and that exporting won't work. Rather, it means the market reality is such that your original plan won't work and thank goodness you were smart enough to develop contingency plans.

Last, free trade agreements improve foreign market access for exporters, promote economic growth, and create jobs. Study active FTAs in advance of selecting an export market and preparing your export business plan to see how they will benefit your organization. Factor that information into your decision-making process accordingly. For example, NAFTA is the FTA among Canada, the United States, and Mexico serving to remove most barriers to trade and investment in that region.

UNDERSTAND MARKET CONDITIONS

Once you have a good idea of what you want to export and where, you can fill out your picture of market conditions by answering questions like these (this is a list I put together for a client):

1. Who will buy your product and why?
2. What is the size of the market?
3. Who is your competition?
4. How new is the product to the market you have selected?
5. Are there growth opportunities in the market?
6. What do the country's demographic profile, economy, and mass culture look like right now?
7. Are there demographic, economic, or cultural trends that will shape the market in the future?
8. Does the government help or hinder the sale of imported goods? For example, are there any barriers to entry or to sales within the market?

9. Will the country's climate or geography present logistical problems for sales of your product of choice—for example, selling chocolates to hot and humid Bali?

10. Does the product have to be adapted to that market by way of a physical reconstruction, a new package, or a change in servicing practices?

11. Does the product have the same use conditions in the international market as in the home market?

12. Does the product require personal after-sales service and, if so, can you provide it in the prospective market?

Use your own business sense and add to the list. Once you actually start research (refer to Chapter 4), more questions will arise. This is all part of the process of turning your vague ambitions into a concrete export business plan based on market realities, so the smarter your questions and more upfront your answers, the better your chances of success.

Three Types of Export Business Plans

Now you're ready to get organized and create your own plan. To keep the process manageable, let's look at three different types of sample template plans, each with distinct advantages for business people with different needs. Pick the one that works best for you, keeping in mind that you can shorten the analysis while keeping the major components of the plan intact.

- The back-of-the-napkin export business plan (suitable for born-global entrepreneurs)
- The traditional-export business plan
- The Laurel export business plan

The Back-of-the-Napkin Export Business Plan

The back-of-the-napkin export business plan is for folks who are big on ideas and pressed for time and want to get to market fast. While it's typically short and sweet, it serves a better purpose than having no export business plan at all. A back-of-the-napkin export business plan can be as simple as explaining what the business does, what you want to do next export-wise, and how you are going to get there (who is going to be on board). It might look like this:

1. "We make the absolute-best purple widgets on the planet."
2. "We will export purple widgets."

3. "We will export purple widgets to France."
4. "We will consider making other type widgets, say in red, if a customer in France is large enough to justify the change."
5. "Suzy, Ted, Mike, and I will work on this initiative."
6. "We will export, at a minimum, twenty thousand purple widgets within the first year."
7. "We will not reduce efforts from our domestic business to apply them to the export business."
8. "We will figure out how much money we need and when we need it."
9. "We will finance the exports of purple widgets with profits from our domestic business."
10. "We will find our own customers directly via our Web site, blog, and Facebook."
11. "We will consult with our banker to provide payment options on all export sales."
12. "We will have fun in the export journey to success!"

Add a Web site link to show what the business does and provide an executive summary that includes the founder's bio and the key team members, and you're done.

The Traditional Export Business Plan

It's important to have a business plan, but you don't have to reinvent the wheel to create one. One place to visit and bookmark online is the Small Business Administration's "Export Business Planner" (http://www.sba.gov/export-businessplanner). It is a free, customizable tool for small-business owners who are exploring exporting. When you are using the planner, you can refer to Getting Started: Creating an Export Business Plan. It outlines the following (in Chapter 124, we guide you on market research so don't overly challenge yourself if you can't answer all the questions at the initial planning stage):

1. Profiling Your Current Business
    a. Identify current successes.
    b. Determine competitive advantages.
    c. Evaluate companywide commitment.

2. Conducting an Industry Analysis
   a. Find export data available on your industry.
   b. Research how competitive your industry is in the global markets.
   c. Assess your industry's international growth potential.
   d. Research government market studies.
3. Identifying Products with Export Potential
   a. Select the most exportable products/services that your company will offer internationally.
   b. Evaluate the product/services(s) that your company will offer internationally.
4. Marketability: Matching Your Product/Service with a Global Trend or Need
   a. Classify your product.
   b. Find countries with the best-suited markets for your product.
   c. Determine which foreign markets will be the easiest to penetrate.
   d. Define and narrow down those export markets you intend to pursue.
   e. Talk to your US customers or other companies who are doing business internationally.
   f. Research export efforts of US competitors.
5. Determining Market Expansion Benefits/Trade-Offs
   a. Assess the benefits to exporting.
   b. Determine the trade-offs to exporting.
6. Identifying Markets to Pursue
   a. Select the top three most penetrable markets (see the sidebar at the end of this list).
7. Conducting an Export Marketing and Sales Analysis
   a. Come up with an overall marketing strategy.
   b. Figure out sales strategies.

c. Write a detailed product or service description.

d. Map out the product life cycle.

e. Make a list of copyrights, patents, and trade secrets.

f. Determine research and development activities.

8. Short-and Long-Term Goals

    a. Define short-term goals.

    b. Define long-term goals.

    c. Develop an action plan with timelines to reach your short-term goals.

In summary, the most difficult aspect in developing an export business plan is determining the demand for a product or service offering in a foreign country. It's one thing to know a product can be sold in a market—after all, that's why you selected a particular market—but it is a totally different ballgame when it comes to forecasting how much you can sell and over what time frame. Assume that the demand for a product develops in direct proportion to the economic development in each country. This might be a useful way to think about it, especially when data might be unknown.

WHERE DO YOU WANT TO GO?

Keep your analysis of markets that you want to pursue to one page and break it into four manageable parts (use a, b, c, and d below). The purpose of this exercise is to establish a broad scope for your research-market analysis but not so broad that you overwhelm yourself. Try to begin with the end in mind: where do you want to go and how will you know that you have arrived?

A. Select the top-three most penetrable overseas markets that appear to have the best potential for your product or service offering. You can conduct market research online; meet in person with an international trade expert (see the SBA's "US Export Assistance Centers": http://www.sba.gov/content/us-export-assistance-centers); or test your product or service by exhibiting at a local trade show. Trade shows give you access to potential customers from all over the world without you having to analyze a thing. For example, if you sell hardware tools and exhibit at a hardware show and find that you get a lot of interest from attendees from a particular foreign market, such as Australia, you would know there must be a market there, because why else would these attendees be asking for information? From there, you can address those inquiries, learn as you grow, and conduct further research.

B. Analyze the market factors and conditions in each of the selected countries. Delve into each country further by reviewing cultural attributes, geographical characteristics, political stability, demographic characteristics, market size, and growth rates. The goal here is to conduct a sound assessment of a foreign market. What might the barriers be? What makes it a good market to enter? How will the local culture influence the sales of your product or service offering? Such in-depth market research information is necessary to make sound marketing decisions and it must be done with each new market entry.

C. Determine the pros/cons to conducting business in each market. Look at potential language barriers, legal restrictions, logistical challenges, and payment problems that might get in the way of doing business in a particular market. Include all relevant variables in your assessment. Do an analysis of your company's own strengths and weaknesses in a selected market. Will your product or service offering be in the low-, middle-, or high-end pricing level? Is there a similar product or service offering currently available in the selected market? If so, who is making it? Where are they based? Can you compete? Why would you? How would you? The more pros you have for entering a new market, the better your chance for success. If you can draw on the perspective of a native (better yet, an actual prospective customer) of the country where you are keenly interested in doing business, do so. Nothing beats an on-the-ground assessment.

D. Select one market to get started! Now you are ready to interpret your findings in light of the stated objective: where do you want to go and how will you know that you have arrived? (This gets back to the back-of-the-napkin plan.) At this juncture, you should have enough data and experience (from going to trade shows, for example) to decide which market is best for you to begin in. Hold off on the other two countries and don't start doing business with them until after you have a proven success with the first overseas market. If the first selected market doesn't work right away, say after six months or a year, move on to market No. 2, and so on. Don't muddy the waters. You don't want to do too many things at once because you will end up not doing any of them right.

The Laurel Export Business Plan

The following plan—I'll call it the Laurel export business plan (LEBP)—has worked well for many of my clients. You can focus on each section heading and then build out accordingly based on the questions I pose and comments I make. What many clients experience as they develop an export plan is the eureka moment: "I can do this!" The trick is to craft a plan that suits you and can absorb economic shifts and shocks along the way yet still allow for you to achieve successful results. And it can't hurt for you to use both the traditional business export and Laurel export plans to develop yours.

Tip It is important to identify where the cash will come from to support your export operation. Conduct a complete audit of your cash situation so you are not surprised later on to learn you need more money than anticipated to reach a new overseas market. Face weak links and potential problems before you are knee deep in a fantastic opportunity.

---

1. *Introduction*: Compose an explanation why you should export and what your company wants to gain from exporting. Your answers will serve as your guiding light and foundation for your entire export business plan.

2. *Executive Summary*: Specify your long-term financial and nonfinancial vision for developing an export business. Think three, five, and ten years out. This part shows clarity of purpose, direction, and intent. It is an understanding of the company's identity and a short, concise picture of the company in the future. Think of it as an entire business plan in miniature.

3. *Strategic Leadership*: State your leadership ability clearly. Do you have what it takes to drive results for your export operation? (Refer to Chapter 1 for a refresher on the global mindset.) The business owner must have the ability to set direction, make decisions, and provide long-term planning.

4. *Company Description*: Explain what do you do and why are you good at it.

5. *Target Export Market:* Identify your customers in _____ (pick a target export market). Think about what would motivate them to pay for your product or service and if they will be able to afford to pay for your product or service. Drill down to a more precise view of your target audience.

Caution Are you crystal clear on who your customers are and why they use your product or service? If not, go back and do a major rethink!

---

6. *The Competitive Analysis (Market and Customer):* Distinguish how your product or service is unique, and explain briefly why people in a selected export market would buy it. Do you know the strengths, weaknesses, strategies, opportunities, threats, and financial status of your top five competitors? Spell them out.

7. *Marketing and Sales Plan:* Detail and clarify how you will effectively and efficiently reach the people with whom you want to connect through your business (direct, indirect, intermediary sales, trade shows, e-commerce, mobile, etc.). Ensure existing local customers are not neglected! Are your products and services suitable for an export market or will major modifications be required? This part should be strategic in that it outlines specific action steps to achieve future sales goals.

Tip Utilizing market and customer intelligence determines a company's ability to perceive and adapt to changes in the global marketplace. The more homework you do, the better the chance you have to achieve desired results.

---

8. *Operations Plan:* Figure out how you will support the business strategies through internal operations, systems, and organizational structures. Describe key factors to use in your business in finding solutions and in meeting the wants and needs of customers, suppliers, employees and other key influencers. If exporting a product, how will it get made? Do you have the capacity to produce and deliver?

9. *Information Technology Plan*: State how you will leverage technology to take advantage of the export marketplace. Will your export business be heavily dependent on technology? List your business's strengths and weaknesses in the information technology area. IT will support your company's business processes and decision making and, at the same time, give it an extreme competitive advantage in the global marketplace. Plan the parts of your business you will use technology for (order taking, mailing lists, social media, finances, e-commerce sales) and how you will use it.

10. *Logistics Plan*: Outline how you will get your product or service to the chosen export market.

11. *Management Structure*: Identify the people and experts in your business who will implement your plan and exceed your goals. Compile a management team section that describes who is on your team and what expertise each person brings to the table. This section should also include an analysis of strengths and weaknesses in the team and what might be missing.

12. *Future Development*: Tailor your business plan by defining future milestones that are in line with your desired goals. Describe your vision for your business, including your exit strategy.

13. *Financials (Export Budget)*: Analyze your available resources (human, material, and financial) to determine how you will support export initiatives. Get together three types of financial statements: a cash-flow statement, an income statement (also referred to as a profit/loss statement), and a balance sheet. Set budget targets and develop pricing strategies. Confront your company's finances squarely. You want your export business to be sustainable over the long term.

14. *Strategy Implementation*: How will you follow up, review, and measure results? Have you set a timeline? Home in on a detailed action plan for execution.

Tip Have your export dream team (EDT) review your plan so that they can seek external sources of advice, test it, and hold you accountable and responsible for implementing it.

As your export business grows, you will become more aware of external factors that influence your business plan, which will allow you to develop ways to manage and adapt to them. These external factors might include: import regulations, exchange rates, availability of finance, new or unexpected competition, and disruptive technology and logistics, to name just a few. As mentioned earlier, anticipating change and adapting to it requires strategic leadership as well as Backup Plans B, C, and D.

Summary: Leaving You with Fun and Export Adventure on Your Mind

You should express and experience the passion you have for exporting in the crafting of your export business plan. If that enthusiasm is not there, reconsider what you are attempting to do. It might not be the right time. Individuals e-mail me on a weekly basis saying, "Here's what I want to do in the export market . . . ." Then they ask me: "Will it work?" My response: "I don't know. It depends on you." (Reread Chapter 1!) This brings us back to the goal of this chapter: creating an export business plan that meets your needs and serves the life of your business.

Now that you know what is involved, craft your own export business plan and use it as a tool for building your export business—and don't forget to maximize profits! Look at it regularly, revise it when necessary, and pay attention to the reality of the market. It will sharpen what you are doing, why you are doing it, and help you define and achieve professional and personal goals.

CHAPTER 3

Prepping For Exports

Legal, Financial, and Logistical Considerations

> *This is the company of the future. Forget about "outsourcing." In today's hyperconnected world, there is no "in" and no "out." There's only "good, better and best," and if you don't assemble the best team you can from everywhere, your competitor will.*
>
> —Best-selling author and *New York Times* columnist Thomas Friedman (2012)[1]

Now that you've set up your business plan, it's time to delve a little deeper into assembling your export company. The next step is tackling the essential details of a sound legal, fiscal, and logistical operation. You'll be faced with obstacles ranging from expanding your enterprise, protecting your company, and choosing a product name and other intellectual property to opening a bank account in your home country, sourcing financing, and dealing with special tax situations. Not all of these issues will come into play immediately, but you will do well to familiarize yourself with the framework in which you will be operating right from the start.

Although the expansion of any business tests us on numerous fronts—from hiring the right people to covering fixed expenses and revenue generation—expanding internationally through exports performed primarily via the Internet challenges us in a whole new way that could potentially interrupt the viability of a business. When reengineering your business from local to export-ready, you must take into consideration bullet-proofing processes, additional laws governing intellectual property, hiring and firing, contracts, and marketing and financial management, as well as settling international disputes.

Prepping for export success boils down to careful planning (refer back to Chapter 2 on crafting a business plan), being proactive in seizing opportunities, and holding transparent discussions with trusted advisors on where you are headed to ensure every move you make is done with confidence and leads to greater growth and prosperity for your business.

Note   I am not an attorney, banker, logistics expert, or accountant. The information in this chapter is based on experience and extensive research and should not be construed as an official plan on how something is done. Before proceeding with an action plan, consult with a specialist, just as I would.

Line Up Your Export Dream Team

One of the first things you should do before officially setting up your export business, or if you are an established enterprise and haven't done so already, is to find yourself a good lawyer, a knowledgeable accountant, savvy banker, and logistics expert, each of whom should specialize in international transactions. They are your export dream team (EDT). You may feel that you can't afford to pay for these professional services, but in truth, you can't afford to do without them.

The Fab Four: Lawyer, Accountant, Banker, Logistics Expert

A qualified lawyer, well versed in international trade and the Internet, will protect you from those who would take advantage of your inexperience in the global marketplace or from unknowingly perpetrating violations yourself! Any one of the big national law firms, such as Baker & McKenzie; Skadden, Arps, Slate, Meagher & Flom; Foley & Lardner; and Latham & Watkins, will be able to advise you on intellectual property issues, the Internet, mergers, acquisitions, and reorganization. The larger the law firm, the greater the overhead and the higher the hourly rates you will be expected to pay. Be aware of this starting out, and if you can't afford it, go elsewhere to make your investment more cost effective.

Tip   To find a good lawyer, ask around and research, research, research! You'd be surprised at how asking a simple question to your accountant, banker, or successful small business peer group—"Who do you use for legal representation?"—can help you home in on following up and getting a solution. Strike a balance of likeability, specialized experience, and affordability that meets your needs. You can also find additional assistance from FindLaw.com and Lawyers.com.

A good accountant specializing in international taxation will help maximize your cash flow, limit your eventual worldwide tax exposure, and protect you from double or triple taxation scenarios. The big accounting firms such as EY and Deloitte have offices in nearly every country in the world and can offer you a broad variety of global services, but they'll cost you. A work-around is to find a smaller accounting firm that specializes in international accounting and taxation matters for small businesses.

A well-versed banker can help you finance an export sale, guide you in structuring competitive payment terms (including online options), or even advise you on risk factors before you transact business in a new overseas market. The large banks such as J.P. Morgan Chase, Bank of America, BMO Harris Bank, PNC, and Citicorp have an unmistakable identity and usually have small business banking divisions as well as branch offices worldwide.

Tip Even though the thought of using the *big* bank guys might intimidate you, once you are a customer—and that could be only the basis of depositing $250 to open an account—you are entitled to free consultations with the international banking experts to help you better manage your export business.

A seasoned logistics expert (refer to Chapter 9 on transport options) will help you minimize the risk, complexity, and cost of transporting products worldwide. Big logistic firms such as UPS, DHL, and FedEx transport products worldwide, prepare specialized export documentation, build shortcuts in standard export shipping processes, monitor shipments, and offer guidance on regulatory issues involving compliance and trade. Freight forwarders often serve the same purpose, but they do so on a more-niche basis (by industry or geographic location). They too organize shipments to get goods from one point to a final destination. Any of these types of organizations are effective and serve as an architect for transport. Before you send your product off on a boat, get comfortable with one point person to help you navigate the choppy waters and ask her about her resources and whether she has people on the ground in the country where you desire to conduct business. And, as always, have a backup logistic provider in case something goes awry in a country where business is booming.

Start Small

For your legal, accounting, and banking needs, I suggest you start out with a smaller firm that can attend to you on a more personal and economical basis. Many founders of small boutique law firms, for example, acquire their experience working for a number of years at a big international law firm prior to starting their own business. To keep overhead costs and client fees low for small business owners, they focus on the highly specialized practice areas that are in high demand, such as Internet law, global trademarks, and international franchising. The benefit of contracting a smaller firm to satisfy your needs is threefold: prior big corporate experience at a fraction of the cost, affordable rate structure, and specific expertise.

When a question is too tough for your small firm to handle, let them outsource it to a larger firm with a more developed international presence. That way, you can stick to your budget and your small firm will stay in charge of your legal or accounting operations. But when you reach the point where you're outsourcing more than in-sourcing, it's time to make the jump to one of the big guns! The large international firms employ individuals of many nationalities who are well versed in the laws, professional ethics, and regulations of the countries in which they operate and well positioned to serve your interests. Expect to require more extensive and sophisticated information about the countries you export to as your business grows, particularly if you do a lot of business in any one of them.

Your lawyer, accountant, banker, and logistics expert are vital to the success of your export strategy. They should be considered the charter members of your EDT. As you will see, they often work in concert to keep your new enterprise in the most advantageous legal, financial, and logistical position possible.

Tip I strongly encourage you to set up an export advisory board (EAB) at your company to help you tackle tough challenges, cut costs, expand rapidly, get key introductions that lead to significant business down the road, and solve problems before they fester. Unlike a board of directors, an EAB does not have authority over your business. It is purely there to offer advice that you can take or leave. If you don't know how to establish an EAB, conduct an Internet search with the keywords "How to create an advisory board." Then, follow the suggestions pertaining to exporting. The advisory board will serve in addition to your EDT because it will not charge you for consultations nor does it have any vested interest in your business other than to help you grow. Your attorney on the EDT should draw up a simple contract. What's in it for people that will encourage them to join your EAB? Perhaps a small annual fee (stipend), gift card, occasional dinner, or excellent connections to high-level people with common interests will motivate them to jump on board!

Legal Considerations

Protecting a trademark in the United States—whether it's your own company name, a product, or your supplier's product name—is a very complicated procedure best handled by a very competent attorney.

Protect Your Intellectual Property

When you are considering adopting a trademark, you or your attorney must perform a search to see if anyone is using that mark on a similar product or service. If you discover that someone has beaten you to it, you then have to find out when the other party began using the mark and if it is currently in use. If it is not, you have to determine if you can have the rights to it. You may find out that another firm is using the same mark but on a totally different product or service. For example, you might have trademarked the name Violetta for your line of purple bird feeders, only to find out that another firm has trademarked Violetta for their line of candles. In either case, you'll need legal advice as to your right to use the mark.

Most trademark and patent registrations are made through the commissioner of patents and trademarks in Washington, DC. After you have taken the necessary steps to protect your design or mark on the domestic front, you will have to start the process all over again in the country in which you are about to do business. Particularly if you are registering marks in multiple countries, it will be crucial to have an attorney who specializes in international intellectual property management. Always discuss fees in advance because this process can be very costly.

Patents and copyrights need the same attention. You never want to see anyone, anywhere in the world, take what you have created and put their name on it.

Legal Protection in the Online Environment

International domain name protection requires specific skills, experience, and legal governance, so it is best to find a lawyer who is familiar with Internet Corporation for Assigned Names and Numbers (ICANN). You should manage domain names as carefully as any other intellectual property within the firm.

Domain Name Protection: Part of Your IP Protection

You can secure a domain name on your own in minutes (try NetworkSolutions.com or GoDaddy.com), but the international use and scope of it may not apply worldwide. Furthermore, registering a domain name does not necessarily create rights to a trademark. For example, let's say I register laurelpizzas.com as a domain name in the United States. After securing the domain name, I cannot assume that I also own it as a trademark and that the same domain is available in China (`laurelpizzas.com.cn`). That is where an international lawyer becomes invaluable for protection, maintenance, and enforcement of the domain name as it relates to your international business brand.

Well before deploying an attorney, a good exercise to go through when you start up or launch a new product or service via an established enterprise is to ask yourself two questions: How important is the domain name or mark to me? Is it a part of my core business? You'll be surprised at how those two questions force you to home in on what really matters to you on legal protection (think along the lines of Twitter, Facebook, and Apple—they all started out small). If something is central to your organization's growth, you better protect it, patrol it, and keep it updated and scalable.

A lot of online legal-environment protection will come into play based on where you are headed with your business and how the Internet factors into your overall business strategy (all the more reason to deep dive into Chapter 2). Budget accordingly and allocate resources to get the appropriate legal protection you need. To avoid the "I never saw it coming" experience, discuss with your international attorney in great length about protecting your products and services, including online properties and Internet strategy, and all aspects of trade dress—which refers to the *look and feel* of a product—before exporting them overseas. You'll be glad you did.

■ **Tip** *The Guide to Law Online*, published by the Library of Congress, is a portal of Internet sources of interest to legal researchers. It also serves as an annotated compendium of Internet links. It's an excellent source for laypeople who don't have a legal background but want to develop an understanding of a country's legal system before entering into it and contacting their own attorney for advice. Every direct source listed in the guide was successfully vetted before being added to the list. To access it, head to http://www.loc.gov/law/help/guide/nations.php.

Other Legal Considerations: Labor Laws, Contracts, and Agreements

Labor laws can vary overseas. You may find your export business growing by leaps and bounds, which is the goal of this book—to allow you to hire more American employees to support your exports and possibly even hire more people where your customers are: overseas. If that is the case, consult with your attorney and accountant to determine the best course of action based on the labor laws of the country you are contemplating entering and to fully understand the legal and tax consequences.

I would be remiss if I didn't highlight the fact that it is nearly impossible to run an export business without creating some form of contract or agreement covering the following: exclusive distribution and supplier agreements , a joint venture, partnership, or licensing agreement, to name just a few. Think of it this way: every time you are about to enter into a relationship overseas that requires a long-term commitment and your company is on the line (e.g., could help you grow or take you down), consult with an attorney to compose one of these items to protect your interests.

Opening Your Bank Account

Opening up your company's first business bank account is as simple as 1-2-3—just don't forget to mention that you plan to export. If you are an established enterprise, skip this section unless you want to be sure you've got everything covered. You'll want to set up and maintain your account in an organized fashion, because once you begin to receive money and pay bills, your statements will become the foundation of your accounting system.

Find a bank in your home country that has an international department (preferably one with extensive expertise on letters of credit), a strong worldwide presence, and that can provide strong personal service because you will need it. Further, look for a bank that offers twenty-four-hour online access from your desk or from a secured Internet line anywhere in the world and a mobile-payment feature with industry-leading security, including proven state-of-the-art encryption software. Online banking allows you to quickly view account balances, monitor transactions, identify current foreign exchange rates, and send and receive payments—all specifically designed to increase efficiency and cost effectiveness at your business. Before you visit your bank, call or e-mail the branch and ask what you need to bring with you to open an account. Here are some of the documents you will typically be required to bring: personal identification, such as a driver's license or passport; business papers showing your type of organization, such as a copy of your business license, certificate, articles of incorporation, and corporate seal or corporate resolution; and a copy of one of your most recent utility bills (to verify your mailing address). It is also helpful to have several hundred dollars or so for the initial deposit, so that you can get your account activated right away.

Be sure you have good rapport with your banking officer. He will play a very important position on your EDT!

Banking in and with different countries can be a challenge. Choosing an international bank that is networked to branch offices worldwide and has relationships with other banks in the countries you intend to do business spares you having to open an overseas account and allows you to transact business in the currency of your choice. Further, choosing an international bank with a relationship to a bank in Japan will also allow you to save money by hedging extreme Yen–US dollar fluctuations. There will be also be times when you are unsure as to what currency you should pay in or be paid in (see Chapter 11). Other times, you might make a payment to an independent contractor in one country via PayPal or Square and not know if you should withhold taxes. In some circumstances, the issue of withholding taxes may be reduced or eliminated altogether by a tax treaty between two countries. How will you know? That's where your team of export specialists, in this case your international banker, is ever so vital in keeping you informed and handling all that comes before you on a case-by-case basis.

Maximizing Tax Benefits for Your Multinational Business

Once you've got an organization set up and an accounting system that makes sense for the way you want to run your business, you'll discover that your global growth will affect your financial planning. Depending on your form of organization, overseas business will present you with a whole new set of accounting and tax issues. Yet the name of the game will remain the same: minimize taxes, maximize profits.

At some point, ambitious as they may now seem if you're new to the export scene, scenarios like the following will become your reality:

- You generate income through a salaried employee who resides in the country in which you do business.
- You generate income from an export intermediary who conducts business in a foreign country.
- You generate income from exports worldwide.
- You generate income through the writing of an export-success article for a highly acclaimed blog in China.
- You generate income through your e-commerce site from individuals the world over.
- You generate income through a service export you are providing to a company in Bangladesh.
- You generate income from mobile payments made through PayPal, Google Wallet, and Square.

You are probably beginning to see how an accountant with international expertise becomes indispensable. You wouldn't want inappropriate accounting either to diminish the income you derive from any opportunities like these or to cause you to run afoul of tax laws. Don't think for a minute that you can apply domestic tax rules to international transactions. For each case, you and your accountant must ask the following questions: How are these business arrangements treated from a tax standpoint? Are you required to pay any domestic taxes? Are you required to pay any taxes on profits earned in a foreign country? Are you required to pay taxes online and, if so, where and to whom? If you need to transfer assets to a foreign entity, how do you do it? Will your exports involve any intercompany pricing rules or complex foreign currency provisions? Are you better off, from a profit or cash-flow standpoint, seizing a particular opportunity or passing it up? And, a very important question to ask you accountant, when you are involved in large cross-border transactions, how do you avoid double taxation? In the United States, for example, as a boost to businesses operating overseas, the government offers a reduction on national taxes based on the taxes you pay abroad, which is referred to as the US Foreign Tax Credit. Use the list as a discussion point with your international accountant. It will serve you well as you explore virgin overseas territories.

More Ways to Guard Your Bottom Line

Be aware of the several other traps (and opportunities) awaiting exporters that follow.

Trade and Customs Duties

Planning and managing customs duties plays an important role in pricing your export product so that it is profitable. First, pay attention to how your product is classified (see Chapter 10 to find out how to determine your product classification), because that classification will affect what duties are imposed and thus make or break your chances of exporting it at a profit. Be sure to get your classification in writing from transportation and logistics experts and then check with them later on to see if there is ever a time when you can reduce or defer duties or even have your products cross borders duty-free.

US customs duties vary widely based on where a product is primarily made, the valuation of the goods, and the destination country. The duties raise revenue for the federal government and protect domestic producers. There are three different types of duties: ad valorem, specific, and compound.

- *Ad valorem duties* are assessed as a percentage of the value of the goods, in the form of either a transaction value or what you would pay in the country of origin. Always try to keep your invoice value at a net sales price. Don't write up your invoice with commissions or transportation factored into your selling price or you may end up paying a much higher duty!

- *Specific duties* are assessed on a fixed-basis per-unit price, such as ten cents per kilogram or forty cents per item, regardless of the transaction cost.

- *Compound* or *mixed duties* combine the bases of ad valorem and specific duties. For example, a shipment might be assessed at 5 percent of the transaction plus ten cents per unit. This works well on very high-priced items.

Keep in mind that certain countries offer privileges on some imports. Before you export, check with US customs or your local department of commerce to find out the duties for your product and if your product is eligible for any breaks.

You should also inquire with your tax accountant about foreign trade zones (FTZs) and how they might help you reduce or eliminate customs duties. An FTZ is a domestic US site that is considered to be outside the country's customs territory and is available for use as if it were in a foreign country. A US company can accelerate the process of duty drawbacks or tax rebates in one of these zones or even have a product imported, assembled on site, and reexported without any duties, taxes, or local ad valorem taxes being charged. In addition, there are duty drawbacks, which allow you to recover duties paid to US customs on exported merchandise, but you must perform feasibility studies to determine how this procedure might apply to and benefit your business.

For example, if a product is manufactured in the United States out of imported raw materials and then exported back out of the country, the imported materials used might be eligible for a duty drawback, less 1 percent to cover customs costs. The passages of US Free Trade Agreements enacted in more than twenty countries (i.e., the North American Free Trade Agreement [NAFTA]; the Dominican Republic-Central America-United States Free Trade Agreement [CAFTA-DR]; and the Trans-Pacific Partnership [TPP, in negotiation]) along with bilateral free trade agreements (i.e., Singapore, Australia, Jordan, Israel) have brought about many favorable developments in the area of customs duties as well. Your accountant should keep you posted.

Interest-Charge Domestic International Sales Corporation

An interest-charge domestic international sales corporation (IC-DISC) can increase your cash flow, provide a reduced taxable base at the export level, and even in certain instances provide a lower effective tax rate. To qualify for an IC-DISC, you must form a corporation (such as an S corp or a closely held C corp) that exports and produces or manufactures US export property (e.g., fabricated metal products and electrical machinery equipment) inside the country. It must consist of a minimum of 50 percent US content, which is sold primarily outside the country. IC-DISCs are "paper" entities and can defer commission payments of up to $10 million, a limitation that was intended to restrict IC-DISC activity to smaller businesses. According to Joseph Englert, president and founder of Export Assist, the IC-DISC acts as a commission agent on the export sales of the parent company. The commission income of the IC-DISC is calculated based on the combined taxable income and expenses related to the export sales of the US exporter and the IC-DISC.[2] Consult with an international accountant to determine whether you should look into an IC-DISC for your business.

Summary

From the time you start out to the time you reach the mature stages of your export company, your EDT of international legal, accounting, banking, and logistic experts can add value and help create and maximize profit opportunities for you and allow you to succeed in the dynamic worldwide marketplace. Our discussion here is only an introduction to the legal, financial, and logistical issues that will affect your export business, a starting point for your long-term planning and a demonstration of the absolute urgency of getting the very best advice. Do not be bashful about consulting with your experts! As your business expands, the issues that impact it will become more complex and sophisticated. The more questions you ask, the more you will build your own expertise—and become a valuable export player in your own right.

Now that you have seen how to line up professional advisory support and build a solid management foundation from which to grow, let's turn to a practical concern: picking the best foreign market for your product or service.

Notes

1. "Thomas Friedman: Hyperconnected," Gawker, last modified January 31, 2013, http://gawker.com/5980150/thomas-friedman-hyperconnected.

2. Joseph Englert, "Interest Charge Domestic International Sales Corporation," AICPA Store, last modified October 27, 2011, http://www.cpa2biz.com/Content/media/PRODUCER_CONTENT/Newsletters/Articles_2011/CorpTax/InterestChargeDomesticInternationalSalesCorporation.jsp.

CHAPTER 4

Exploring Your Territory
How to Research and Pick the Best Foreign Market

> Only 1% of the businesses in the U.S. today actually export. So that's a big part for our inspiration, to make it easier and easier for companies to compete in the global environment.
>
> —UPS Chief Financial Officer Kurt Kuehn[1]

Once you've decided on a product or service to export, you've got to find an export market where you can sell it profitably. At this point, I am assuming you know what you need to do to get export ready based on the results of the export readiness questionnaire you took in Chapter 1. As for market research, it can be a slow, painstaking, and tedious chore, but as you add to your knowledge, by tracking the movement of goods and tapping into the world's networks of purchasing and distribution, you will create your own living and changing map of international trade that will serve you throughout your export business.

There are a variety of methods by which a company can locate the best—meaning the right—potential foreign markets for its product or service. This chapter outlines a range of efficient methods for researching export markets, focusing on where to get export-market data and intelligence, and how to use it.

Since you will be consulting a variety of resources, you will want to take some time to plan your approach. In this chapter, I offer you ways to nail down specifics about your product, your consumer, and the market conditions necessary to support healthy sales of your product—all of which will help you to identify a hot target market when you move on to your research.

You will be assembling information about two kinds of customers: the everyday citizen who buys goods for personal use (B-to-C) and the various high-volume traders who buy goods from you to sell to other businesses (B-to-B). I will provide you with numerous ways to find out about both kinds of customers, so that you can determine what modifications, if any, will be needed to prepare the product for your target markets. You'll find that there are dense networks of information and support, largely government sponsored, for every aspect of the development of your export business. Most of these sources of assistance are easily accessible online and within the reach of even a modest operating budget. Once you have a good idea of where and how to direct your marketing efforts, you can create an action plan to get your export program underway.

■ **Caution** In the words of the late Steve Jobs: "Some people say, 'Give the customers what they want.' But that's not my approach. Our job is to figure out what they're going to want before they do. I think Henry Ford once said, 'If I'd asked customers what they wanted, they would have told me, 'A faster horse!'" People don't know what they want until you show it to them. That's why I never rely on market research. Our task is to read things that are not yet on the page."[2] Keep Jobs's remark in mind as you conduct your market research, and use gut instinct, humanity, and commonsense as you research data. But don't get analysis paralysis where you keep researching but never take action. That's the worst outcome. And never forget the end user—the customer—for that is who buys the products and services.

Market Research—a Dreaded Chore, a Powerful Tool

One of the tasks I dreaded while getting my business underway was conducting market research. I hated it because it cost both time and money. When I promised a potential supplier that I would study a foreign market to determine whether it would be receptive to the product, I would rack my brain about (a) how I would go about it and (b) how I would go about it inexpensively!

Sometimes you'll get lucky and an inquiry will land in your e-mail inbox pointing you right to an ideal market for a product. For example, you might have a friend who runs a company in Botswana and loves a certain type of sandal but can't find it there. He contacts you and asks you to source a supplier of the shoe or an equivalent product. You now have a country (Africa) to export to, a potential buyer (your friend's company) to sell to, and a product (a sandal not available in Botswana) to offer. Furthermore, now that you know that these sandals or anything like them are not sold in Botswana, you've been alerted to an untapped market that you can develop on a larger scale. But don't take these windfalls for granted. If you want to keep the orders coming in, you're going to have to ramp up your social media conversations and go out and approach customers. Market research tells you where customers can be found.

Your first market research project is usually the toughest because it's all unfamiliar terrain. But once you have searched out the data you need in order to predict how a specific type of product will sell in a specific geographic location, you can use the information over and over again as a guideline for exports of similar products in the future. As you build your personal information database on global markets and learn to keep yourself up to date on developments in international trade, it will become less and less of a chore to determine where to take your product. You will find that market research is a powerful tool for exploring and taking control of your export territory.

Get Yourself Organized

There is no getting around the fact that market research is *not* a tidy, linear process! It involves several closely related objectives: to put together a working profile of your actual consumer or end user; to determine if the country's market conditions (its economy, demographics, level of political stability, trade barriers, distribution system, competition, transportation, and storage, etc.) will favor or hinder your product's success; and to identify the people who will buy your product from you (consumers, wholesalers, importers, etc.). Before you consult your resources, I recommend that you sit down with pen and paper or PC (it can be a tablet if you prefer), and try the following procedures to help you structure the task. The idea here is to establish a few attractive or promising directions for your investigations and to clarify exactly what kinds of information you'll be looking for.

Choosing Your Market—Pleasure, Profit, Competitive Advantage, or Challenge?

In Chapter 2, I talked about the various motivations that might guide your choice of a product to export. When deciding where to concentrate your sales efforts, the same range of motivations comes into play. You should choose a market that intrigues you, presents a competitive advantage, or offers a challenge and then consider products that you might want to sell there. You will be visiting this market frequently and getting to know its people intimately, so, just as you should pick a product that will delight you for years to come, you should plan on exporting to a country that delights and fascinates you. If you are enthralled with French culture and you are excited at the prospect of cracking that market, then you want to sell France. If you have dolls to sell, you should sell them to France. It's a place to start! But use commonsense: Don't ignore other countries that offer good prospects for your dolls, and don't expend too much time and energy on your first-choice market if it turns out to be a poor prospect. The trick is to find the right market.

Tip Even though in Chapter 2 I talked about selecting a product that is wildly successful on the domestic front to export, don't overlook the possibility and opportunity of selling products that are less successful in the United States, as they could be in high demand elsewhere. Say you manufacture two different types of dolls—one that uses high-end materials and is very expensive and the other low end and quite inexpensive. The glamorous high-end doll sells magnificently in your local market, but the moderately priced doll is more appealing and affordable overseas. The only way to discover this is through extensive research of foreign countries.

If you start your market research and find out that there's no demand for dolls in France, you can always move on and pick another market. But stick to dolls because that's what you manufacture and are comfortable with and knowledgeable about. Unless you've exhausted all of the options on your product of choice, it's best to stay as close to your original plan as possible—entertaining too many possibilities can put you off track and cause you to lose your confidence and enthusiasm.

If easy profits with minimal effort and exercise of business ingenuity are your priorities, you can just use your domestic market as a model. If you take a careful look at where, to whom, and why a product is selling well in your country and then locate markets abroad with similar demographics, chances are that the demand will be similar. A bonus: minimal product modification, if any, will be required.

Segmenting Your Product and Market

Another important aspect that will help you focus your research is categorizing or segmenting your product and target market by making lists of the relevant factors. Take the dolls, for example. What type of dolls are you going to export? Baby dolls? Antique? For boys? For girls? Talking? Education? Under each product segment, list the categories of likely customers until you reach the end user for your product. Once you determine who your customer is, what she buys, when she buys, how often she buys, and why she buys, you've got a customer profile. For example, your customers for girl's dolls might include manufacturers, wholesalers, independent doll shops, big box stores, and e-commerce platforms, as well as private citizens. Push your lists as far as you can—it might take anywhere from one to ten categorizations before you can reach optimum segmentation.

Use a format like this for your list:

1. I'm going to export: _____ (product)
2. Specifically these types: _____ (type of product), _____ (type of target customer), _____ (type of buyer).
3. I'm going to export to: _____ (country)

Your completed list might look like this:

1. I'm going to export "dolls" (product).
2. Specifically these types: "educational dolls" (type of product), "for girls ages seven to ten" (type of target customer), "to importing wholesalers of educational toys and direct via e-commerce" (type of buyer).
3. I'm going to export to "France" (country).

Through this exercise, you will sufficiently narrow down search categories so that you are ready to conduct a search via Google, Bing, or Yahoo. You will also be ready to send an e-mail to a trade officer to ask a specific question or set up an appointment with the Small Business Administration or US Export Assistance Center for help. Refer to your list and refer to it frequently to keep you on track.

Will Your Product Succeed in Your Market of Choice?

Once you have a good idea of what you want to export and where to, you can fill out your picture of market conditions by answering questions like these:

1. Who will buy your product and why?
2. What is the size of the market?
3. Who is your competition?

4. How competitive can you be?
5. How new is the product to the market you have selected?
6. Are there growth opportunities in the market?
7. What do the country's demographic profile, economy, and mass culture look like right now? (Its macroeconomic indicators such as GDP growth, employment, and birth rates will give you an overview of the state of the economy and population.)
8. Are there demographic, economic, or cultural trends that will shape the market in the future?
9. Does the country's government help or hinder the sale of imported goods? For example, are there any barriers to entry or to sales within the market?
10. Will the country's climate or geography present logistical problems for sales of your product of choice? For example, selling chocolates to countries with warm climates such as in Brazil.
11. Does the product have to be adapted to your target market by way of a physical reconstruction, a new package, or a change in servicing practices? (See Chapter 6 for more details on preparing your product for export.)
12. Does the product have the same use in the international market as in the home market?
13. Does the product require personal after-sales service and, if so, can you provide it in the prospective market?

Tip Many new exporters look at where their competitors are exporting to and then investigate country and industry reports to identify the export trends and growing markets for their product or within their industry. Trade associations, US government online portals, and reports from other global organizations are an excellent source for this type of information. Because Canada and New Mexico border the United States and are a part of NAFTA, they are a good starting point for new exporters.

Use your own business sense and add to the list. Once you actually start your research, more questions will arise. This is all part of the process of turning your vague ambitions into a concrete strategy based on market realities, so the more smart questions you ask and answer, the better your chances of success.

Exporting Essentials | 45

Once you have narrowed down your options and answered all the questions, take the following steps, focusing on nine key areas (many of which—numbers 4 through 6—can be accomplished through the helpful guidance of a good logistics specialist):

1. Conduct a country assessment that examines the country's geographic, demographic, economic, cultural, political, and legal systems and infrastructure.

2. Perform a market assessment that examines the size, characteristics, and projected growth of the target market.

3. Examine your competitors' products, prices, marketing methods, and distribution channels.

4. Find out if there are any licenses or certifications needed to export to the country (refer to Chapter 13).

5. Learn about any tariffs and import regulations that will affect you (see Chapter 9).

6. Classify your product using one of the following commodity classification codes: Harmonized Tariff Schedule (HTS), Schedule B number (refer to Chapter 9), North American Industry Classification System (NAICS), or Standard International Trade Classification (SITC). Each of these classification systems allows you to assign a six- to-ten digit code to commodities so that trade data can be collected and analyzed in a consistent manner. For help with any of the terms or concepts, visit export.gov's "Trade Data & Analysis" (http://export.gov/trade-data/index.asp).

7. Determine how you will distribute your product or service (using an agent, distributor, wholesaler, or e-commerce fulfillment—more in Chapter 8).

8. Figure out your global competitive advantage. What are you bringing to the marketplace that no one else has or can offer?

9. Test demand. Do a trial shipment to an interested customer, exhibit at a trade show, participate in a catalog-only show, or utilize a foreign-partner matching service. All of these methods allow you to sample test the market, determine interest, and find out whether people will buy your product.

> **Tip** Don't rely entirely on the amount of visitors to your online platform as a predictor of the e-commerce market demand for your product or service offering. Google's Adwords program can give you an idea of how many monthly searches there are for specific keywords, say "tablet cases," or phrases that relate to your product. A high volume of searches for one specific term does not necessarily ensure high market demand for your product, but it does provide a good starting point. Once you understand the market demand for products similar to yours, you can tailor your own Web site to meet the demands of consumers who may have an interest in your product. But again, this is all tied more to e-commerce and doesn't necessarily indicate the demand of those who don't use digital for purchases.

Export Market Data: Where to Get It and How to Use It

The following resources offer a wealth of information on international trade. This list is not in any particular order; I recommend that you begin with whichever of your chosen resources is easiest to access. Once you've begun acquiring a body of knowledge, you'll have a better idea of where to direct your search. There are both physical locations and Web sites that offer information on international trade.

Physical Locations

We'll start with the physical locations where you can go to obtain information on international trade. Most of them are run by federal government organizations and have multiple branches in all of the states.

Small Business Administration

One of the most important places you should go, and many people's first stop, in order to seek high-powered export advice is your local Small Business Administration (SBA) office or the equivalent government-sponsored small business support group in your country. When you hit the bookshelves there (many directories are available online, but in person you have the benefit of the assistance of real people), you'll see directory after directory with intimidating titles like *Report FT 410* (the census), *HS Code Directory*, *Trade Profiles* (WTO Statistics Database), and so on. Luckily, the staff can help you navigate through them. Many of the people working at these organizations are retired from high-ranking positions in the corporate world and enjoy offering their years of experience to help others get a start. It's best to come armed with concrete questions to help them help you. Write down exactly what you want to know and what you want to use it for. Don't just throw up your hands and ask, "I want to export a product somewhere, can you assist?"

The export assistance available from the SBA includes training seminars and legal advice as well as answers to your questions. All export programs administered through the SBA are available through local branches. The SBA also serves as an administrative center for small business development centers; loan programs (funded by private lenders and backed by the government); and services for businesses owned by minorities, veterans, and women. Be sure to ask if you are eligible for these forms of assistance. In addition, each branch typically houses a business library, a computer center for business owners who don't own their own equipment, and an office of the Service Corps of Retired Executives (SCORE). The staff of SCORE, who work under the SBA's umbrella, can match up small businesses with mentors who have experience in foreign trade and help new or experienced exporters develop an export strategy.

Department of Commerce

Another stop should be your local branch of the Department of Commerce (DOC), which houses nineteen different Export Assistance Centers (EACs; find one by going to http://export.gov/eac/index.asp) in the United States that link to one hundred US cities and more than eighty countries worldwide by providing a comprehensive global network. The mission of the EAC network is to deliver a comprehensive array of counseling and international trade services to US firms, particularly small- and medium-sized ones. The EAC offices have the appearance and feel of a private-sector export consulting firm yet it is a federal agency that partners well with state resources and organizations that promote exports. Addresses and phone numbers for all district offices are yours for the asking. The centers give you access to the services of the US DOC, the International Trade Administration (ITA), the US Commercial Service, the Export-Import Bank of the United States, and the US Small Business Administration. Although the programs the organization offers are geared mostly toward experienced, export-ready companies looking to enter new markets, it also offers a boatload of trade and finance assistance to established small- and mid-sized businesses. One-on-one counseling is available. One of the simplest and handiest resources is the pamphlet *A Basic Guide to Exporting* issued by the US Government Printing Office (it can be purchased from http://export.gov/basicguide/). Although the guide focuses on exports from the United States, it also offers global advice on what is required to export from any point in the world. If the guide is not specific enough for you, check with the government programs that facilitate trade in your own country.

In addition to previously mentioned services, the DOC offers expert advice on export administration, trade adjustment assistance, travel and tourism, and minority businesses, to name just a few. Be sure to ask somebody about your specific situation, even if you don't see it covered here. More likely than not, there's someone who can help you. If not, you will be directed to other government service offices that can.

The following list is a sampling of information and services the DOC offers:

- Exporting seminars, webinars, podcasts, conferences, trade missions, and exhibitions
- Offering financial aid to exporters
- Providing information on emerging international-trade opportunities
- Furnishing information on export documentation requirements
- Exporting statistics
- Supplying readings on international trade
- Distributing information on licensing, patent, trademark, and protectionist practices abroad
- Providing counseling on general export marketing issues
- Offering services to help you make cross-border contacts and find agents and distributors (see Chapter 7)

US Commercial Service—An Exporter's Gold Mine

Ever wonder who gathers all that information on trends and actual trade leads? It's the US Commercial Service (USCS; http://export.gov/worldwide_us/index.asp; to find the USCS local office near you, head to http://www.trade.gov/cs/states/csinyourstate.asp). This wonderful resource is an exporter's gold mine.

There are more than 1,400 trade professionals, all eager and waiting to help you go global, who are working in USCS's 128 commercial offices, located in US embassies and consulates in more than seventy-five countries. Most of them have international experience, so they know what it takes to do business in the country in which they're stationed. They put their invaluable understanding of local culture and prospective customer contacts at the service of the small business owner interested in entering overseas markets.

I used this resource within the first couple of weeks of starting my business. It proved extremely effective. I faxed the American embassy with a specific question: I was seeking a list of reputable food-importing wholesalers that specialized in high-volume product movement throughout Japan. Within twenty-four hours I received a reply from an agriculture trade officer indicating that a list was being forwarded by airmail (well before the days of e-mail). When I received it, I was excited about its potential and began contacting the companies right away. It was an ideal way to get started.

Here are just a few of the services the USCS overseas staff will provide at no charge:

- Customer lists
- Sales representative and other agency-finding services
- Background checks on companies overseas
- Business counseling

Keep in mind that most state governments offer overseas business resource centers to help the small business executive tap into new markets. Check into these as well as the USCS—they usually work in tandem.

Web Sites Brimming with Trade Statistics

There are also many Web sites that offer a wealth of trade information.

TradeStats Express

TradeStats (http://tse.export.gov/TSE/TSEhome.aspx) provides the latest annual and quarterly trade data, including national trade data and state export data.

USA Trade Online

The Foreign Trade Division of the US Census Bureau hosts USA Trade Online (https://usatrade.census.gov/), which allows you to access current and cumulative US export and import data for more than nine thousand export commodities and seventeen thousand import commodities.

Market Research Index

Hosted by export.gov, Market Research Index (http://export.gov/mrktresearch/) provides a step-by-step guide on how to get started in market research. In addition, you can access the Market Research Library run by US Commercial Service (http://www.buyusainfo.net/adsearch.cfm?search_type=int&loadnav=no), which comprises more than one hundred thousand industry- and country-specific market reports authored by specialists working in overseas posts.

BusinessUSA

BusinessUSA (http://business.usa.gov/) is a centralized, one-stop platform designed to make it easy for businesses to access services to help them grow (through exporting) and hire, regardless of where the information is located or which agency's Web site, call center, or office they go to for help.

United States International Trade Commission

The Web site of the United States International Trade Commission (http://www.usitc.gov) aims to administer US trade-remedy laws; provide the president, the United States trade representative (USTR), and Congress with independent quality analysis, information, and support on matters relating to tariffs and international trade and competitiveness; and maintain the Harmonized Tariff Schedule of the United States. Its goal is to contribute to the development of a realistic US trade policy.

USEmbassy.gov

Run by the US Department of State, USEmbassy.gov: Websites of US Embassies, Consulates and Missions (http://www.usembassy.gov/) provides links to the Web sites of the diplomatic organizations in many countries and features business information specific to those countries.

World Trade Organization

The World Trade Organization (WTO; http://www.wto.org/) is an organization that focuses on opening up trade and sorting out trade problems as they arise. It is a forum for governments to negotiate trade agreements and a safe haven for them to settle trade disputes. It operates a system of trade rules.

Other Federal-Export Assistance Resources

There are also a handful of other organizations designed to assist you with federal exports.

Export-Import Bank of the United States

The Export-Import Bank of the United States (Ex-Im Bank; http://www.exim.gov/) is a government agency that is responsible for assisting the export financing of US goods and services through a variety of loan guarantees and insurance programs (see Chapter 11).

Foreign Agricultural Service

The Foreign Agricultural Service (FAS) of the US Department of Agriculture (http://www.fas.usda.gov/) provides a network of counselors, attachés, trade officers, commodity analysts, and marketing specialists to assist in making contacts overseas. Check with your state or regional department.

Additional Resources

There are also various other agencies that may come in handy during your search for federal-research assistance. Although you probably will not need to contact these agencies at the outset of your operations, you should know about them. They are: The Overseas Private Investment Corporation (OPIC; http://www.opic.gov/); the US Department of the Treasury (http://www.treasury.gov/Pages/default.aspx); USAID (the US Agency for International Development; http://www.usaid.gov/); and the Office of the US Trade Representative (http://www.ustr.gov/about-us/trade-tool-box/us-government-trade-agencies). Most of these resources are available through the office of your local chamber of commerce or Small Business Administration. Check the Web sites for further information.

Local Colleges and Universities

Another important resource is the colleges and universities in your state. Contact them to see what type of international assistance they offer to small businesses interested in expanding overseas. You'll find that nearly every major university offers what is referred to as a university outreach or partnership program, which extends university resources to individuals, groups, and communities. During the past few years, most campuses have focused on international development opportunities, offering services such as trade assistance, promotion of state exports, and trade research. Southern Illinois University Edwardsville (http://www.siue.edu/business/itc/), Michigan State University (http://globaledge.msu.edu/), and Bradley University (http://www.bradley.edu/academic/colleges/fcba/centers/turner/sbdc/), for example, all have programs in place. Michigan State University also offers a great resource called MPI (Market Potential Index: http://globaledge.msu.edu/knowledge-tools/mpi) to evaluate the potential of emerging markets as well as DIBS (GlobalEDGE Database of International Business Statistics: http://globaledge.msu.edu/knowledge-tools/dibs) that allows you to choose from thousands of variables in order to generate reports that synthesize and evaluate data from reliable sources.

In addition, many state and private educational institutions offer courses in exporting or going global. They may even cosponsor international trade seminars with federal agencies or private-sector organizations. If you cannot find a school in your area that offers this type of service, be sure to search the Internet.

Business Intelligence Companies

For those who find visiting agencies in person too intimidating, time consuming, or just plain old fashioned, the following business intelligence companies arm you with critical and competitive information on US waterborne trade activity through an online searchable trade database, covering international trade activities throughout the world, for a fee: PIERS (http://www.piers.com), Datamyne (http://www.datamyne.com), Zepol (http://www.zepol-com), and ImportGenius (http://www.importgenius.com).

■ **Tip** A little-known publication that is a huge source of trade data is the *Journal of Commerce* (JOC; http://www.joc.com). The magazine offers everything from a listing of the top hundred US exporters (including the top ten states exporting to China) to import/export trade leads and international trade news. What can you quickly glean from the data? Let's say you see a lot of container shipments being exported to Brazil. Why is this happening? What is the commodity? What should you be looking at or doing relative to that kind of movement?

Other Places to Look for Market-Research Help

The following resources and tools offered by organizations provide advice and insight as well as statistics on international exporting:

Foreign Trade

Produced by the US Census Bureau, Foreign Trade (http://www.census.gov/foreign-trade/) is responsible for issuing regulations governing the reporting of all export shipments from the United States. It is the official source for US export and import statistics. If you're searching for import or export statistics, information on export regulations, commodity classifications, or a host of other trade-related topics, this is the place to get the information you need.

The Export Practitioner

The Export Practitioner (http://www.exportprac.com/) is a monthly magazine devoted to providing news and analysis about the export-licensing requirements and the law-enforcement activities of the commerce, state, and treasury departments. The information provided in the advance reports help you better understand an issue and, at the same time, avoid costly legal troubles.

Ease of Doing Business Rankings

The Doing Business site, run by the International Finance Corporation and the World Bank, ranks economies on their ease of doing business, on a scale from 1 to 185 (http://www.doingbusiness.org/rankings). A high ranking on the Ease of Doing Business Index means the regulatory environment is more conducive to the starting and operation of a local firm. The index provides a bird's-eye view on the potential of exporting to a given economy, too.

The World Factbook

The World Factbook (https://www.cia.gov/library/publications/the-world-factbook/) is a reference guide produced by the Central Intelligence Agency that provides detailed information on history, people, government, economy, geography, communications, transportation, military, and transnational issues for 267 world entities.

US and World Population Clock

Produced by the United States Census Bureau of the US Department of Commerce, the US and World Population Clock (http://www.census.gov/popclock/) is a continuously updated population estimate based on earlier census figures, which serves as the leading source of quality data about the nation's people and economy.

World Bank Atlas Method

The World Bank Atlas Method (http://data.worldbank.org/about/country-classifications/world-bank-atlas-method) uses the Atlas conversion factor to minimize exchange-rate fluctuations in the cross-country comparison of national incomes.

Euromonitor International

Euromonitor International (http://www.euromonitor.com/usa) provides market research, business intelligence reports, and on data in strategy research on consumer markets.

eAtlas of Global Development

The *eAtlas of Global Development* (http://www.app.collinsindicate.com/worldbankatlas-global/en-us), produced by the World Bank, is a sophisticated online interactive tool that maps and graphs more than 175 indicators from the World Bank's development database. It allows users to easily and quickly transform data into customized visual comparisons across time, countries, and regions.

International Trade Statistics Yearbook

The *International Trade Statistics Yearbook* (http://comtrade.un.org/pb/) is a multivolume publication produced by the United Nations Statistics Division and the Department of Economic and Social Affairs that is featured on the International Merchandise Trade Statistics Web site. The yearbook provides information on the world trade of individual commodities in 2013 and features world-trade tables covering trade values and indices.

Bureau of Economic Analysis

A US Department of Commerce affiliate, the Bureau of Economic Analysis (BEA; http://www.bea.gov) promotes a better understanding of the US economy by providing timely, relevant, and accurate economic accounts data in an objective and cost-effective manner. The bureau's goal is be the world's most respected producer of economic accounts.

Binational Societies, Councils, and Trade Associations

There are also binational groups that will put you in touch with citizens of a country where you'd like to do business. You can search the Internet for the local branches. NAJAS (National Association of Japan-American Societies; http://www.us-japan.org/); the US-China Business Council (https://www.uschina.org/); and the US-India Business Council (http://www.usibc.com/), for example, all promote bilateral trade between the United States and the respective countries and also provide a stimulating social forum for people with common interests.

Check with your state to see if it has a foreign-relations or export council. Organizations like these usually assemble at least once a month, offering a forum for discussion about how to facilitate better international relations and expand trade.

Contacts made through business colleagues and associations can often also prove invaluable to exporters. Many states have associations that focus strictly on promoting world trade. Check with your local chamber of commerce to see which of these associations have chapters in your area and sit in on a meeting—and then sign up.

Additional Instant Resources

There are a number of additional online services that specialize in information about particular foreign markets, especially news about fast-breaking market opportunities in fast-changing parts of the world. When you use these services, don't forget to keep your segmentation schedule and your market-issues list close at hand.

- In addition to the previously mentioned ease of doing business rankings, the Doing Business site (http://www.doingbusiness.org/), run by the World Bank Group and the International Finance Corporation (http://www.ifc.org), provides objective measures of business regulations for local firms in 185 economies and selected cities at the sub-national level.

- When all else fails, you can go back to the days of picking up the phone and call the US Department of Commerce Trade Information Center at 1-800-USA-TRAD[E] (1-800-872-8723).

Creating an Action Plan

Once you've spent some time getting a picture of the international market for your product, you'll want to make a plan for how you're going to put your new knowledge to work. It's best to tailor your plan to your day-to-day operating style or that of your organization. If you are action oriented and like immediate and tangible results, then structure your export plan so that you'll see regular results or responses. If you are more methodical and conservative in your business habits, then structure your export plan to produce degrees of progress over a longer period of time.

Setting goals that will allow you to operate comfortably will generate regular signs of progress. For example, let's say you have no export business at present. Your goal might be to generate US$12,000 in international sales during one year. That's US$1,000 a month, or US$250 a week. When you break this annual goal down into regular increments, it begins to look reachable. There is no point in setting overambitious goals.

Tip Are you already exporting? Where to? Expanding into new markets is the next logical step. If you're currently exporting to Ireland, for example, then the United Kingdom might be a good complementary market to enter. Are you conducting business in Canada? Then try Mexico (due to NAFTA) since it's close in proximity to the United States. It's likely that similar conditions exist in other nearby markets too, indicating that your product or service could also be successful there.

Above all, your plan must be manageable for the person or persons who actually have to implement it. If you are beginning your export program as part of an existing company, it is particularly important to get and keep a top-to-bottom companywide commitment to the export project.

Once you determine the style in which you want to conduct your export activities, the sales goals you hope to attain, and how fast you want to achieve results, then draft your plan. Start with a short, specific statement that gives a comprehensive view of your program—you can break this down into more specific steps later. A simple plan might look like this:

- All Alone Becky New to Exporting, Inc.

   "I am going to e-mail product offerings to all the customers on the lists I've compiled. At the same time, I am going to ramp up marketing efforts via all social networks. I hope to receive a dozen inquiries within two weeks and at least one order within a month. If my results are not achieved within this time frame, then I will contact the appropriate government agencies and begin plans to participate in a trade show."

If your company has a larger budget and more staff resources, your statement might look more like this:

- ABC Conglomerate Exporting, Inc.

   "We are going to allocate 10 percent of our company's net profits to developing foreign markets. An export team will be appointed within three months. Informational and promotional brochures as well as pricing schedules suitable for exporting purposes will be developed during the following three months. Advertising and trade show activities will be implemented thereafter."

Summary

As you can see, preparing market research doesn't have to be elaborate. It just has to be broken down into a series of manageable courses of action to be carried out during an estimated period of time. As you implement your plan, monitor it closely and expect to adjust it along the way to meet your objectives. And remember: the most important element of the plan of all is to keep trying!

So far, you've begun to learn about international markets for your product, to tap into the enormous network of export assistance that's available to you, and to plan how you're going to put these resources to work. Now you're ready to take more ambitious measures to get in touch with serious players looking to buy what you've got to sell. If you want to catch their interest, though, you must first make sure that the product you have selected for export meets the target market's local conditions. The following chapter gives a rundown on all the details you need to consider as you prepare your product for export.

Notes

1. "Measuring Global Growth and Trade," Craig Poole, *Upside: The UPS Blog*, last modified May 24, 2013, http://blog.ups.com/2013/05/24/measuring-global-growth-and-trade/?.

2. Walter Isaacson, *Steve Jobs* (New York: Simon & Schuster, 2011), 567.

CHAPTER 5

Preparing and Adapting Your Product for the Export Marketplace

> *You may have heard the story that Coca-Cola translated into Chinese meant "bite the wax tadpole." (Some think it's an urban legend.) In fact, it's true, but the translation didn't happen in the way you might think."*
>
> —Phil Mooney, Coca-Cola Conversations[1]

Many business owners believe it is only packaging that has to be adapted in the overseas marketplace. That's a mistake. Adapting your product to meet the needs of an overseas market is a considerable undertaking and will likely require a substantial investment of time and money.

Chapter 5 | Preparing and Adapting Your Product for the Export Marketplace

In the following pages, I talk about how packaging and other product characteristics play a vital role in enabling international sales and what factors to consider when preparing your own product for export. I also include case study examples to better understand the process that goes along with modifying a product to succeed in the export marketplace.

This phase of business is very important because there are differences in both the cultural and physical environments across countries. You should expect that to some degree you will have adapt your product to sell it outside domestic markets before you make your first sale. You'll be well situated to tackle this phase after you have availed yourself of the market information resources outlined in the previous chapter, consulted with local government market experts, and communicated with various sources overseas: prospective customers, wholesalers, agents, embassies, and so on.

Studying competing products in the country where you wish to do business is a great way to target what works in that market. If you cannot visit the country and scan store shelves yourself, get in touch with the American Embassy and see if it can apprise you of what products are comparable to yours.

When it is not possible to sell the standardized products and services, a small business must adapt its product if it wants a global business. And although the changes might involve satisfying foreign countries' regulatory requirements, the biggest test is always with the end user—the customer—because that's who ultimately buys your product or service. If customers turn their noses up at your offering, even if you get regulatory approval, there will be no sales. Always keep the customer at the top of your mind and have empathy for others' point of view; it will lead to ideas for meeting cultural differences.

Case Study: Hershey's Yo-Man Satisfies the Sweet Tooth of Chinese Consumers

Hershey is currently introducing a candy to China. Known in English as the Lancaster and in Chinese as Yo-Man, it is a condensed-milk candy that Hershey expects will gain it a healthy share of an estimated ¥7.5 billion (in Chinese currency, which is equivalent to $1.2 billion) Chinese market. Premium-milk candy is considered the fastest-growing segment in China's candy market.

This is Hershey's first launch for a new brand beyond the US market. Hershey's goal is to expand its overall international sales to 25 percent of its global sales by 2017, up from its current 10 percent, which includes brand extensions and acquisitions. The company wants China to be its second-biggest market within five years.

Yo-Man will be manufactured in China by a local confectionary company in Hunan Province. Milk for the candy will be imported. Creating a new brand, and one that is specifically tailored for the Chinese market, is a good bet for

Hershey. The company could have just as easily sold its Hershey Kisses and other related branded items without making any changes to the products, but that would send a message to the Chinese consumer that Hershey doesn't care enough to suit that population's particular taste buds. Or worse, the company might turn off the audience entirely by that move—forever—and open sweet opportunities for its competitors. It's a perceptive judgment call, and Hershey has decided not to take a chance wondering *what if* and instead is doing what is right for the Chinese market, its budget, and its resources.

Checklist to Prepare Your Product for Export

So how do you go about getting your product ready for a foreign market, much like Hershey has done? Grab a sample of your export-ready product, get out your tablet to keep you organized, and let's run through some rules of thumb to prepare your own product for export:

1. *The name of your brand or product might work well in your local market but could have negative connotations in a foreign market's local language.* For example, in the 1950s, there was a Swedish car magazine called *Fart*, which in Swedish means "speed." To Americans, however, the title meant a good laugh. Check to see what the translation of your brand's name means in the language of the country you are about to enter. If you don't, you will end up with a fiasco like Chevrolet had on its hands when it introduced its new automobile called the "Nova" in Venezuela—which in Spanish means, "Doesn't go!"

2. *The colors of your packaging need to take into account cultural sensitivities.* What do the colors connote in the country of destination? Vibrant, attention-grabbing red is often thought to signify warning or danger in the United States, but in Chinese culture it represents good luck. A slick black package with touches of embossed gold or silver conveys elegance and sophistication in the United States and some newly industrialized countries, but in certain parts of Africa, for example, it suggests death! Even if your design principles have been foolproof for products to be sold in the United States, expect to have to scrap them and start fresh when it comes to marketing products abroad.

3. *Look at the overall packaging and labeling design of your product.* In addition to your color choices, your illustrations and graphics need to be appropriate, appealing, and understandable to your end user. If there is any possible way you can get opinions on your package design from actual consumers in your target market, do so. Would they buy your product on the basis of the way it looks? For example, if you put a smiling face on your package, but they take the purchase of that particular product quite seriously in their country, would your labeling be seen as trivial, cheap looking, or even offensive? Details like this matter, and they need to be thoroughly researched and addressed before shipping anything of significant value to a foreign market.

4. *The size or quantity of your product itself needs to match the export country's expectations.* Your product's size might be perfect by US standards but way too large in Japan, where the size of the typical household is very small. One Whopper may feed one American, but that same burger sold in France may make a lunch for two, or the extra burger might be tossed in the trash. If too much of your product will go to waste, it's not economical or convenient for your consumer, and they won't buy it.

CASE STUDY: GIVE CUSTOMERS WHAT THEY WANT

One of my past clients manufactured a very successful premium ice cream. Supermarkets throughout the United States could barely keep the decadent treat in their freezers because the demand was so great. The company wanted to build on this success by expanding internationally. It chose Japan as its entry point into the international market. The Japanese are exacting about quality and would appreciate this premium ice cream, it was thought.

The test shipment fell flat.

What happened? My client looked deeper into the Japanese culture and discovered some very important differences between Americans and Japanese. First, Americans prefer gallon-sized containers, while the Japanese prefer individual-sized containers, which fit better into their smaller freezers. My client also discovered that the ice cream had too much sugar for Japanese tastes.

The company tried again; this time using a reduced-sugar recipe in individual-sized containers and shipping a twenty-foot freezer container to Japan monthly. Over time, that one freezer container a month grew to ten a month, and the company's business in Japan was assured.

5. *Weights and measurements vary from country to country.* You must label your product according to local standard measurements. The metric system is considered the global standard, but double check.

6. *The standard CE mark, which ensures consumer safety, is required on many products sold in EU countries.* A manufacturer that has gone through the conformity-assessment process may then affix the CE mark to the product. If you plan to do business in a country that is part of the EU, look into the benefits of securing the union's approval, which will make your product appear safer in your target audience's eyes.

7. *Look at how and where the product is sold.* Do most consumers like to make their purchases online in your export country? Or do they prefer to go to a local convenience store to make their purchases? It's not about doing it your way. It's about doing it in a way that the consumers of the home country prefer. Take the French cosmetics company L'Oréal, which is breaking the rules but with the hope of big payoffs. In Brazil, where women prefer door-to-door sales, L'Oréal will not be using that approach. Instead, the company hopes its sales will increase by staging beauty advisors in stores where the company's products are sold. Jean-Paul Agon, the CEO of L'Oréal, is convinced the market will grow and that direct sales will become less popular. Is he attempting to make Brazilian women forget about that part of their culture? Only time will tell. Door-to-door vending is a long-standing custom in Brazil that has ushered millions of Brazilian women into the middle class. Some 2.5 million women, out of a total female workforce of 42 million, earn a living by doing direct sales in Brazil.[2]

Tip To cash in on growth in emerging markets, Facebook is making adjustments to its social platform as it expands internationally. According to the *Wall Street Journal*: "[India] has about 100 million Internet users mostly through desktops. But the real focus for digital companies will be on the group of 900 million-plus mobile-phone users, most of whom will get Web access for the first time over the coming years."[3] Think that Facebook will adjust and accommodate those folks? More than likely it will, especially if it fuels its own growth. Look for investments by Facebook that target lower-end feature phones as well as translations to Hindi and other languages.

Chapter 5 | Preparing and Adapting Your Product for the Export Marketplace

8. *Will you need to put a bilingual label on the outside of packages?* Canada requires a French-English label. Finland requires a Finnish-Swedish one. Most Middle Eastern countries require it to be in Arabic-English. You must find out! For some destinations, the first order or trial shipment requires only a sticker on the outside of the package in the language of the importing country. Generally, this sticker should state the importing agent's name and address, the weight of the package in the country's standard unit of measurement, an ingredient legend, and the expiration date if applicable.

Caution Even a close translation of your product's name might not be close enough—"Jolly Green Giant," for instance, translates into Arabic as "Intimidating Green Ogre."

---

9. *Be careful of the cultural significance attached to the number of units you place in a box.* Anytime you have a relatively small number of products packed showcase style in their box, check beforehand to make sure the quantity is not considered unlucky in the overseas market. Some countries, particularly in the West, find seven to be a lucky number and thirteen to be unlucky. In Japan, the number four is the sign of death, so packing anything four to a box will be the kiss of death for your marketing venture! (Not that you need to worry too much about the number of cookies in a single box.)

10. *Put pictures of your product on the label of your package.* A picture tells a thousand words. When Americans read "pizza" on the outside of a box, they know what's inside. But will they know what it means in New Caledonia? Probably not. Keep this in mind when you develop packaging for worldwide sales. Illustrations are acceptable, two-color pictures look nicer, but four-color photography on the label shows it like it is. Put yourself in the shoes of the prospective customer. If you don't know what's being sold, why buy it? Get visual: Images speak every language.

11. *Don't skimp on packaging material.* If your packaging is behind the times in the United States, don't think you'll be able to unload it in the world market. Customers worldwide appreciate innovation and cutting-edge technology, and they *expect* it from the United States. Don't let your customers down. Keep informed on what is the newest and best in your packaging category.

Exporting Essentials

CASE STUDY: KEEP AN EYE ON THE COMPETITION

My company used to export all-metal tins of gourmet nut snacks to Southeast Asia. We thought we were well received, until one customer asked why we didn't package our snacks like a major competitor did: that company used a composite of tin and cardboard, which was safer and lighter—desirable qualities in Southeast Asia. Once we found a supplier that could manufacture the composite tin, we ordered enough labels for both the domestic and international markets. Listening to that one customer and making that one change grew our sales in Southeast Asia more than 30 percent year over one year.

12. *Look for ways to extend current product applications.* This is where a few months of actually living in a foreign country would really pay off. It would teach you how the locals do things and what they need to be able to do things better. You may find that if you changed the speed of a kitchen mixer, a food item in China would be made better and faster than ever before. Or you might want to reconfigure an existing vacuum attachment and it would be perfect for some out-of-the-way corners in Sri Lanka. Before you set out to do business in a particular country, ask some simple questions: How do the people there like to spend their time? What are their favorite foods? How do they clean their homes? How are their clothes laundered?

13. *Make sure your electrical products are suitable and compatible for international use.* If your wired product is not adjusted to the electrical standards in your target market, you'll have all sorts of problems, especially if you have already shipped the unacceptable product! A good resource you should know about is *Electric Current Abroad* (http://www.trade.gov/publications/pdfs/current2002FINAL.pdf), a publication of the US Department of Commerce. It provides everything you need to know about electrical standards worldwide. If for some reason you don't find the information you need, contact your local chamber of commerce or a government official in the country where you are about to do business.

14. *How will you handle warranties, guarantees, consignment sales, and service calls overseas?* Anticipate what it will take to put one of these features in place not locally but globally. Can it be done? If so, map out the logistics from start to finish and determine who will be responsible. If it's not feasible, then don't offer it.

15. *Determine how the physical environment affects your product.* Humidity, high energy costs, poor water supply, extreme hot or cold temperatures, or poor infrastructure can affect how your product holds up and works in a new market. You may only need to adjust your product to withstand a damaging environment, but if it's a lot more than that you should choose a market that's a better fit. If there are no roads to move your product, you can't get anywhere. Period. Consider the differences between your home market and the foreign market. For example, when air conditioners are exported to Egypt, they must have special filters and the coolers must be sturdy enough to handle the thick dust and heat of Egyptian summers.

16. *Determine how the cultural environment affects how you market your product.* When Unilever bought Slim-Fast in 2000, it wanted to expand the company's market that existed outside North America, which accounted for more than 90 percent of its sales at the time. Unilever wanted to increase Slim-Fast's revenues fivefold by 2003. The company's strategy was to plug Slim-Fast into its global marketing and distribution system.[4] According to Smriti Chand Marketing, "When Slim-Fast was first launched in Germany, its ads used a local celebrity. In the U.K., testimonials for diet aids may not feature celebrities . . . . [Also] in the U.K. banana was the most popular flavour but this flavour is not sold in continental Europe."[5] This demonstrates the cultural effect each country has on a product and how vital it is to adapt to all the countries you export to in order to ensure that consumers love the product. Be aware of local customs and be willing to understand and accommodate any differences that can cause misunderstanding.

17. *Local product regulations need to be scrutinized.* In order to sell a product in retail stores or elsewhere, some countries require a statement on the product that indicates where it was made. Check with your prospective customers or a logistics specialist to determine if a country-of-origin label (see Chapter 13), for example, is required by law before you export a product to a foreign country.

Summary

It would be smart to determine if the anticipated export sales of your product will outweigh the expense of adapting it to the country's standards and to project how long will it take to recover the costs. You may find it more realistic, at least initially, to export your products to countries that will accept them as they are. From there, you can always grow and expand from your successes at your own pace. But keep a long-term perspective: being willing to make strategic changes to your product (a crucial attitude) will open doors to many more international markets. The risk is minimal compared to the risk of maintaining the status quo.

Tip   It's crucial for your company to remain what it is (be it German, American, Japanese), but develop an understanding and willingness to accommodate cultural differences that exist. Follow that path, and great success in the export marketplace will come your way.

Now that we've spent a good deal of time looking at getting your product ready for export, we'll shift our attention to exporting a service.

Notes

1. "Bite the Wax Tadpole," Phil Mooney, Coca-Cola Conversations, last revised March 6, 2008, http://www.coca-colaconversations.com/2008/03/bite-the-wax-ta.html.

2. "To L'Oréal, Brazil's Women Need New Style of Shopping," *Wall Street Journal*, Christina Passariello, last modified January 21, 2011, http://online.wsj.com/news/articles/SB10001424052748703951704576091920875276938.

3. "India, A New Facebook Testing Ground," Amol Sharma, *Wall Street Journal*, last modified October 20, 2012, http://online.wsj.com/article/SB10000872396390443749204578048384116646940.html.

4. "Unilever's Slim-Fast Goes From Juggernaut to Afterthought," Matthew Boyle, *Bloomberg*, last modified January 15, 2013, http://www.bloomberg.com/news/2013-01-14/unilever-s-slim-fast-goes-from-juggernaut-to-afterthought.html.

5. "5 Major Product Communications Strategies Used in International Marketing," Smriti Chand Marketing, YourArticleLibrary.com, accessed October 24, 2013, http://www.yourarticlelibrary.com/marketing-2/5-major-product-communication-strategies-used-in-international-marketing/5834/.

CHAPTER 6

Preparing Your Service for Export

Laughter is America's most important export.

—Walt Disney

You don't have to be a manufacturer to export. As you take your business into the digital age, you'll find that keeping ahead of the competition takes more than just getting your product into world markets. You'll also need to export superior services to cultivate additional strength. In this chapter, I'll discuss exporting a service and how it differs from exporting a product. In addition, I'll provide a brief look at services that have the best potential for export success, a list of the best international market prospects, and a couple of case examples.

The United States is the largest exporter of services in the world. Export.gov indicates that more than two-thirds of US small- and medium-sized exporters are nonmanufacturers. Business services alone—such as financial products, software publishing, and telecommunications—employ more than double the number of US workers in the manufacturing sector. And these jobs are not just ordinary blue-collar positions. They are white-collar services that involve high wages, high skills, high technology—and high growth! Because of this, the United States is likely to retain these jobs.

According to the *Wall Street Journal*, "Nearly a third of all U.S. exports this year [2014] will be services—everything from higher education to software to tourism. In 2013 America ran its 20th consecutive surplus in services trade with the rest of the world, a record $231.3 billion driven by a record $699.4 billion in services exports according to the Bureau of Economic Analysis."[1] During the next five years, 87 percent of world economic growth is forecasted to take place outside of the United States, according to the International Monetary Fund.[2] Service exports are vital for high economic growth.

And there is every indication that the growth will continue in the years ahead, with many countries currently emerging from a period of economic weakness and showing a strong demand for American know-how as well as American-made goods. As long as countries' local currencies remain fairly stable and technology continues to advance, this demand will continue to rise, notwithstanding the ups and downs of the US dollar. Service exports typically don't face tariffs, as goods sold overseas often do.

AN EXAMPLE OF A SERVICE EXPORT: HUNTINGTON BANK PROVIDES EXEMPLARY SERVICES

Take Huntington Bank, the winner of the 2013 President's E Star Award for export service. Presented by the Department of Commerce's International Trade Administration, the award is the highest recognition any US entity can receive for supporting export activity. Huntington was recognized as demonstrating a sustained commitment to the expansion of exporting by offering manufacturers the ability to finance foreign buyers who want to buy American products. The bank also developed an export-finance capability by actuating its delegated lending authority under the US Export-Import Bank Working Capital Program. Huntington has provided a mix of international services, trade services, and foreign exchange since the mid-1970s. The bank also received the E Star Award in 1982.

There are, however, some nontariff barriers that do exist for service exports, such as safety standards, customs procedures, and regulatory hurdles (specific to investment trade), that can make it difficult but not insurmountable for an attorney, accountant, designer, or architect to work abroad.

Still, exporting a service attracts customers because the service usually offers original knowledge—and knowledge is power these days. People are starting new e-ventures every day, purely on the basis of a business model offering superior know-how and great ideas. Disseminating that knowledge aggressively and at a profit worldwide is a winning formula for global success. With technology advancing at lightning speed, and worldwide communications becoming faster and easier with every passing day, now is an ideal time to consider this business avenue.

Fact According to the *Wall Street Journal*, "Services are much more important than hitherto believed. They account for about 40% of international trade on a value-added basis, double the total that shows up in balance-of-payments statistics."[3]

Exporting a Product vs. Exporting a Service: Is There a Difference?

Throughout this book, we have focused on exporting a product—one that you can see, hold, easily assign a monetary value to, and transport from Point A to Point B. Exporting a service, such as one that is business-oriented, professional, technical, financial, or franchise- or insurance-based, requires a somewhat different approach. Here's a quick rundown of the differences between a product and a service that affect the export process (again presenting the table we looked at in Chapter 1 in order to jog your memory):

Product	Service
Tangible	Intangible
Visible	Invisible
Measurable	Immeasurable
High perceived value	Low perceived value
Transportable—freight costs	Transportable—negligible freight costs
Negligible human interaction	High human interaction
Low maintenance	High maintenance
High standardization	Negligible standardization

To revisit our discussion in the first chapter, you cannot see or touch a service, it's invisible,—and you often cannot assess its true value until after you have used it and discovered all the resulting benefits. A service is in many ways a tougher sell than a product, either at home or abroad. Each of the listed ways in which services differ from products creates a marketing challenge for the service exporter, perhaps the most crucial being the need to convince a distant customer to buy your service sight unseen and without any real idea of how he will benefit. This is why a service business depends first and foremost on people. Of course, when you export a product, you are also relying on a whole string of people to do their jobs—bankers to help you get paid, freight forwarders to move your goods, local distributors to get your product on store shelves—but exporting a service demands a special emphasis on human interaction, both at home and abroad.

People Power Drives Your Service Exports

Selling a service successfully requires even more people power than selling a product. A service export requires direct interaction with your customer, not just initially but for the duration of the service contract. And for some services, of course, the quality of the interaction with your customers is exactly what they're paying for. This is why people with superior communication skills, diplomacy, and—this can't be emphasized enough—acute cultural awareness are the single-greatest asset for delivering a quality service export. Having the technology in place to deliver the service is important, too!

Tip Never increase customer expectation, such as offering free expedited shipping or a discount on work, to the point where you cannot deliver on your promises! That does not make for a satisfied customer. It creates a ticked-off customer who never returns.

Which Services Are Best for Export?

As with a product, if your service is a success locally, it is a likely candidate to be successful elsewhere—but you'll need to do appropriate research to choose the new market most likely to respond well. (Also, just as with your product export, check the Export Administration Regulations [EAR] that can be found at the US Bureau of Export Administration [BXA] beforehand to find out if you need an export license [discussed in Chapter 13] to perform your service abroad.)

Your service should, of course, be relatively unique and difficult to come by in your target market. Services like a manicure at a beauty salon or a last-minute oil change at a car dealer, for example, are essential, but they are unlikely candidates for export because the skill level required to do them is very basic, plus the services themselves lack novelty. It's all too easy for local operators to duplicate these services, so why should customers seek them beyond their own borders?

According to export.gov,[4] the following highly skilled and specialized services offer infinite export opportunities because they are in demand worldwide:

- *Architectural, construction, and engineering services:* This sector requires special skills in operations, maintenance, and management with expertise in specialized fields, such as electric power utilities, construction, and engineering services. "There is this huge infrastructure boom where these big, fast-growing economies are going to need to build out their roads, sewers, telecommunications networks, factories, airports, harbors, you name it," says J. Bradford Jensen, an economist at the Peterson Institute for International Economics. "All those projects require armies of architects, engineers, project managers, financial insurers. These are all the kinds of tradable services that we have an advantage in providing."[5]

- *Financial services:* These services include banking, insurance, securities, leasing, and asset management. US financial institutions, for example, are very competitive internationally, particularly when offering account management, credit card operations, and collection management.

- *Commercial, professional, technical, and business services:* This sector encompasses accounting, advertising, public relations, design, and legal and management consulting services. The international market for those services is expanding at a more rapid rate than the US domestic market. It is estimated that there are already 2.4 billion Internet users worldwide—but that figure represents only about 34 percent of the world's population.

- *Education and training services:* Management training, technical training, and English language training are areas in which US expertise remains unchallenged.

- *Entertainment and media:* Films that are made in the United States and music that is recorded in the country have been very successful in appealing to audiences worldwide.

- *Environmental services:* The United States is the largest producer and consumer of environmental technologies in the world. Environmental technologies are generally defined as the goods and services that generate revenue on the basis of environmental protection (pollution), assessment, compliance with environmental regulations, pollution control, waste management, design and operation of environmental infrastructure, or provision and delivery of environmental resources.

- *Healthcare*: "Healthcare is a steadily growing industry with an approximate value of $117.4 billion exported from the U.S. in 2011, which has risen almost 26% since 2007," according to export.gov. "With the recent rapid growth of emerging markets such as Brazil, Russia, India and China there exists a tremendous opportunity for U.S. companies to successfully expand into the international arena."[6]

- *Retail and wholesale trade*: The wholesale trade sector is made up of establishments engaged in wholesaling merchandise. The retail trade sector comprises establishments engaged in retailing merchandise and may include integral functions such as packaging, labeling, or other marketing services.

- *Supply chain and distribution*: The United States wants to secure a more efficient and integrated approach to supply chain issues, which will involve leveraging the capabilities and resources of the US distribution network to bring competitive service offerings to other world markets.

- *Telecommunications and information services*: The United States leads the world in marketing new technologies and enjoys a competitive advantage in online services, computer consulting, and systems integration. This sector includes companies that generate, process, and export e-commerce activities, such as e-mail, funds transfer, and data interchange, as well as data processing, network services, electronic information services, and professional computer services.

- *Travel and tourism*: This is the largest single category of service exports within the United States. According to the National Export Initiative, "In 2012, more than 66 million international tourists visited the United States, generating an all-time record of $168 billion in revenue—an increase of 10 percent from 2011. Travel and tourism accounted for 8 percent of all U.S. exports and 27 percent of all service exports in 2012."[7] The industry is diverse and encompasses services in transportation, lodging, food and beverage, recreation, and purchase of incidentals consumed while in transit.

- *Transportation, shipping, distribution, and logistic services*: This sector encompasses aviation, ocean shipping, inland waterways, railroads, trucking, pipelines, and intermodal services, as well as ancillary and support services in ports, airports, rail yards and truck terminals.

There are also other services, such as passenger fares and royalties and license fees, for instance, that can be exported. For more information, visit the "Trade Data Basics" page on the International Trade Administration Web site at http://www.trade.gov/mas/ian/referenceinfo/tg_ian_001872.asp#service.

Top Service-Export Destinations by Volume

The Bureau of Economic Analysis indicates the following are the top ten countries receiving the largest amount of service exports from the United States[8]:

- Canada
- United Kingdom
- Japan
- China
- Ireland
- Mexico
- Germany
- Switzerland
- Brazil
- France

Targeting the countries that are known to be the most receptive to US service exports will allow you to capitalize on the strengths of particular countries, adapt accordingly, and succeed.

WHERE TO GET HELP

The same agencies that can help you get your product-export business up and running can advise you on marketing your service internationally. Start with the US Department of Commerce. If appropriate, it will direct you to export councils, US export assistance centers, or trade-development industry specialists. If, by some chance, these export-specific agencies are unable to help you, ask them for a referral to other government organizations or private-sector companies that have experience in service exports.

Chapter 6 | Preparing Your Service for Export

> ▪ **Caution** Don't get paranoid about how you are going to get paid on a service export. It's true that since a service doesn't have a form of collateral, financial institutions may be less willing to provide financial support to your company. However, many public and private institutions will provide financial assistance to creditworthy service exporters. Ask. By the way, try my method: Ask your customers for one-third of the payment upfront, one-third in the middle of the project, and one-third upon completion. This can be secured through your bank, provided you ask for help, have a legitimate business opportunity, and a good credit history.

Planning for and Overcoming Market Barriers

Whether you are exporting a product or service, it is a given that you will have to confront numerous market barriers—governmental, practical, cultural, and economic. These barriers can be quite challenging, not to mention extremely frustrating, to a new-to-export service company. To overcome them and beat out the competition, you will need to plan on being aggressive and persistent and taking longer to establish a business presence than you may have expected to have to do. If you cannot make any progress despite your best efforts, you may find you need to target another region or country for your export operation. Let's get acquainted with the barriers:

1. *Government*: Red tape, bureaucracy, bribes, infringements of copyrights, trademarks or patents, and special rules that only the natives seem to know about—these are just a few of the government-generated barriers you'll encounter. For example, you might discover that your target market has a labor regulation stating that whenever there is a locally funded project, local experts must be hired for any specialized services that are required. Or there might be restrictions aimed at a specific industry, like accounting, which tends to rule out foreign participation. Sometimes you will make dozens of solicitations that will go unanswered—and you'll never know why. The most notorious barrier is the governmental regulation that locals never comply with even though, for some reason, they've never caught. However, when you try to export, the regulation is enforced just rigorously enough to leave would-be exporters out of the trade loop. These slippery, elusive protectionist practices are very real, and they may well end up compelling you to take your business elsewhere.

2. *Local practice and custom*: Before you export your service, you must conform to global industry standards. If your service depends on scientific accuracy, for example, you need to perform any calculations using metric measurements and notation. If you don't, your proposal might get ignored because of your lack of compliance with local practices. Presenting your proposal in the local language is an obvious necessity if you want it to be read and understood. If you don't know the language, hire someone who does and get a high-quality translation.

3. *Cultural differences*: Sometimes differences between the types of media used in different cultures can present barriers if not used in a way valued by the other culture. Look closely at the photographs and print copy for an advertising campaign you are about to launch abroad, examine the materials you are about to use for an interior design project, and think through the pictures you have selected for your client's Web site. Are any of these items offensive in any way? If they are, then edit accordingly. If you don't know, find out from someone who does before you implement the service package.

4. *Economic*: One surefire giveaway that your target country is economically unstable is the situation where you are locked solidly into a deal and then find out that your customer is slow to pay or doesn't pay at all! Also, watch out for infrastructure factors that may apply in another country, such as astronomical prices for land, making it impossible to start a building project; undrinkable water, making it impossible to open up a tourist bar; or electrical service that is so scant and unreliable that additional power generators are needed to keep things running smoothly. All these factors present very serious barriers for your service business.

Seven Ways to Launch Your Service

When you set out to enter a market with your service export, you will face four critical questions: How are you going to get a foot in the door? How are you going to get noticed by prospective customers? How are you going to keep your foothold once you're there? And how are you going to do it all inexpensively? Here are some ideas that may help you answer all four questions:

1. *Create new working relationships.* It may take a new working relationship to get your service business underway in another country. For example, in preparation for its upcoming IPO, Twitter is aiming to expand its international footprint. It will use its Dublin location as a main hub for expansion into other European countries and will double its existing workforce of a hundred people by 2014.[9] Twitter has even started sending key executives from its San Francisco headquarter office to markets it desires to enter, such as France and Singapore, to spearhead global growth. You should use a similar strategy when you export a product and it is extra important to do in launching a service business: find out who's already operating where you want to be, see what they can do for you, and figure out how you're going to make it an attractive proposition.

2. *Consider an acquisition, joint venture, partnership, or franchise.* You can purchase, jointly own, partner with, or assign rights to a company that is operating in a country where you wish to do business. Discuss with your tax and legal advisors. If you can't work out one of these relationships, try working for the company as a consultant first, and then attempt to obtain an equity stake.

3. *Expand your services to your existing domestic clients that have a global presence.* One of the simplest ways to get a foothold in international markets is to follow your local customers to their international branch offices instead of starting an independent base of operations from scratch. It means a lot less risk for you, especially financial risk. If you'd like to try this route, find yourself a good confidant within a firm for which you are serving as a consultant. He can notify you well in advance of any future projects that may involve crossing national boundaries.

4. *Approach foreign companies operating in the United States.* If you have not yet performed a service for a global conglomerate, look for one that can take you where you want to go. If it has a presence in the United States, it is highly likely that it has already selected other foreign sites for further expansion.

5. *Learn the language of your target market.* You will have an incalculable advantage if you already speak your prospective customers' native tongue. You can at least be sure they will understand you! Try marketing your expertise in the area where your parents or grandparents were born. If you mention your ancestral ties to a prospective client, it may enhance her comfort level with you and make her more receptive to your solicitation.

6. *Seek representatives or agents.* Look for local professionals who perform a similar but noncompeting service, train them, and then hire them on a consultancy basis. Make sure your expertise adds value to their service package and vice versa—perhaps you can offer their specialization to your customers in the United States. It can be a global-sales and profit booster for you both as well as a relatively simple and inexpensive program to launch.

7. *Become a virtual consultant (also known as teleconsultant).* Market your knowledge and skills via telecommunications such as e-mail, Skype, Twitter, business apps, or the Internet. Don't dismiss any medium as obsolete—each has its own place in the business of global interaction and each will enhance your power to communicate, making you more efficient and responsive to your global customers. And don't forget to use digital platforms for marketing. For example, design yourself a Web site where private individuals as well as companies can read all about your service. Anyone who responds is a potential client!

An Example of a Service Export: A Wildflower-Nursery Business that Also Exports a Service

Neil Diboll runs Prairie Nursery (http://www.prairienursery.com/store/), a nursery that sells wildflowers and other native plants that many people dismiss as weeds. These products are tough and well suited to climates like the Midwest in the United States, where temperatures in May, for example, can swing anywhere from as low as 40°F at night to as high as 80°F during the day.

Think Diboll can export a service tied to the nursery? You bet. And that's exactly what he has done so that he can operate a company that is more than a nursery. His team offers garden designs and customized advice that can be purchased from anywhere in the world, provided that person has access to the Internet. If you want an ecologically grown green roof or a backyard meadow, he will consult with you remotely or virtually via the Internet. Many product-based businesses have complementary services that can be exported.

To get the word out, use images—they have no language barrier. Every time Diboll does a great job creating a new garden for a client, he can take a picture and share it via Instagram, Pinterest, Facebook, and Google+. That's how his work gets discovered and how his service becomes in demand worldwide!

INTERNET MARKETS SUPPORTED BY GOVERNMENT

Here is a listing of Internet markets where commercial service officers can help guide you in Internet sales. What this means is that if you have a service export, you can receive greater support in each of these countries via the Internet[10]:

- Brazil
- Canada
- China
- Czech Republic
- India
- Japan
- Malaysia
- Mexico
- South Korea
- Spain

Summary

As technology continues to grow, the market for service exports is only going to get bigger—making us all the more responsible and accountable for knowledge outcomes. Countries would benefit from adopting policies that increase service exports, improve productivity, and promote service-export performance. Breaking into export markets is a major achievement, but it's what you do once you're there that makes all the difference in whether you'll be an also-ran or an industry leader. Remember: if you're working hard on customer service, as I've been encouraging you to do, you're already a service exporter. See how far you can take it—and how far it can take *you*.

Next, let's take a look at one of the most important topics in the book: how to find customers outside of your country.

Notes

1. "The Free Trade Way to Job Growth," accessed October 23, 2014, http://online.wsj.com/articles/matthew-j-slaughter-the-free-trade-way-to-job-growth-1412250623.

2. "NUSACC: Trade Outlook, accessed October 29, 2013, http://www.nusacc.org/knowledgebase/trade-data-tpid=14&stid=26,27&pid=192.php.html.

3. "The Red-Tape 'Spaghetti Bowl' Hurts Trade: One Country Producing a Good from Start to Finish for Export? The Idea Is Obsolete," Razeen Sally, *Wall Street Journal*, last modified May 28, 2013, http://online.wsj.com/news/articles/SB10001424127887324310104578509103306337848.

4. "Chapter 9: Exporting Services," access date October 29, 2013, http://export.gov/basicguide/eg_main_043087.asp.

5. "Should the U.S. Focus on Exporting Services?," New York Times, *New York Times*, last modified April 11, 2012, http://india.blogs.nytimes.com/2012/04/11/some-urge-u-s-to-focus-on-selling-its-skills-overseas/.

6. "Health Technologies," export.gov, accessed October 25, 2013, http://export.gov/industry/health/.

7. "Fact Sheet: National Export Initiative," Commerce.gov, United States, Department of Commerce, last modified May 24, 2013, http://www.commerce.gov/news/fact-sheets/2013/02/19/fact-sheet-national-export-initiative.

8. "Cross-Border Trade in 2012 and Services Supplied Through Affiliates in 2011," US Department of Commerce, Bureau of Economic Analysis, U.S. Trade in Services (PDF file), accessed October 29, 2013, http://www.bea.gov/scb/pdf/2013/10%20October/1013_international_services.pdf.

9. "Twitter to Double Its European HQ Ranks," Mike Isaac, All Things D, accessed October 25, 2013, http://allthingsd.com/20130927/twitter-to-double-its-european-hq-ranks/.

10. "Top Internet Markets FAQ," export.gov, accessed October 25, 2013, http://export.gov/sellingonline/eg_main_020794.asp.

CHAPTER

7

Finding Cross-Border Customers

> *The purpose of a business is to get and keep a customer. Without customers, no amount of engineering wizardry, clever financing, or operations expertise can keep a company going.*
>
> —Theodore Levitt, a late marketing professor at the Harvard Business School[1]

Finding customers for your export product and services can be accomplished through a range of programs, largely government sponsored, including trade shows, trade missions, and related trade-networking services. I'll introduce a number of these services to you and explain how you can take advantage of them.

This section is one of my favorites because, as Levitt says, you can't keep a company going without customers, and most books on international trade never provide a specific course of action on how to find them. I've been in your shoes and know the struggles that come with starting an export venture, so use me as a resource to help you get started. Get out your customer compass (sounds like a great new product idea!), and let's go. I want this part to be fresh, fun, relevant, and accessible to everyone everywhere.

Define Your Cross-Border Customers

As we discussed in Chapter 4, the goal of the export research you did is to help you select a likely market for your products, envision your end user, and refine your product or marketing strategy, if need be. This usually involves learning the demographics of your targeted consumer in the country you are about to enter and considering how to reach them in the most efficient manner.

Caution By now, you better know what is important to a consumer when she makes a purchasing decision related to your product or service, because if you don't (and if Theodore Levitt were alive today, he would most likely agree), your best intention will not satisfy, nor woo, the extremely selective, busy, and value-conscious visitors to your online properties.

Learning about consumer trends is another means of helping you to determine where your product belongs and predict how successful it will be. Another goal of your research has been to assemble information about your first tier of customers—in other words, the intermediaries or end users who will actually purchase your product. Regardless of whether you are selling direct or indirect, your customers will tend to fall into one of five categories, which I will get to later.

However you move your product, it's important to be aware of how many intermediaries will be involved in getting your product or service to your consumers. Each one will add his markup to the price of your product in order to earn his due profit. You need to take this into consideration when you price your product, so that it won't end up being excessively expensive by the time it actually hits store shelves or arrives at a consumer's door. The most attractive import won't be able to compete with local products if it costs more than a consumer is willing to pay.

There are five different categories of customers I will talk about in this chapter: the distributor or importing wholesaler, the overseas agent or representative, the overseas retailer, the overseas end user, and the trading company.

Let's start first with the large-volume customer.

Distributor or Importing Wholesaler

A distributor buys products from you (the seller or exporter in this case) in large volumes, and then warehouses, distributes, and resells them to its customers. It also takes care of after-sales service. It is the most common first-tier buyer you will find and can offer the most efficient and profitable way to get your product to the consumer.

> **Note** Don't get too bogged down with titles and terminology. They vary from country to country. In Japan, for example, distributors are referred to as wholesalers.

When evaluating prospective distributors, look for the following critical characteristics:

1. They trade in the geographic areas where you want to sell your product.
2. They have experience in importing, selling, marketing, and promoting your type of product.
3. They have distribution channels in place that will reach your targeted consumer.
4. They distribute products that are similar to yours but are noncompeting.
5. They are large enough in size to accomplish the desired results.
6. They have the financial strength to meet the demands of your business over the long haul.
7. They have a substantial number of sales outlets and a record sales performance.
8. They have facilities to warehouse your products.
9. They have a reputation in the marketplace for scrupulous honesty, reliability, and regular customer service.
10. They deliver the kind of after-sales follow-through you'll be proud to have associated with your product.
11. They understand local culture, know how to negotiate the ins and outs of government regulations, and might even have helpful political connections.

After you find a distributor or two that match this criteria, I recommend that you meet with each one—preferably in person, or via Skype if you are conserving expenses—and decide which one comes closest to sharing your views on market penetration.

You will be establishing an important and long-term relationship, ideally, and that means you should find out everything you can about them well before you structure any contract. When you interview them, use the following list of questions as a guide:

1. How long have you been in business?
2. Can you share a few success stories about similar yet noncompeting products you have sold?
3. Have you represented other foreign companies? Explain what you did.
4. How long has your relationship lasted with the top three companies you represent?
5. How will our line fit in or complement your existing portfolio of products?
6. What's your game plan for building our brand in your country?
7. Do you have good market coverage, including a trained and educated sales force?
8. What specific territory, customer type, or product range are you interested in covering (either exclusively or nonexclusively)?
9. Can you deliver on pre-agreed sales targets?
10. Where do you see our brand in three, five, and ten years?

Tip Conducting serious due diligence on a distributor who intends to buy a large volume from you consistently over the course of years can spare you from headaches later on. You don't want to doubt your partner throughout the relationship. The relationship should be fluid, trusting, adventurous, and growth oriented.

Prequalifying Distributors

Once you have found a distributor, how do you prequalify it beyond your interview process to ensure that it is a reputable organization? These helpful resources will give you some tips:

1. *Country Riskline Report:* (http://www.dnb.com/risk-management/international-risk/14909183-1.html). A Dun & Bradstreet (D & B) service that provides an in-depth analysis of political, commercial, and economic risk covering of doing business in a single country.

2. *The Million Dollar Database:* (MDDI; http://www.mergentmddi.com). Also put out by D & B, this database provides a flexible gateway to a database of 1.6 million international business records from outside the U.S. and Canada.

3. *USEmbassy.gov: Websites of U.S. Embassies, Consulates, and Diplomatic Missions:* (http://www.usembassy.gov). This Web site provides a list of US embassies in other countries. Contact the one in the country in which you hope to do business and run your prospective customer's name by the people there, just in case they know anything. You'll be surprised at how willing they will be to help.

4. *International Business Credit Reports from Experian.com:* (http://www.experian.com/b2bglobal). Experian provides global information on a wide range of businesses from more than 225 countries. The suite offering consists of three products: the *United Kingdom Risk Report,* the *European Company Report,* and the *International Developed Report.* Pricing varies based on the complexity of the inquiry and the country.

5. *ICP:* (http://www.icpcredit.com/). International Company Profile provides international credit-status reports, company profiles, and business information on companies all over the world, especially in the emerging markets. Pricing varies based on the region and delivery time but generally starts around US $75.

Once you have qualified several prospective distributors and found a good one that can carry out your export action plan, you're ready to discuss an export business contract. Consult with your international attorney to set up a contractual agreement that establishes terms of mutual cooperation and assures you of an exclusive market, product type, or customer type for a specified period of time with defined sales performance targets. Commit to a minimum of one year so that you have time to see how well you and the distributor work together. You should also monitor sales performance closely during this time. If sales are satisfactory and both parties are agreeable, you can extend the agreement as often and as long as you wish. As Harris says, clearly defining the sales quotas and performance targets is essential because failure of the distributor to meet the minimum for a certain period might result in termination, which could later become your way out if the relationship is not working.

Overseas Agent or Representative (Importer)

An overseas agent works on a commission basis (ranging from 2.5 to 15 percent) to locate buyers for your product, which is considered indirect exporting (more in Chapter 8). It involves selling to an intermediary, who in turn, arranges the sale of your products either directly to customers or to importing wholesalers. Once a buyer is found, however, customer service and all transaction logistics, including setting up payment and arranging transportation, become your responsibility. The agent oversees your work, stays in close contact with the customer, and will step in to assist on behalf of either party if needed. The advantage of this type of working relationship is that you have a fair degree of control over price and who your customers are.

Since overseas agents, sometimes considered foreign country brokers, typically have a vast knowledge of a target market along with solid relationships with customers, they can easily identify and exploit opportunities for your enterprise—from tracking demographic trends, to announcing radical customer shifts, to identifying emerging hot new products in any given country. The trick to working effectively with agents or reps is to stay in close contact by e-mail, telephone, or Skype and set expectations in writing right at the outset.

To find agents, work with the US Commercial Service, check online sourcing platforms such as Alibaba (http://www.alibaba.com) and Global Sources (http://www.globalsources.com), inquire with the international trade team at your bank for recommendations, reach out to industry trade-show executives who have access to the exhibitors and buyers who attend, and conduct a search via the Internet—by typing in "Sales agent, UK, pet supplies," for example. Many of the ways to find an overseas agent are similar to those that I will look at in Chapter 8 in my discussion of export management companies (EMCs).

Note Using a company's own sales force will exert the most international control, but often for small businesses it is at a cost that is not affordable. Using overseas agents, representatives, and distributors is a prudent stepping-stone for testing the market and learning whether your product and services can be sold successfully first through someone who knows the market better than you do.

Overseas Retailer

You can sell your products directly to overseas retailers, such as department stores, supermarkets, or mail-order houses on either an exclusive or nonexclusive basis. However, retailers are generally small in size, service only a regional location, and have limited warehouse space. This means that their purchases are usually small and they can only give your product limited geographic distribution. Larger retailers like Costco, Walmart, and Sears have the capability to import directly but rarely do because of the challenges it presents (local culture and tastes vary from country to country), so you will still need to appoint a local agent or distributor to service the local on-demand needs of the small and big firms alike.

Alternatively, small businesses with ties to major domestic retailers (Toys "R" Us, Costco, and Target, for example) may also be able to use them to sell abroad. Many large American retailers maintain local buying offices and use these offices to sell abroad when practical.

Overseas End User

You can sell your products directly to certain types of end users, such as hospitals, universities, or original equipment manufacturers. They, in turn, may resell your products to their customers or incorporate them into their own manufacturing processes.

Buyers can be identified at trade shows, through international-trade publications, or through your local US Export Assistance Center (http://export.gov/eac/). When you sell directly to an overseas end user, you are responsible for shipping, collecting payment, and after-sales service unless other arrangements are made.

Trading Company

As I note in the next chapter, you can sell your products directly through a trading company, which resells them to its customers. Trading companies such as Jardines (Hong Kong) and Mitsui & Co. (Japan) have long histories as import intermediaries in the development of international trade between countries. They are virtually identical to export management companies (EMCs), but they tend to function on a more demand-driven basis; that is, the demand of the market compels them to buy specific commodities. Trading companies usually have long-standing customers for whom they source products on a regular basis and these customers can be located not just in one country but all over the world. Nowadays, some people refer to trading companies as global B-to-B traders that specialize in one commodity and in one market with strong logistics capabilities. (An example would be eTransWorld [http://www.lexecongroup.com/etransworld.php].)

Trading companies, better known in Japan as *sogo shosha* companies, are useful for establishing contacts or making introductions for you, but they are rarely qualified to do extensive marketing of your product. This is because they tend to be huge, loosely structured organizations that lack both the appropriate investment funds and the focused commitment to bring a product to market. Their efforts show very little continuity, which means poor repeat business. If you use a trading company and it develops some business for you, consider meeting the customers it finds in person, taking responsibility for the sales, and doing the marketing and distribution yourself. It could be a great way to lay the groundwork for future direct sales.

Note Many large trading companies maintain buying offices in the United States and use these offices to sell abroad when practical.

Now that you know who your customers are, let's talk about how you're going to meet them.

Making Customer Contacts—Composing Your Inquiry

When a large-volume customer, such as an overseas wholesaler, contacts you or you contact him either by snail mail or over the Internet, always respond promptly and completely. Include the following materials and information:

1. *A cover letter*: It should establish your credentials as a reliable and reputable supplier in the industry. I always suggest e-mailing a scanned, signed copy of the letter and then sending the original via airmail, especially if you have attractive letterhead and marketing materials. (If snail mailing, attach your business card.)

2. *Product specification and pricing sheets*: These should provide enough information for the customer to make an intelligent decision as to whether or not he wants to continue communicating with you. Your letter to the customer might look like this:

Dear [Name of Customer]:

Thank you for your interest in our _____ product line. We have enclosed product catalogs and special export pricing for your review. Additional information can be found at our Web site called _____, located at _____, on our Facebook page at _____, on our LinkedIn page at _____, and on our Google+ page at _____. You can visit us on Twitter, too: _____.

Our company was established in 1974 and has been serving customers worldwide with quality products since then. We have the manufacturing capacity to keep up with demand. In addition, we only require a fourteen-day lead time to produce any quantity you might wish to order.

We look forward to your reply and the opportunity to do business with you.

Sincerely,

[Your Name]

Your goals here are very basic: to identify yourself, to reference the inquiry, to provide the information requested, to establish yourself as a solid, reputable institution, and to respectfully express your interest in entering into a relationship with the company. A lot of this information might already be featured on your Web site, but when it comes to specifically tailored information, such as pricing, it's best to respond directly and with a personal touch.

I've already discussed a number of sources from which you are likely to obtain lists of likely customers in the course of your market research. Start e-mailing inquiries to the customers on your lists and keep adding new names. Meanwhile, the following are some high-powered services and activities that can put you directly in touch with people who are actively seeking products like yours.

Next, I'll cover some valuable US Department of Commerce's International Trade Administration programs that help companies succeed in export markets around the world.

Gold Key Matching Service

Start with the most useful program: the Gold Key Matching Service (http://export.gov/salesandmarketing/eg_main_018195.asp), a US Commercial Service.

Chapter 7 | Finding Cross-Border Customers

For a small company with a reasonable budget, the Gold Key Matching Service (GKMS)—which is run by the US Department of Commerce, US Commercial Service—is one of the most efficient ways to meet with prescreened potential cross-border business associates, whether you are seeking an agent, distributor, or joint-venture partner. The service arranges individual meetings, most taking place at the US embassy in the host country. Many companies say that this is a wise investment because you pay only for your airfare, lodging, and entertainment and have a series of productive meetings already set up.

Many businesses could benefit from learning more about the GKMS. Every year, the US Commercial Service helps thousands of national companies navigate the challenges of exporting goods and services worth billions of dollars. Located in 109 cities across the United States and in US embassies and consulates in more than seventy-five other countries, its global network of trade professionals opens doors that no one else can. First and foremost, it can connect US companies with international buyers worldwide. After all, isn't that what you are after: *finding customers the world over?*

The GKMS will also help you with:

- Creating custom market reports and industry briefings to target the best trade prospects and opportunities with the help of trade specialists

- Conducting market research that pertains to a specific country and examines cultural issues, analyzes market potential and size, and includes market-entry strategies for your product or service offering

- Performing due diligence on foreign competitors

- Setting up appointments with prospective trading partners in key industry sectors

- Conducting effective debriefings with trade specialists and assisting in developing appropriate follow-up strategies

- Booking international travel, accommodations, interpreter service, and clerical support

- Arranging participation in trade shows sponsored by state and federal agencies

---

Tip If you are operating on a shoestring budget and cannot afford to travel internationally, the GKMS also offers a video service whereby you can receive all the same benefits but you meet your potential business partners via videoconferencing instead of in person. Inquire.

Gold Key Service in India

Let's say you are interested in visiting India with the intention of eventually doing business there. (In 2012, the United States saw exports of nearly $42 billion to India, an almost 8 percent increase over 2011.[2]) First, you would need to brush up on India (to do this, you could go to http://export.gov/india/doingbusinessinindia/index.asp) and then review the "Frequently Asked Questions" and look at "I am an American company and want to export to India. Where do I start?" (http://export.gov/india/frequentlyansweredquestions/index.asp). Next, you would get in touch with the Gold Key Service for India (http://export.gov/india/servicesforu.s.companies/goldkeyservice/index.asp), which will assist you in identifying attractive opportunities tailored to your business and arrange appointments with prescreened key players in the Indian market.

The service can help you set up appointments with your choice of agents and distributors; importing wholesalers in your industry; key governmental officials; service experts (e.g., bankers, consultants, and lawyers); potential Indian partners' trade associations; joint venture specialists; and major end users. It's up to you and what your business needs are. GKS makes it easy to enter the market and does most of the work, if not all, at a modest fee.

Fees vary depending on company size and the scope of service, but for standardized services they typically are as follows (the prices are as of 2013): $700 for a small- to medium-sized company; $350 for small- to medium-sized new-to-export companies that are using the service for the first time; and $2,300 for a large company.

Other Helpful US Government-Sponsored Programs

The Gold Key Matching Service isn't the only useful program. Here are some of the others.

The US Export Assistance Centers

The US Export Assistance Centers (EAC; http://www.sba.gov/content/us-export-assistance-centers) are staffed by professionals from the Small Business Administration (SBA), the US Department of Commerce, the US Export-Import Bank, and other public and private organizations. They can provide the help you need to find reputable distributors to compete in today's global marketplace.

Trade Leads Database

The Trade Leads Database (TLD; http://export.gov/tradeleads/index.asp) contains prescreened, time-sensitive leads and government tenders gathered through US Commercial Service offices around the world. You can search leads and receive notification when new leads are posted.

Platinum Key Service

The Platinum Key Service (PKS; http://export.gov/salesandmarketing/eg_main_018196.asp) allows US companies to take advantage of longer-term, sustained, and customized US Commercial Service assistance on a range of issues. The service can include a range of issues including but not limited to identifying markets, launching products, and developing major project opportunities. Ongoing service is available for six months, one year, or a specified time frame based on the mutually agreed upon scope of work.

International Buyer Program

The International Buyer Program (IBP; http://export.gov/ibp/) recruits thousands of qualified foreign buyers, sales representatives, and business partners to US trade shows each year, giving exhibitors an excellent opportunity to expand business globally.

International Partner Search

International Partner Search (IPS; http://export.gov/salesandmarketing/eg_main_018197.asp) will put its trade specialists, located in more than eighty countries, to work finding you the most suitable strategic partners. All you do is provide marketing material and company background information, and IPS does the work!

Business Intelligence Companies

No matter what business you are in, you will benefit tremendously from studying your competitors and working to lure their customers by offering better products or services. The following business intelligence companies offer searchable trade databases, covering international trade activities throughout the world, for a fee. They are a fantastic source of tracking what companies are exporting and to where.

As you review these sites, you must know what to look for. For example, if you want to export refurbished computers, study your competitors to find out: Are they growing? Do they have websites, blogs and other social media platforms? Do they make the news? Are they global? This doesn't mean copying every move they make. It means analyzing what your competitors are doing and then understanding why they are doing it so that you can tap into lucrative opportunities just as they are—but with a better, stronger, or new-and-improved version.

Find out where all their exports are going. You can either steal away business from them by exporting to the same location, provided you have a competitive advantage or a better value proposition (vastly improved quality, design, or price on a refurbished computer, for instance), or you can predict where they might go next and enter that market before they do. (Tread carefully here because you are on your own, carving out a new unproven market—can you do it profitably?)

If you duplicate a competitor's strategy, tweak it to accommodate your strengths and then execute it better. And don't forget to utilize the transparency of social media and social networking. See what people are saying about your competition. If there is a thread of discontent, capitalize on it with a new product or differentiate an existing product in the market where the competitor is weak. Two critical key points: Find out what works, and do it better. Find out what doesn't work, and avoid it. A few good sites to review your competitors and their strategies are the following:

- *PIERS*: (http://www.piers.com). Whether you need to conduct market research, generate sales leads, or find buyers, PIERS is a comprehensive source of US waterborne import and export trade data online.
- *Datamyne*: (http://www.datamyne.com). This site provides real-time data about US exporters and export movement.
- *Import Genius*: (http://www.importgenius.com). This site provides real-time data on containers that enter the United States.
- *Zepol*: (http://www.zepol). This site helps you find sales leads of US importers and exporters by geographic region, shipment volume, and carrier.
- *Journal of Commerce*: (http://www.joc.com). The JOC provides trade data and offers everything from a listing of the top hundred US exporters (including the top ten states exporting to China) to import/export trade leads and international trade news.

> **Tip** Revisit Chapter 4, because all the market research resources I list there can also help you find customers—from the Small Business Administration, to world trade centers, to American embassies. All you need to remember is to ask: "Help me put together a list of potential customers for _____ (fill in your product or service offering)."

Other Ways to Snag Customers Worldwide

You can do all the social networking in the world to find potential international buyers for your product or service offering, but one surefire way to corral people to one central location in person is to exhibit at a trade show. You can do this either locally or internationally.

Domestic (Local) Trade Shows

A good first step and a low-cost way to generate international sales—for both the large volume customer and Everyday Joe—is to exhibit at a domestic trade show in your industry that offers an "international buyer" exhibit area. This will allow you to keep your transportation expenses to and from the show low. If the show's local, you can even drive to it and sleep at your own home each night.

It may sound counterintuitive to make international sales without leaving the country, but the fact is that international buyers are attracted to large trade shows in the United States. And let's not forget the draw of Las Vegas, Chicago, Miami, and other big trade show venues.

For example, many years ago, I exhibited at the International Home & Housewares Show in Chicago, where I am based, to tap into its international buyer audience and number of global member benefits. Afterward, I was able to use the directory in order to prospect customers.

After you generate national interest and sales success, you can think about exhibiting overseas at a show that brings in worldwide buyers in your industry. From there on, others in your industry will expect to see you there every year as long as you're in business. If you exhibit once and then disappear, they'll think you gave up on the market or went out of business.

For a listing of domestic trade shows, many of which will be within driving distance of your city, visit the ExpoPromoter Web site at http://www.tradeshowsusa.com/.

International Trade Shows

When you decide to exhibit internationally at a trade show, you incur transportation, food, hotel, and exhibition-related expenses. Yet those additional costs are often more than offset by the potential of finding customers on the ground from all over the world.

Many big international trade shows offer a US Pavilion, where the actual cost of the exhibit is subsidized by our government, offering a substantial discount from the regular exhibit rate (inquire with your state's US Export Assistance Center). The pavilions are strictly for the American exhibitors. Market experts from the US Embassy are typically on hand at the show to help national firms makes connections and further establish themselves in a new market.

For a listing of international trade shows, try these sites (but also conduct a web search on your industry—automotive, technology, or food, for example—to find out when and where the next overseas trade show will take place):

- *Trade Show News Network*: http://www.tsnn.com/
- *BizTradeShows*: http://www.biztradeshows.com/
- *EventsEye*: http://www.eventseye.com/
- *export.gov*: http://export.gov/eac/trade_events.asp

Tip The US Commercial Service has what is called a trade fair certification program. It is a cooperative arrangement between private-sector trade show organizers and the US government for the purpose of organizing a US pavilion. The goal is to increase US exports and expand national participation in overseas trade shows.

Government-Sponsored Trade Mission

Trade missions serve US firms that want to explore and pursue export opportunities by meeting directly with potential clients in their respective markets. They typically offer one-to-one meetings, networking events, site visits, briefings, and media coverage.

Certified Trade Missions (CTM; http://export.gov/ctm/index.asp) are overseas events that are planned and organized by private- and public-sector export-oriented groups outside of the US Department of Commerce. They are designed for new and experienced exporters to establish sales and set up representation abroad at a low cost. CTMs typically bring representatives of US companies into contact with potential agents, distributors, joint venture partners, licensees, local businesses, and government contacts.

Binational Societies, Councils, and Trade Associations

As I discussed in Chapter 4, it is important to search the Internet for local binational groups that will put you in touch with customers in the country where you'd like to do business. The National Association of Japan-America Societies (http://www.us-japan.org/), the US-China Business Council (https://www.uschina.org/), and the US-India Business Council (http://www.usibc.com/), for example, all promote bilateral trade between the United States and their respective countries and also provide a stimulating social forum for people with common interests. In addition, they can help with prospecting for export customers. You just need to ask.

Check with your state to see if it has an export promotion agency, or a foreign relations or export council. Organizations like these usually assemble at least once a month and offer a forum for discussion about how to better facilitate international relations, expand trade, and acquire new customers.

Contacts made through business colleagues and associations can often prove invaluable to exporters. Find someone who is successfully exporting and doesn't compete with you, and buy her lunch and pick her brain. Many states offer associations—such as The International Trade Association of Greater Chicago (http://www.itagc.org/), Monterey Bay International Trade Association (http://www.mbita.org/) and Miami Valley International Trade Association (http://www.mvita.org/)–that focus strictly on promoting world trade. Check with your local chamber of commerce to see which of these associations have chapters in your area and sit in on a meeting—then sign up.

All of these are ways to scout for new, promising customers in export markets and each can be a valuable source of knowledge.

Tap Local Clients for Their International Reach

One of the easiest ways to quickly enter a new foreign market is to partner or form an alliance with a company (it could be a client—Brother International, IBM, or American Express, for example) who is more powerful than you and is already conducting like-minded yet noncompeting business in that market. Before you consider this avenue, I caution you to consult with tax and legal advisors to learn what type of partnership you should form, if you form one at all, what compliance issues need to be addressed, and whether or not you will be required to file tax returns in the host country. Please note that not all partnerships need to be formalized. Sometimes a trusting relationship and a handshake is all it takes to get started.

Most companies decide to partner because they sense that there is great synergy between two specific companies—a mutual need and a desire to share risk in achieving a common objective. I'll go into more detail about partnerships and alliances in Chapter 8 when I discuss methods of exporting, but for now I'll just say that partnering can open doors to new markets by enabling the acquisition of export customers at a faster rate. Inquire with your global clients. Ask for an introduction to the individual who heads up the in-country office. Take it one country at a time.

> **CASE EXAMPLE: PARTNER WITH A DOMESTIC CLIENT THAT HAS A GLOBAL PRESENCE**
>
> When I first started exporting foodstuff, I contacted one of the largest Japanese trading companies in the world: Mitsui & Co. The company had a local office in Chicago and did a significant amount of exporting to Japan. I approached the company about piggybacking my products with those it carried. Since I had the suppliers and the company had the established distribution channels and customer base, it was a good match. By combining my company's gourmet food items with Mitsui's beef products, we were able to provide extra value to customers throughout Japan. We went on to export container loads of product every month for many years. That experience taught me the importance of partnering in growing a business internationally—especially for small businesses!

Summary

Finding customers for your export product and services can be easily accomplished through a wide variety of methods, government-sponsored programs, trade shows, trade missions, and related trade-networking services. You can even advertise to acquire customers. But it's not simply one tactic that will bring export customers to your door. It's several different things in combination, and each part must be done exceptionally well.

As a result of your diligence, you will get customers. Now, we're on to the easy part—determining your best export-sales strategy. How will you serve your customers?

Notes

1. Theodore Levitt, *The Marketing Imagination* (New York: Free Press, 1983).
2. "Doing Business in India—the Second Fastest Growing Market in Asia," export.gov, last modified June 10, 2013, http://export.gov/india/doingbusinessinindia/index.asp#P10_896.

CHAPTER 8

Methods of Exporting
Direct, Indirect, and Collaborative Sales Channels

> [Be] prepared to change your strategy or combine several options as your business needs evolve. By opening your mind to the full range of possibilities, you broaden perceived opportunities, sharpen your strategic decisions, and enhance global performance.
>
> —Pankaj Ghemawat, Anselmo Rubiralta Professor of Global Strategy at IESE Business School in Barcelona, Spain[1]

There are several factors to consider when determining whether a direct, indirect, or collaborative sales strategy is best for you—the most important are the extent of your resources, the degree of control you wish to exercise over your export ventures, and other in-country issues. The following analysis will help you to make a decision that is tailored to your needs.

First, let me emphasize that timing is everything. Readiness to seize an opportunity is more important than having your whole strategy nailed down beforehand. If you get a promising inquiry for your export product, go for it. Don't analyze it to death until after you've responded to the inquiry. If there's one thing I'd like you to take away from reading this particular section and entire book, it's the exporter's habit of action: It's better to do something—anything—that will put you in the export marketplace than to expend enormous amounts of time researching and debating options and wondering what other people would do if they were in your place. When an opportunity comes, you must be ready to operate via any sales channel, be it direct, indirect, or collaborative.

Methods of Exporting

Let's look at the two primary methods of exporting: direct and indirect.

Direct Exporting

Direct exporting means you export directly to a customer interested in buying your product. You are responsible for handling the logistics of shipment and for collecting payment.

The advantages of this method are:

- Your potential profits are greater because you have eliminated intermediaries.
- You have a greater degree of control over all aspects of the transaction.
- You know who your customers are.
- Your customers know who you are. They feel more secure in doing business directly with you.
- Your business trips are much more efficient and effective because you meet directly with the customer responsible for selling your product.
- You know whom to contact if something isn't working.
- The feedback you receive from your customers on your product and its performance in the marketplace gets to you faster and more directly.
- You get slightly better protection for your trademarks, patents, and copyrights.
- You present yourself as fully committed and engaged in the export process.
- You develop a better understanding of the marketplace.
- As your business develops in the foreign market, you have greater flexibility to improve or redirect your marketing efforts.

The disadvantages of direct exporting:

- It takes more time, energy, and money than you may be able to afford.
- It requires more people power to cultivate a customer base.

- Servicing the business will demand more responsibility from every level of your organization.
- You are held accountable for whatever happens. There is no buffer zone.
- You may not be able to respond to customer communications as quickly as a local agent can.
- You have to handle all the logistics of the transaction.
- If you have a technological product, you must be prepared to respond to technical questions and to provide on-site start-up training and ongoing support services.

Indirect Exporting

Indirect exporting refers to selling your products to an intermediary, who in turn sells them either directly to customers or indirectly to importing wholesalers. The easiest method of indirect exporting is to sell to an intermediary in your own country. When selling by this method, you normally are not responsible for collecting payment from the overseas customer nor for coordinating the shipping logistics.

An export management company (EMC) is one such intermediary. A good one will, in all respects, act as a global extension of your own sales-and-service presence—more or less executing your intentions on behalf of the product. These companies offer a wide range of services but most specialize in exporting a specific range of products to a well-defined customer base in a particular country or region. For example, one of these companies might specialize in exporting agricultural products to restaurant customers in Europe. An EMC is highly market driven, representing your product along with other companies' noncompeting products as part of its own import "product line" aimed at the customer base it has created. Generally, it buys the product from a manufacturer and marks up the price to cover its profit. This is called a buy-resell arrangement. Other common compensation structures include commission and buy-and-resell, start-up payment, project fee only, fee plus commission, and buy-and-resell. An EMC will carry out all aspects of the export transaction. Fees vary depending on the services rendered and risks accepted but can range anywhere from 1 to 7 percent of sales value.

Finding a good EMC is not that difficult. You can conduct a search through Google or Bing with the keywords "Export management company" to access a list of them. For each company, make note of how long it has been in business, the number of employees it has, the products in which it specializes, and the countries to which it exports. Start your own select list of companies that export products that are similar to yours but don't act as competition to it. Then consult the following resources for more referrals to add to your list:

- *A local trade association with an international focus:* Attend a few meetings and talk some shop—somebody's bound to know of an EMC or even run his own.

- *The international division of your bank:* The division is likely to have an inside line on which EMCs are reputable and doing well.

- *A conference or trade show that specializes in a particular industry, such as agricultural, construction, or hunting and sporting goods:* Attend a show or even consider exhibiting so you can access a list of exhibitors and buyers who attend. As you walk through the show, ask questions. Find out who is using whom for export movements.

- *As always, your local Chamber of Commerce or small business assistance center:* It generally knows who has been in the export trading business for a while. At the very least, it can point you to a good exporting resource.

- *Freight forwarders:* They might be able to provide you with the names of EMCs that use their service. Because you probably haven't made a sale at this point, you probably don't have a working relationship with a transportation company. Ask someone you know who uses a freight forwarder regularly.

You might also use the services of an export trading company. ETCs are virtually identical to EMCs, but they tend to function on a more demand-driven basis, according to which the demand of the market compels them to buy specific goods or commodities. They usually have long-standing customers for whom they source products on a regular basis. For example, they might get a request from a customer to find a supplier of canned corn who can provide twenty container-loads a month for a given number of months. The ETC will then seek out a reputable manufacturer that can handle the demand at an economical price and arrange for the transport of the goods to the customer. You can track down a good ETC using the same channels recommended above for finding an EMC.

Indirect exporting can also involve selling your products to an intermediary in the country where you wish to transact business, who in turn sells them directly to customers or other importing distributors (wholesalers). Under these circumstances, you will not know who your end consumers are. When selling by this method, you are normally responsible for collecting payment from the overseas customer and for coordinating the shipping logistics. In some instances, the overseas agent might request that it be allowed to handle the shipping, usually because it receives special transportation rates from carriers with whom it has done volume business for years. In this case, you will need to arrange for the cargo to be ready by the shipment date. You must still collect payment from the customer, but your actual involvement in the transaction is minimal. It is nearly as easy as a domestic sale.

The advantages of indirect exporting are:

- It's an almost risk-free way to begin.
- It demands minimal involvement in the export process.
- It allows you to continue to concentrate on your domestic business.
- You can learn about export marketing as you go rather than needing to master it immediately.
- Depending on the type of intermediary with which you are dealing, you don't have to concern yourself with shipment and other logistics.
- You can field-test your products for export potential.
- In some instances your local agent can field technical questions and provide necessary product support.

The disadvantages are:

- Your profits are lower.
- You lose control over your foreign sales.
- You very rarely know who your customers are and thus lose the opportunity to tailor your offerings to their evolving needs.
- You are a step removed from the actual transaction causing you to feel out of the loop.
- The intermediary might also be using your product to test the market for her own products that are similar to yours, including ones that are directly competing with it. They might be selling their products to the same customers instead of providing exclusive representation.
- Your long-term outlook and goals for your export program can change rapidly, and if you've put your product in someone else's hands, it's hard to redirect your efforts accordingly.

Questions to Use for Deciding on the Method of Exporting

Only you can determine which strategy suits your needs. Your choice will depend on your goals, your available resources, and the type of business you run. I do recommend that you choose the method that makes you most comfortable and lets you focus on your own core competencies or business priorities, so that you aren't wasting your energy worrying that something isn't working. At the same time, though, I think I've made my bias in favor of direct exporting abundantly clear—it's the only way to maximize control, profits, and market presence. I urge you to move in that direction as soon as you feel able.

Tip If at all possible, go the direct marketing route. It's the best way to learn, grow your presence in the market, and maximize profits.

Let's start with a list of questions to consider before you decide which method of exporting will be best for you:

1. *How big is your company?* A larger company will have more people power to dedicate to the task of achieving direct sales than a small firm or a solo operator, who may find the indirect route to be more readily within his reach.

2. *How big do you (or your company or division) want to get?* If you want to be the size of Siemens International someday, tackling direct sales now will help you build the foundation for that blockbuster future. But even if you prefer to continue doing business as a one-person operation, you'll want to establish some direct channels as your business develops.

3. *How much time and money do you have?* If you have deep pockets and all the time in the world, then you have nothing to lose by selling direct. If time is of the essence because you don't have unlimited funds, indirect channels are more likely to bring you a fast sale.

4. *Will your product require extensive on-site training and support?* Look at Apple, one of the world's largest producers of smart phones. It wants to maintain a reputation not only for making high-quality, expertly designed products but also for improving its customers' lives. The only way to express this commitment to them is by staying right in their faces all over the world and constantly improving upon and updating existing products. Would Apple rely on

local agents or set up a joint venture to cultivate the high degree of customer satisfaction it's after? Unlikely. The more complex and technical your product, the greater the importance of on-site customer service. In Apple's case, this involves retail stores featuring only its own products, staffed by highly trained company employees. But if you're exporting a product that comes without instructions, you'll do your customers no disservice by going indirect.

5. *Do you feel like you know what you're doing and where you want to go? Do you have a strong heart, mind, and stomach?* If you can honestly answer yes to these questions, then go direct. If not, start off indirect and slowly move into developing collaborative relationships.

Caution Early in my career, I worked with an export trading company that purchased goods from my company so it could export them to Japan. I, in turn, was acting as an export trading company for the manufacturer, who thus had two intermediaries between itself and its foreign customers. Imagine the high retail price the consumer paid once the product landed in his country! If you are two or three times removed from a direct relationship with your customers, think twice—or even thrice!—about how you might get to them directly. After all, the name of the export game is to generate your own network of customer relationships. The sooner you begin building this foundation, the sooner you will have a flourishing export business.

In-Country Factors that Can Affect Your Distribution Choice

To ensure you make an intelligent decision regarding whether to export directly or indirectly, confront the following issues. Going in with your eyes wide open will help enable success in an overseas market.

- *Your potential costs and profit margins can help you determine whether it is more profitable to sell directly or indirectly.* In some emerging countries, competition in large cities is so fierce that costs are low and margins thin. On the other hand, particularly in rural areas, the lack of capital can cause just a handful of big, established companies to grow significantly, often gaining monopolies. Hence, the large companies in these areas get away with charging higher prices and achieving wider profit margins. As a potential exporter, determining the competition you will face will help you figure out whether selling directly will truly be profitable, or if it makes more sense to do it indirectly.

- *The competition you face in your export area can affect your choice of entry.* Is the market you are about to enter saturated with lots of competitors? Will you end up a "me too"-type product with no key differentiator to spur sales? Or do you have a value proposition (better pricing, design, or quality, for instance) that will disrupt the market and allow you to become a market leader?

- *The length of a sales channel can affect distribution choice.* In Japan, for example, the traditional distribution system adds many layers to get a product transported to a consumer. In this country, perhaps it would be better to work directly with a big retailer than to go through an importer that might sell to three other intermediary companies to get the product in the hands of the end user.

- *The reach or availability applied to your product line can affect whether it is profitable to bring it into a new market.* Is there an existing distribution system for your type of product in the country you are exporting to or must it be established? Does the government have any restrictions to direct sales on your product line, sales to intermediaries, or limitations on licensing requirements? The more established the system for bringing your product into the country and the fewer restrictions, the less time and labor will be required to export the product.

- *The channel of distribution affects how a product enters a market.* If there is no distribution system to be found in an export country or it is blocked, it will be impossible to enter the market. Or perhaps your product can only be sold door to door or through street stands and the country you wish to enter does not support that method of selling.

- *The product inventory needs to be handled, paid for, and stocked.* Nothing is worse than having lots of interest and demand for your product, only to find out later that it is out of stock at the factory. Get a feel for power, control, and competition in a market. If you see or hear of any distribution company dominating a market (distributing to many middlemen across the country), it's a sign that it will be a tough market to crack unless you get that company on your side. Go elsewhere.

- *Barriers to enter a country, whether real or imagined, can influence a market-entry strategy.* Certain economic or political trade controls and restrictions can cause impediments to an import. Two of the key controls are tariff and nontariff barriers set up to reduce imports that might compete with locally produced goods. It's a form of protectionism. Others include: embargoes, sanctions, export license requirements, entry time restrictions, restrictive government policies, high entry and exit costs, and weak infrastructure.

- *Distance can matter.* According to Pankaj Ghemawat, writing in the *Harvard Business Review*, "By distance, I don't mean only geographic separation, though that is important. Distance also has cultural, administrative or political, and economic dimensions that can make foreign markets considerably more or less attractive."[2] Make sure you evaluate the many dimensions of distance and how they can impact opportunities in a foreign market, allowing you to decide whether it will be profitable to export directly to a country.

The bottom line is: you need to spend as much time as you need surveying the market before you decide on your method of exporting.

Other Methods to Entering an Export Market: Collaborative Sales

Now that we've looked at direct or indirect exporting, let's examine other means for entering an export market: global strategic initiatives, or what I refer to as collaborative sales. Each of these new styles of selling enables you to enter an overseas market faster to expand your existing sales or operations into a foreign country. And none of them are mutually exclusive. Rather, these options should be considered along with, or in addition to, direct and indirect exporting. You can, for example, export if a market permits it and has a licensing arrangement in place or form a joint venture. Once you form a new relationship, you reduce domestic dependence and increase export revenues and profits worldwide. I'll start with the most widely used initiative first and then drill down as best I can from there.

Tip All global strategic initiatives involve an attempt to achieve outcomes that are acceptable to all parties involved. Keep it clear in mind what you are seeking to gain from the initiative, select the right type of relationship, and choose a partner whose contribution will enable you to achieve those goals. Most important, seek international legal (for agreement help) and financial advice. Consult with your export dream team before taking formal action.

Partnership

If you've gotten about as far as you can on your own in charting your export strategy, it's a good time to consider partnering with another company that is located in a foreign country where you are already doing business or would like to be doing business. First, it's important to understand exactly how a partnership works and what it can and cannot do for you.

A partnership is a commitment (voluntarily made) by parties to work collaboratively rather than competitively to achieve mutually desired results in a complex endeavor. A partnership does not necessarily involve a formal contract. It can be formed with a handshake and be based purely on trust. "You do this. We'll do that." Done.

Partnerships can be project based, narrowly defined, or spelled out with a definite time frame. It depends on what needs to be accomplished. If the arrangement is relatively long in duration, say five to ten years, some refer to that as "strategic partnering."

In a partnership, each side knows and commits to the goals of the project and to those of one another, but independence is generally retained. In other words, each party may individually suffer or gain from the relationship.

The biggest downside or disadvantage to a partnership is conflict resolution or the question of who takes responsibility should a crisis arise. The biggest advantage is you can get a partnership going rather fast by minimizing risks while maximizing your leverage in the marketplace.

Global Strategic Alliance

There is no precise definition of a global strategic alliance (GSA). There have been many different versions put forward by thought leaders with the focus on what it achieves. In my experience, a GSA is usually established when a company wishes to edge into a related business or new geographic market—particularly one in a country where the government prohibits imports in order to protect domestic industry. Strategic alliances can come in all shapes and sizes—from an informal business relationship based on a simple contract to a licensing or joint-venture agreement that spells out what needs to be done. Typically, these alliances are formed between two or more corporations in the same or complementary businesses, each based in its home country, for a specified period of time. They are formed between a group of companies that would benefit equally from the partnership. The arrangement can create a win-win environment—or a big-time lose—for all parties. The common goal, however, is for all parties to achieve their objectives more efficiently, at a lower cost, and with less risk than had they acted alone.

The cost of a GSA is usually shared equitably among the corporations involved, and the alliance is generally the least expensive way for all concerned to form a partnership. An acquisition, on the other hand, offers a faster start in exploiting an overseas market but tends to be a much more expensive undertaking for the acquiring company—and one that is likely to be well out of the reach of a solo operator. While a global strategic alliance works well for core business expansion and utilizing existing geographic markets, an acquisition works better for immediate penetration of new geographic territories. Hence, an alliance provides a good solution to export marketers that lack the required distribution to get into overseas markets.

A GSA is also much more flexible than an acquisition with respect to the degree of control enjoyed by each party. Depending on your resources and the type of relationship you form, you can structure an equity or nonequity alliance. Within an equity alliance, each party can hold a minority, majority, or equal stake. In a nonequity alliance, the host-country partner has a greater stake in the deal and thus holds a majority interest.

Yet the right choice of a partner is arguably more important than how the alliance is structured. When it gets down to business, you want a partner who will have an active contribution to make and who is flexible and able to resolve conflicts as the alliance evolves. Even more important, however, is that you have a clear idea of what you are seeking to gain from the alliance and that you have chosen of a partner whose contribution will enable you to achieve those goals.

What do alliances look like? Starbucks, once a small business, opened its first store in Seattle in 1971. Since then, it has created more than seventeen thousand stores in more than fifty-five countries. It was strategic partnerships that enabled it to advance a lot of its growth. "Starbucks partnered with Barnes and Noble bookstores in 1993 to provide in-house coffee shops, benefiting both retailers."[3] A couple of years later, Starbucks partnered with Pepsico to bottle, distribute, and sell the coffee-based drink Frappacino.

In 2010, Intuit, which serves millions of small businesses around the world with its financial software, and Nokia (soon to be a part of Microsoft), which sells hundreds of millions of devices each year, announced an alliance to develop and deliver an innovative new mobile and web-based marketing service. This service has catered to small businesses around the world, bringing their respective expertise to bear for a wider audience than had they not partnered up.[4]

Forming an Alliance: Where to Look

You might be surprised to find that you can build mutually advantageous alliances with some unlikely allies. Many companies make conscious decisions to form partnerships with complementary or even competing companies that can offer them a market share in countries they have been struggling to break into for years. South Korean technology company Samsung and American-based Best Buy, for example, have entered into a broad global strategic alliance that involves setting up 1,400 ministores selling Samsung products in Best Buy and Best Buy Mobile locations across the United States. The locations feature Samsung's laptops, connected cameras, and accessories, giving Samsung a presence in Best Buy locations, previously held only by Apple. By using their complementary strengths and expertise, these companies ensure their mutual survival and foster continued growth in their respective industries.

Even if you're not an international technology company or one of the world's leading retailers, you can follow the example set by Samsung and Best Buy and see which of your contacts, colleagues, peers, or competitors in the international market might have compatible needs and objectives. You'll probably feel most secure with a company that you already have a reasonably long-standing business relationship with, especially if you have achieved substantial sales growth together. It could be your distributor in Athens, a manufacturer that took on distribution of your product in Vietnam, or that trading company in Japan that can't keep up with consumer demand. Any one of your contacts with a problem you can solve or a need you can fulfill might serve as a potential partner.

Advantages of a GSA

There are many specific advantages of setting up a GSA. It will allow you to:

- Get instant market access, or at least speed your entry into a new market
- Exploit new opportunities to strengthen your position in a market where you already have a foothold
- Increase sales
- Gain new skills and technology
- Develop new products at a profit
- Share fixed costs and resources
- Enlarge your distribution channels
- Broaden your business and political contact base
- Gain greater knowledge of international customs and culture
- Enhance your image in the world marketplace

Disadvantages of the GSA

There are also some inevitable trade-offs of a GSA to consider:

- Weaker management involvement or less equity stake in the larger company
- The dreaded market insulation—an inability to see the realities of the market—due to the local partner's presence
- Less efficient communication within the company
- Poor resource allocation
- Difficult to keep objectives on target over time
- Potential loss of control over such important issues as product quality, operating costs, employees, and customer service.

  For example, if you enter into a GSA with even a little less equity stake—say, 49 percent—you lose managerial control. You may end up with that equity percentage because the host government only allows up to 49 percent for an outsider, because you could only negotiate that amount, or because you were willing to accept a minority stake in exchange for gains (e.g., responsibility for R&D) that you thought important during the negotiation phase. Whatever the reason, what are you going to do if profits plummet, product quality deteriorates, or customers are dissatisfied? You do not have enough interest in the venture to take action. Your 49 percent can swiftly depreciate when it comes to exercising any control. In any partnership, the majority-interest holder tends to dominate, putting its needs first and its partner's last. The ideal situation is a fifty-fifty partnership, which allows both parties to share the decision making. If you do settle for a minority interest, make sure you maintain enough control to accomplish your objectives in the target market.

Caution There are always exceptions to the fifty-fifty partnership being the ideal scenario. In the United States, for example, there can be advantages to a business having 51 percent ownership by women or minorities. This can be used to gain contracts or preferential treatment in the marketplace. The Small Business Administration, for example, offers many special programs and services to help women business owners who have 51 percent or more stock ownership succeed.[5]

It's also critical to explore all the legal and financial implications before entering into an alliance with an overseas company. Seek legal counsel from those who are well experienced in international trade, acquisitions, joint ventures and divestitures and ask them to go over the best- and worst-case scenarios with you. You should hire counsel both in your own country and in the host country for maximum protection of your rights. You are not only seeking to ensure the fundamental integrity of the partnership but also to work out crucial entitlements and obligations, such as copyrights, trademarks, patents, taxes, antitrust, and exchange controls.

You will also need to keep informed about the host country's political and economic stability. Get in touch with the local economic development offices within that country. They should be able to assess the country's future investment climate and to provide you with past, present, and future growth trends. This will give you a better idea of what kind of risks you will incur, if any, if you go ahead with the alliance.

As an exporter, it's only a matter of time before you consider a GSA as a logical step in expanding your business. It's not enough to expand domestically; that is not an exporter's core business. Your core business is the world. Up until now, you may have single-handedly cemented strategic alliances with a network of agents and distributors to maintain access to markets worldwide, but you are currently finding that this is no longer enough to remain competitive. You may feel that you've gotten about as far as you can on your own and want to explore alternatives for kicking your export business into high gear. You're prepared to exchange a limited measure of creative control if it will get you established in highly lucrative new business territories.

So you've decided to create a GSA. Now what?

Negotiating a Deal for the GSA

In negotiating a deal for a GSA, your main concern should be that you and the other party share the same goals and see the deal-making process in the same light.

During the initial phase of negotiations, rather than discussing an agreement point by point, you might be better off outlining in draft form how you would like the joint venture to work. This keeps the draft-in-progress simple and provides a tangible way for the other side to see your ideas. Then expand on each point in your outline and make sure that each party understands the objectives and implications. You can accomplish this by presenting each issue in draft form and having a representative from each side write a synopsis of her understanding of it. If there are any discrepancies or disagreements, you can clear them up at this point, prior to putting together a final draft agreement.

After you submit your draft, it's up to the other party to make a counterproposal that sets out its own conceptual framework for a GSA. This method allows for shared control of negotiations and gives the parties an opportunity to offer alternate ways of setting up the venture. With each proposal and counterproposal, the parties will narrow the gap and come closer to a viable agreement.

Retaining Autonomy and Independence

A good GSA allows for both parties to retain a fair degree of autonomy and independence with minimal restrictions on complementary business opportunities. Ideally, the two parties will form a whole that equals more than the sum of its parts. So, it's important to spend a significant amount of time getting to know the party with which you are considering joining forces.

Problems usually occur when there is poor communication between parties or when there is a staggering difference in strengths and management philosophies. Without a clear-cut mission statement that clarifies goals or objectives from the beginning, things can take a disastrous turn when business gets well underway. For example, it might initially seem that an alliance between a company that has a stronger management team and one with a weaker one offers enormous opportunities for the weaker partner, but in the long run it turns out that the weaker party becomes a drain on resources, forcing the stronger management team to carry the entire weight of the alliance. In the end, the strong partner buys out the weaker one. It's a no-win situation.

To have a reasonable chance of success, the merging parties should both have three vital elements: (1) good communication skills, (2) matching corporate cultures, and (3) matching corporate philosophies. If you do not see these elements operating during the time of negotiations, you never will. Cut your losses and look for a more compatible partner.

Considering the GSA: What Can We Learn?

Before you decide to enter into a GSA, make an excruciatingly honest appraisal of your own goals, strengths, and limitations. Determining at the outset if you're really ready to form an alliance or not and what you can realistically expect to accomplish will save you losses down the road. Appraise your potential partner just as carefully. And remember, no two deals are alike; the final structure of any alliance depends on what each party has to offer the other and what each hopes to gain.

Expect cultural factors to complicate the smooth running of business. For instance, if your partner-to-be behaves in a way you experience as flat out weird in that it goes against the grain of your own culture, factor that in and consider it very carefully while you are reviewing the upside and downside of the deal. This odd behavior could mean trouble waiting to happen. Picture yourself living with the alliance you've made for a long, long time. Make sure you can live with your partner before you sign on the dotted line.

As a longtime independent businessperson, you might approach such an arrangement with ambivalent feelings and dread the potential headaches of working out all the details. But if the arrangement is structured properly, thoughtfully, and equitably, a GSA can pay off handsomely for both parties in terms of greater growth, higher profits, and excellence in export business. I recommend that you review and consider all the options I have talked about and then harness your newfound skills and direct your efforts exactly as you see fit.

Joint Venture

Just as GSAs allow companies with complementary skills to benefit from one another's strengths, a joint venture can do the same. When two companies invest money into forming a third jointly owned enterprise, that new enterprise is called a joint venture. For a joint venture to work, there should be a nice give-and-take, a codependency, or a shared management arrangement. The joint venture can receive market knowledge (customer and distribution, for example), assets, and financing from both parent companies without altering the condition of the parent company. The new venture is an ongoing enterprise whereby the parent companies—"parents"—own the joint venture and share in the profits (or losses) it generates.

A joint venture spells out a defined project that each of the respective parties involved agrees to and carries out. Again, I repeat: Not only do the parties share in the venture's profits, but they also share in the losses. Each parent company has an equal voice in controlling the project, which means there is more than one parent. Oftentimes they each can be powerful and visible.[6]

■ **Tip** Oracle founder Larry Ellison recently purchased the Hawaiian island of Lanai. He was cited in an interview in the *Wall Street Journal*, saying, "We have the right climate and soil to grow the very best gourmet mangos and pineapples on the planet and export them year-round to Asia and North America. We can grow and export flowers and make perfume the old-fashioned way—directly from the flowers, like they do in Grasse, France. We have an ideal location for a couple of organic wineries on the island."[7] The big question is this: Should Ellison do this on his own or elect to go the sales collaboration route and negotiate with Dole on the pineapple side and Chanel or Estée Lauder on the perfume side? If Ellison is eager to get to market and doesn't mind giving up a piece of the action, collaborating with other companies who have been there, done that will speed up the process. If not, he can launch on his own, take as much time as he wants and reap 100 percent of the rewards. Knowing Ellison, he will go it alone. It'll be fun to watch his progress.

One illustration of how a joint venture might work would be a situation in which you currently export a ton of stuff to a particular overseas market. The importer asks you if he can make the product in his market and reexport to other contiguous markets. That's how the seed is planted. You form a joint venture, and that newly formed enterprise spells out intent, and it starts to service customers in other parts of the world. You continue exporting to the importer, but he has a new obligation or role and vested interest, as you do, in the success of the newly formed organization.

Tip Two classic articles on the subject of joint ventures worth a read are: "How to Make a Global Joint Venture Work," by J. Peter Killing (*Harvard Business Review*, May 1982, http://hbr.org/1982/05/how-to-make-a-global-joint-venture-work/ar/1), and "Launching a World-Class Joint Venture" by James Bamford, David Ernst, and David G. Fubini (*Harvard Business Review*, February 2004, http://hbr.org/2004/02/launching-a-world-class-joint-venture/ar/1).

International Franchising

International franchising is a strategic way to reduce dependence on domestic demand and grow new future revenue and profit centers worldwide. Extending a brand globally through franchising involves a lower risk than doing it through more hands-on exporting, requires minimal investment, and offers a huge upside potential on scaling capabilities. Let's look at what international franchising is, its benefits, examples of companies that have successfully franchised internationally, how to get started in franchising, and where to look for additional help.

What Is International Franchising?

Franchising is a pooling of resources and capabilities to accomplish a strategic marketing, distribution, and sales goal for a company. It typically involves a franchisor—potentially you—granting an individual or company (the franchisee) the right to run a business or sell a product or service under its successful business model and giving the other party the right to be identified by its trademark or brand.

The franchisor charges an initial up-front fee to the franchisee, payable upon the signing of the franchise agreement. Other fees, such as marketing, advertising, or royalties, may be applicable and are largely based on how the contract is negotiated and set up. Advertising, training, and other support services are made available by the franchisor.

Benefits of International Franchising

In addition to entering new overseas markets with additional customers, international franchising can also offer franchisors the opportunity to use what are called foreign-master owners, rather than franchisees. These individuals are typically natives of the country and understand the political and bureaucratic problems in their country far better than any outsider. Foreign master franchise owners pay a hefty up-front fee to acquire a designated geographic area or, in some instances, an entire country, where they operate as a mini- or subfranchise company, selling franchises, collecting royalties, training the owners, and overseeing all other related matters. They can even open units by themselves. In general, a specified number of franchises must be outlined to gain the exclusive right to use the business model in an entire country.

Examples of Successful International Franchising

Domino's Pizza International began serving consumers outside the United States in 1983 when the first store opened in Winnipeg, Canada. Since that time, Domino's Pizza International has extended its global reach to include more than fifty-five international markets, serviced by more than 3,230 stores.

The company claims, "The success of Domino's Pizza outside the U.S. is due to the collaborative relationship between our exceptional franchisees and the corporate team that supports them. Together, we continuously strive to support a policy of 'One Brand—One System' in order to be the best pizza delivery company in the world."[8]

Another fast-food giant, McDonald's, does business in 118 countries around the world. For those countries where McDonald's does not already have a presence (Afghanistan, for example), the company does not have any firm plans to open locations. The company says it is instead focusing on the markets where it already has a presence.[9]

Many of these companies weren't huge when they started their overseas operations, yet little acorns grow into mighty oaks. A friend and colleague of mine, Shelly Sun, CEO and cofounder of Illinois-based BrightStar, has visions of having her company follow such a path: The company was established in 2002 as a full-service health care staffing agency serving corporate and private clients. Sun has big plans to use the franchise model to take her company international. Currently, her firm generates $250 million annually and has more than 250 locations throughout the United States and Canada, and she has plans to expand it further within Canada as well as to the United Kingdom, Australia, and China. She wants to first make sure she has a solid base of franchisees and an equally solid basis of royalties coming in before going global. "If we had expanded internationally prior to 2012, we would not have had the resources to invest in the high level of support, which we believe is indispensable in a successful international expansion strategy," says Sun.[10]

Getting Started in International Franchising

The best place to find out how to get started is the International Franchise Association (http://www.franchise.org). It can help you with the first steps to take and tell you what opportunities are available in the global marketplace. As in any new international expansion, there will be challenges: cultural differences, legal considerations, contract negotiations, and intellectual property issues, to name just a few. For a snapshot on what is involved, see the article "Dealing with the Complexities of International Expansion."[11]

Where to Look for Franchising Help

Here are a couple of resources that will guide you in the international franchising area:

1. *International Franchise Association*: (http://www.franchise.org/). This site is considered the go-to source on anything to do with franchising—from country profiles to international franchising articles and information on international franchising laws.

2. *Franchising World*: (http://www.franchise.org/Franchise-Industry-Fran-World.aspx). The International Franchising Association site offers digital versions of current Franchising World issues and archives of past articles.

3. *DLA Piper's Francast Newsletter*: (http://www.dlapiper.com/us/publications/list.aspx?Title=francast). The Francast Newsletter is put out by DLA Piper. DLA Piper is considered the number one global law firm in the area of franchise law by *Who's Who Legal* and is ranked the top practice in the United States by the respected research firm Chambers & Partners.

4. *Grow Smart, Risk Less: A Low-Capital Path to Multiplying Your Business Through Franchising*: Written by Shelly Sun, this book provides a road map to guide you in franchising your business.

5. *International Franchising: A Practitioner's Guide*: Written by Marco Hero, this book is a practical guide for all those involved in planning and operating an international franchise program, describing a range of topics from in-house counsel, to managing directors, to those in private practice.

Establishing a Foreign Office or Acquiring an Existing Company

When companies want to quickly gain access to markets or a new area of expertise (technology, for example), they usually form a partnership or GSA. They can also open a foreign office or acquire a smaller company with those assets in the targeted market.

To maintain better control of your exports, you can establish a foreign branch office, subsidiary, or joint venture, in which you make the decisions, and staff it with local people, who receive the imported goods (your exports) and see that they are properly distributed to the intended customers and serviced thereafter.

The advantages of this type of arrangement is that the branch office can serve both as the initial link in the marketing channel in the foreign market and can facilitate customer loyalty for the brand. The biggest disadvantage is that you have higher setup costs and the potential for higher credit risks at the beginning stages of operation.

Acquiring a smaller company, on the other hand, offers a faster start in exploiting an overseas market and might avoid getting a trade restriction (which blocks an export or makes it cost prohibitive to sell a product at a profit) but tends to be a much-more-expensive undertaking for the acquiring company—one that is likely to be well out of the reach of a smaller enterprise.

Due to uncontrollable economic factors, many companies can be forced into establishing a foreign branch office if they want to maintain a market presence. This often happens when companies are doing well with their exports in a foreign market, only to discover later on that the government has raised the tariff on their particular commodity from 20 percent to 70 percent. As a result, they must decide to either stay in the market, take the hit, and hope for the best—thereby remaining competitive—or beat the system by acquiring a company in the foreign market that can make and distribute the product, in which case they will enjoy a definite cost advantage by eliminating the tariff. Obviously a lot depends on competition (if you are the only one in a market, you might be able to sustain the tariff increase), customer demand, funding, human resource capability, and long-term outlook.

Whatever route you take, keeping track of regulations that constantly change, not to mention having the experience needed to run an operation and distribute products through the distribution chain, can be complicated. Before you consider this option, check with your international attorney and tax accountant. Make sure the opportunity you see or anticipate justifies the investment.

With ever-changing compliance issues and new country alerts appearing frequently, you will need to be kept informed of issues that can impact your overseas operations. Will your office staff handle this or will you need to appoint an outside person to manage the foreign operation? This is sometimes necessary because seemingly routine tasks, such as issuing payroll or taking care of back-office mail and supplies, can absorb huge amounts of time, particularly when dealing with different time zones, multiple languages, and a wide variety of service providers.

Take into consideration these six points before establishing an office overseas:

1. Who are your core customers?
2. Where is your best talent pool located?
3. What is the legal structure and regulatory climate of the other country like?
4. What are the preliminary tax consequences?
5. How will cultural differences impact your enterprise?
6. Do you speak the language?

Licensing

Where laws prohibit the establishment of a foreign branch office, subsidiary, or joint venture, licensing can prove useful to an exporter. Licensing is different from obtaining an export license, which is covered in Chapter 13.

Licensing is a contractual arrangement where the firm—the licensor—offers some proprietary assets (a trademark, a patent, marketing know-how, technology, or an established production process, for example) to a foreign company—the licensee—in exchange for royalty fees or other kinds of payments. The licensing agreement can be long term or on a per-project basis.

Companies like HP[12] and Oracle[13] license some of their software technology to companies in other parts of the world to jointly create better products, speed up time-to-market, and generate lucrative royalties fees. To allow customers to legally use its images for their projects, Getty Images licenses its stock photos, illustrations, and archival images to individuals and companies worldwide.[14]

Royalty fees for licensing can range anywhere from one-eighth of 1 percent of the gross-sales revenue stream to 15 percent or greater. Before you sign on the dotted line, consider these factors: you must account for currency conversion, how royalties will be paid, geographic jurisdiction, what taxes might be applied, and how progress will be monitored and audited.

Licensing can be very beneficial to small companies that lack the resources to invest in foreign facilities. Compared to exporting, licensing can also offer an entry mode that requires a low commitment of capital and allows you to navigate around import barriers while still providing you with access to markets quickly that might otherwise be closed to imports.

As in all modes of entry into the market, there can be risks with licensing. The biggest one I see is—as the licensor—is serving as a feeder to a potential future competitor. Once an agreement expires, the licensee can run with your idea. That brings us to—once again—the ever-important issue of consulting with your international attorney about how to protect yourself against the risks of licensing arrangements. When evaluating prospective licensees, review the list of characteristics to look for in distributors and the list of questions to ask them provided in Chapter 7.

Summary

When all is said and done, the best strategy for export market expansion is one that makes you feel like you have the whole world in your hands. Although most companies begin their foray into foreign markets through exporting, the best long-term global-market entry strategy is a diverse one—employing direct, indirect, and collaborative initiatives—to ensure you don't rely on one single channel for export growth. The collaborative initiatives we've looked at in this chapter are options to be considered along with, or in addition to, direct and indirect exporting.

Once you've decided what type of exporting method you are going to use, you must figure out how to put the deal together and make the export sale happen. Next, I'll show you how to choose safe, prompt, and cost-effective transport; arrive at an appropriate price-per-product unit; and work with a freight forwarder to prepare your final quotation. Read through these next two chapters carefully and refer back to them often. You want to be on top of all the information you'll need at each stage of the process.

Notes

1. "Managing Differences: The Central Challenge of Global Strategy," Pankaj Ghemawat, *Harvard Business Review*, March 2007, http://hbr.org/2007/03/managing-differences-the-central-challenge-of-global-strategy/ar/1.

2. "Distance Still Matters: The Hard Reality of Global Expansion," Pankaj Ghemawat, *Harvard Business Review*, September 2001, http://hbr.org/2001/09/distance-still-matters-the-hard-reality-of-global-expansion/ar/1.

3. "Examples of Successful Strategic Alliances," Je' Czaja, *Chron*, accessed October 27, 2013, http://smallbusiness.chron.com/examples-successful-strategic-alliances-13859.html.

4. "Nokia and Intuit Form Global Alliance to Create Mobile Marketing Services to Small Businesses," Intuit: Press Releases, September 15, 2010, http://about.intuit.com/about_intuit/press_room/press_release/articles/2010/NokiaAndIntuitFormGlobalAlliance.html.

5. "Guide to Size Standards," SBA.gov, accessed October 27, 2013, http://www.sba.gov/content/guide-size-standards.

6. See "How to Make a Global Joint Venture Work," J. Peter Killing, *Harvard Business Review*, May 1982, http://hbr.org/1982/05/how-to-make-a-global-joint-venture-work/ar/4.

7. "Larry Ellison's Fantasy Island," Julian Guthrie, *Wall Street Journal*, June 13, 2013, http://online.wsj.com/article/SB10001424127887324798904578529682230185530.html.

8. "Dominos Around the World: International Franchising with Dominos Pizza," Domino's Biz, accessed October 27, 2013, http://www.dominosbiz.com/Biz-Public-EN/Site+Content/Secondary/International/International+Franchising/.

9. "International Franchising," the About McDonalds Web site, accessed October 27, 2013, http://www.about-mcdonalds.com/mcd/franchising/international_franchising.html.

10. Shelly Sun, CEO and co-founder, BrightStar, email exchange October 8, 2013.

11. "Dealing with the Complexities of International Expansion," Bachir Mihoubi, International Franchising Association, published in *Franchising World*, March 2011, http://www.franchise.org/Franchise-Industry-News-Detail.aspx?id=53325.

12. "Technology Transfer," HP, accessed October 27, 2013, http://www.hp.com/hpinfo/abouthp/iplicensing/technology/.

13. "Global Pricing and Licensing," accessed October 30, 2013, http://www.oracle.com/us/corporate/pricing/index.html

14. "License Agreements," gettyimages, accessed October 27, 2013, http://www.gettyimages.com/Corporate/LicenseAgreements.aspx.

CHAPTER 9

Transport, Logistics, and Fulfillment Options

The number one thing you can do is figure out how to ship to people globally.

—Joanne Bethlamy, director, Cisco Internet Business Solutions Group[1]

The container is at the core of a highly automated system for moving goods from anywhere, to anywhere, with a minimum of cost and complication on the way. The container made shipping cheap, and by doing so changed the shape of the world economy.

—Marc Levinson, author, *The Box: How the Shipping Container Made the World Smaller and the World Economy Bigger*[2]

People have been trading with each other, between countries, across roads and oceans, for thousands of years. According to the International Maritime Organization, "We live in a global society which is supported by a global economy—and that economy simply could not function if it were not for ships and the shipping industry. Shipping is truly the lynchpin of the global economy: without shipping, intercontinental trade, the bulk transport of raw materials and the import/export of affordable food and manufactured goods would simply not be possible."[3] Since export shipment involves moving goods from one country to another—a somewhat riskier and more complicated enterprise than domestic shipments—it is extra important to find a company that offers safe, reliable, quick, and cost-effective transport services.

In this chapter, I discuss a range of air and ocean transport choices (containerized shipments, for example), including special state-of-the-art vehicles for cargo with special handling requirements, and a variety of methods for loading your export shipment. In addition, I'll introduce you to global freight forwarders, logistics specialists, and third-party logistic providers (3PLs)—the all-around experts who will become an indispensable part of your export transport operation.

The quantity, value, and perishability of your product; your customer's location; how fast the shipment is needed; and how much you are willing to spend will determine which method of transportation you should use. Oftentimes, a compromise among these factors takes place. Product movement between neighboring countries, such as the United States and Canada, is relatively simple and economical, and you can always ship overland by road, by conventional rail, or by double-stacked trains, whichever your customer prefers. Product movement over water is somewhat more complicated and expensive. Accordingly, I'll focus on air and ocean shipping options. I'll also take a look at third-party logistics providers that support e-commerce sales.

SHIPPING HAZARDOUS MATERIALS OR GOODS

Always remember that if you are shipping hazardous material or goods, such as products packaged in aerosol cans or containing dry ice, you must notify your transportation company. This type of shipment requires special transit treatment and is carefully regulated by the US Department of Transportation under the US Code of Federal Regulations, Title 49. These regulations determine which products may or may not be transported via air and offer guidelines for preparing the product for safe export. Whether shipped by air or ocean, hazardous goods must be properly certified, marked, and labeled and must be packed and handled with appropriate care. Should your transport company, freight forwarder, or 3PL provider be unable to guide you through the process of shipping a hazardous product, contact the US Department of Transportation (DOT) or International Air Transportation Association (IATA), or conduct a Google or Bing search with the keywords "Shipping hazardous material internationally" to obtain more information.

Air Transport

Shipping by air used to be an emergency strategy, used only when a customer needed a product immediately, but with the proliferation of international air delivery services such as Federal Express, DHL, UPS, and Airborne Express, it is now easy and economical to move your product around the world, even overnight. You'll generally pay a higher price per kilo than you will for ocean shipment, but in some expense categories you'll actually rack up some savings. For example, packing costs tend to run less for air transport. One major consideration is the weight of your cargo. Are you exporting feathers? If so, air transport would be cheaper, provided you don't use cartons that take up a lot of space. Tractors, on the other hand, should be transported via ocean.

If exporting highly perishable items is your business, you'll want to familiarize yourself with carriers that offer affordable worldwide express shipments of chilled, frozen, and fresh foods, such as seafood, meats, and produce. You will see more and more demand for this service as the market for organic, fresh, and convenience foods expands. I suggest you call the US Department of Agriculture's international marketing office for additional help. It usually has directories, workbooks, and guides to assist exporters of highly perishable products.

The International Air Transport Association (IATA; http://www.iata.org) represents 240 airlines worldwide. When these members reach agreement on a fixed rate, they file a tariff with the US Department of Transportation (DOT; http://www.dot.gov). Tariffs define the rate, rules, and regulations governing air cargo deliveries for a given carrier or conference. Only when an exporter is charged by a shipper a cost that is beyond the maximum amount specified in the tariff (unless it is under a service contract) will she need to notify a regulatory agency to complain.

There are two major types of equipment used in air transport:

1. *Air cargo containers*: These types of containers are loaded by hand or forklift. They come in more than a dozen different styles and sizes.

2. *Air cargo pallets made of wood or plastic (corrugated plastic is used but not recommended) with netting*: These are also loaded by hand or forklift.

Which type of equipment you use depends on the type and quantity of the cargo you are shipping. To determine the absolute best way to ship your cargo, always discuss your situation with your transportation company. And don't forget to find out the distance from your customer's door to the closest seaport or airport. If one delivery destination is closer than the other, you'll save your customer time but not necessarily money in the case of shipping to the nearest airport, because air cargo can be expensive.

The top two considerations when choosing air vs. sea freight are transit time and the cargo itself. It usually takes a product a couple of days to arrive by air, whereas sea freight takes anywhere from twelve to fourteen days. The cargo itself, whether delicate in nature (fine art, for example) or large in size (as is heavy equipment), forces you to make the best decision for your cargo shipment.

Caution   Always check with your shipping specialist to verify the pallet requirements for your destination country. Some countries, for example, require certain types of wood packaging to be treated with chemicals or heat before being allowed into their country.

Ocean Transport

Shipping by ocean takes much longer than shipping by air, but it is nearly always much less expensive. That is why it will generally be your overseas customers' preferred method of transport. Whereas with air shipment, the greater the volume of your shipment, the more expensive it becomes, with ocean shipment a greater volume of shipment actually decreases the cost. Ocean transport is less simple, though, because it involves many more choices that you may know very little about. These include the choice between terminals, vessel types, container loading options, and so forth. You'll have to rely on your transport company to give you advice.

When choosing a transport company, you'll want to find out the following:

1. The frequency that the vessels sail
2. The transit times
3. The reliability measures
4. The ports served by steamship line
5. The company's safety record
6. The computerization for cargo management

The last point, computerized cargo management, is vital these days. You want to be able to track your cargo at any given point. If it gets lost, you want to know that the transport company can find it. Cargo management is an important part of the package you offer your customers—so anytime you find a new and better way to serve them in terms of cargo, jump on it.

Shopping for an Economical Transport Package

Shipping lines—whose vessels are still commonly referred to as "steamships" although the days of steam-powered shipping are long gone—can be classified as either independent or conference. Independent lines tend not to have as many ports of call, which can cause shipping delays. Sometimes, while comparison shopping, you will find an independent line that quotes you a rate that is cheaper than what the conference lines are offering. However, when using an independent line you can't be sure of your shipper's timeliness or reliability.

Conference lines, on the other hand, guarantee similar standards and rates. If you can contract with a conference line on an exclusive basis, rates are usually cheaper than, or at least competitive with, those offered by an independent line. The guarantee on rates during a specified period of time is a savings that you can then pass on to your customer or use to pad your own profit margin. Other types of ocean transport companies that have evolved over the years are NVOCCs, or non-vessel-operating common carriers, and shipper's associations. NVOCCs book space on vessels and then sell the space to shippers with smaller cargoes in smaller-volume units. They consolidate these smaller shipments into container-loads under one bill of lading, and as a result can pass on more favorable rates to the small cargo shipper. You can also take advantage of a larger shipper's economies of scale to move your smaller loads more cheaply. Shipper's associations, similarly, were formed to pull together several different shippers' cargoes to achieve greater volume and hence lower rates.

Don't forget that ocean and air shipping itself is only part of the transport package you'll need to assemble. To get your product to an ocean-going vessel for loading, you must also transport your cargo overland by truck or rail. How do you do this without spending an arm and a leg? The most advanced and efficient transport mode currently available to exporters to handle this problem is intermodal transportation. This is a start-to-finish transport package that takes your cargo from its point of origin to its point of destination (commonly described as "door-to-door") under a single bill of lading. It involves the use of at least two different transportation modes—rail and ocean, for example—to cover the overland and overseas movement of the cargo. The company that offers the package is liable for getting the cargo from the point of origin to the final destination, and it will charge you a "through rate" to do so. The rate represents a substantial savings over what it would cost you to engage separate carriers for each leg of the trip. An added bonus: The company can issue a computer-generated bill of lading within hours of the cargo's receipt at an inland terminal or immediately after the vessel has left port. This means faster turnaround time in collecting payment from your customer. Some intermodal service packages also offer container freight stations, which save you time and drayage (local transportation) costs by bringing their service closer to your door.

> **Tip** With the Internet and the advent of e-commerce sales transactions for B-to-C transactions, most international carriers and third-party logistics providers now offer all-inclusive door-to-door landed costs (meaning they include the price of the product, the delivery charge, taxes, duties, customs, and in a currency your shoppers understand) on single-product shipments delivered to a consumer. In 2009, this was unheard of. What a difference five years makes!

If you are an exporter of refrigerated commodities, most sophisticated transportation companies can offer cost-efficient transport via refrigerated vehicles. For example, there are railcars equipped with individual generators to ensure the preservation of perishable products during transit. Some companies offer what is called a "motorbridge" (trucking) service to exporters of frozen meat and other perishables, which entails a through transportation rate from the producer's door to the customer's door. Other companies offer multipurpose vessels for more cost-effective shipment of noncontainerized cargo, such as tin, tea, equipment, and grain. These vessels are usually smaller in size than those found in a regular containerized ship, allowing them to travel safely through rough seas and narrow channels. They also make the difficult portside dockings at newly industrialized countries easier.

It's imperative to shop around and compare rates to get the best-possible transportation package for your customer. Don't be shy about questioning a transportation company or freight forwarder at length and in great detail about its service and rates. That is what it is there for, and you don't owe them anything until after you've hired them. Always inquire about the latest and most advanced methods for moving goods overseas. Even as you read this, improvements are underway. Keeping current with the transportation industry will help you offer your customers the most innovative and cost-effective service and equipment options.

Break-Bulk and Container Loading

What kind of vessel you choose to ship your cargo, and what special handling, loading or storage apparatus, if any, should be used, will depend on the type and quantity of your goods. Here are a variety of common options and techniques for loading your shipment.

Break-Bulk

Better known as less–than–container-load, or LTL shipment, break-bulk shipment is the most likely option to be used by new exporters, whose first orders are likely to be small. It allows your customer to test the product in his market before committing to a large quantity, such as a full container-load or more. The shipper can still load the goods into a container, but the container will be delivered to a consolidation point (port of exit) where other shippers' goods will also be stowed in the container. The advantage of this method is that it allows smaller, low-volume exporters to have their cargo containerized, although it is not as desirable as a sealed door-to-door container, as I will discuss.

To control the expense of small-quantity shipment, find a transport company that specializes in break-bulk. Naturally, when you are shipping a small trial order and hoping for repeat business, it will be to your advantage to control your customer's costs by offering them the best rate possible. When shipping LTL, you'll need to take extra care in packing and marking your cartons. (I'll discuss carton marking in greater detail later.) Break-bulk shipments are commonly packed using the following materials:

- *Pallets*: Wood pallets must be strong enough to be stacked on racks and reused numerous times. *Never* let your cartons overhang a pallet. Your whole load might collapse! As previously mentioned, some countries require certain types of wood pallets to be treated with chemicals or heat before allowing the shipment to cross its borders. Check with your transportation specialist.

- *Slipsheets*: Used to pull your cargo to the point of loading, these sheets are usually made of fiberboard or plastic. They must be strong enough for the forklift operator to clamp onto and pull. Slipsheets cost less than pallets and eliminate the expense of transporting pallets back to the shipper for reuse. Cartons placed on slipsheets must be cross stacked, shrink-wrapped, or secured with extra-strength strapping.

- *Crates*: Wood crates are still popular with some shippers due to their strength and resistance to humidity, at any temperature and at any point in transit.

All onboard packing aids should be recyclable or reusable. Use the minimum amount of material necessary to protect your product. Pallets, slipsheets, and crates are loaded using the following methods:

- Bulk loading by machine or hand (for bulk commodities, for example)

- Hand loading using individual shipping containers, with or without pallets

- Unit loading using palleted or slipsheet stacks into containers with forklifts

Container Loading

Shipment by container-load continues to be the preferred method for exporting goods because each container is sealed (allowing it to stay closed from the factory door to the customer's door), strong, theft resistant, and stackable. Containers are also easy to load and unload; transport by truck, rail, or ship; and store. The only time the container may be opened while in transit is for the customer's inspection, so the transport of the goods becomes nearly bulletproof concerning safety and pilferage issues.

Note Exporting by container continues to grow. According to trade data produced by PIERS, "U.S. containerized exports were up 5 percent in February 2013 compared to February 2012, reaching 1,011,874 20-foot-equivalent units."[4] PIERS, a database of US waterborne trade activity, says this is the largest year-over-year increase since June 2012, when exports jumped nearly 10 percent.

Containers are available in various volumes and in a number of specialized constructions to accommodate various cargo types. Typically, shipping companies provide containers, but you can also rent or buy them new or used. If you want to do so, try eBay, contact a local shipping company to inquire about used shipping containers, or contact the Container Alliance (http://www.containeralliance.com/), a network of portable storage and shipping container providers.

A container can cost anywhere from $1,500 (used) to $8,000 (new). Rental costs range from $75 to $295 per month. You can also expect to pay delivery and pickup charges on any of these scenarios. The twenty-foot container, the most popular volume, works well for starting up with exports. The forty-foot container is the second-most popular choice. It's important to resist the temptation to overload this larger container or you won't be able to move your cargo over land! For large loads, a forty-five-foot container is an attractive bargain because it gives you a 27 percent increase in interior capacity over the forty-foot unit for the same handling costs. Containers come as large as forty-eight feet, but these are comparatively rare.

Just as you conducted market research on where the best market is for your product using a variety of sources, keeping track of where all your exports are going provides a good basis for asking yourself, "Should we be looking at these markets since there are so many containers going to that part of the world?" Take *The Journal of Commerce*'s annual ranking of the top fifty world container ports for 2012).[5] Here is a snapshot of the top ten container ports, which shows heavy concentration in China (Asia):

1. Shanghai, China
2. Singapore, Singapore
3. Hong Kong, China
4. Shenzhen, China
5. Busan, South Korea
6. Ningbo-Zhoushan, China
7. Guangzhou Harbor, China
8. Qingdao, China
9. Jebel Ali, Dubai
10. Tianjin, China

The port of Shanghai handled 32.5 million twenty-foot-equivalent container units, considered the busiest container port in the world in 2012.

High-cube containers (referred to as HQ; they include twenty-foot, forty-foot, and other measurements) are oftentimes shipped at the same rate as a standard container but offer more cargo space and are typically one foot taller. Garment containers have a movable track system, so that prepressed and prelabeled garments can be shipped on their individual hangers, unloaded, moved right into a showroom, and racked for sale. Open-top containers, designed for awkward, oversize goods, such as heavy equipment, can be loaded from the top by crane. This reduces handling costs. Refrigerated containers come in high-cube and wide-body dimensions and offer temperature-controlled environments that can be monitored by means of an exterior temperature recorder, a central shipboard control, or even satellite transmission. Bulk-hatch containers, used for commodities such as corn and grains, can be loaded from the top or the rear for easy access and minimal handling. Vented containers allow for appropriate ventilation and thus eliminate potential condensation, preventing damage to moisture-sensitive goods like tobacco, spices, and coffee. Flat-rack containers, designed for moving huge goods, such as heavy equipment, lumber, and pipes, can be loaded from the top or the side, thus reducing handling costs. An expandable chassis accommodates a variety of box sizes and allows for easy offloading from ship, to train, to truck.

Tip If you are interested in learning more about shipping containers and who invented containerized cargo (hint: an American by the name of Malcolm P. McLean), read the article "The Truck Driver Who Reinvented Shipping,"[6] and try *The Box: How the Shipping Container Made the World Smaller and the World Economy Bigger*,[7] by Marc Levinson. Both are fascinating reads!

Having shown you what's entailed in getting your shipment underway, I'd like to introduce you to one of my favorite solutions for the shipping phase: the freight forwarder.

The Global Freight Forwarder: Your One-Stop Transport Pro

Global freight forwarders serve as all-around transport agents for moving export cargo, typically transporting it from a factory door to your customer's warehouse or storage facility. Their service saves you lots of time, effort, and anxiety and is available for a very reasonable fee, usually under US$200 per transaction—an expense that you'll include in your price quotation to your customer and recoup when you collect payment. These are just some of the things a freight forwarder will do for you:

- Handle all shipping arrangements on the basis of your specifications
- Take legal responsibility for the shipment
- Pay up-front costs to move the product
- Arrange for a carrier to arrive at your factory door at a specified date and time
- Book space with transportation carriers
- Handle all documentation and see that it is properly processed
- Arrange insurance, if requested
- Present documents to your bank in a timely fashion to meet your payment terms
- Suggest or make on-the-spot packing adjustments, if needed
- Move the product from the factory door to the port of exit, either by common carrier or rail
- Take responsibility for getting the cargo on the vessel in time to sail on schedule, thus enabling you to meet all the terms and conditions of your payment agreement
- Monitor the shipment from beginning to end and keep you informed throughout
- See to it that the shipment arrives safely at the foreign port of entry and proceeds from there, depending on the delivery terms that you quoted to your customer

If you were to undertake the transit of goods yourself, you would probably be overwhelmed by all these logistics, and you would certainly not achieve the savings that forwarders can, given the networks of service providers that they have in place and the volume and frequency of shipping that they do. You can find freight forwarders by conducting a web search using the keywords "Freight forwarders, international transportation" or you can check for listings in trade magazines or other international directories. You should find hundreds of them. In some instances, they will be categorized by the geographic area they serve, the type of commodity in which they specialize, or the transport modes they offer, such as air or ocean—most forwarders offer both. Pick two or three that seem like a good fit for your product and shipping destination. Some may be located near your office or by an airport or port facility that you expect to use often.

The Kings and Queens of International Shipping: UPS, FedEx, DHL, and TNT

Logistic experts UPS, FedEx, DHL, and TNT have long been considered the best in international shipping. Check with each of these companies in regard to their areas of expertise, including whether they not only ship worldwide but also handle fulfillment needs and collecting payments from customers worldwide.

- *UPS Global Trade*: http://www.international.ups.com/
- *FedEx Small Business Center*: https://smallbusiness.fedex.com/international
- *DHL*: http://www.dhl.com/en.html
- *TNT*: http://www.tnt.com/express/en_us/site/home.html

Tip The electronic filing of export information, formerly done with the Shipper's Export Declaration (SED) form, is the system used by US companies to electronically declare exports with the US Census Bureau. The process, now called electronic export information (EEI), is done through AES *Direct* (http://aesdirect.census.gov/). The filing is required for items valued over $2,500 or on products requiring an export license.[8] Most sophisticated carriers can take care of the electronic filing on your behalf for a small fee and provide options for you to self-file or provide your own company's completed EEI. Check with each international carrier. Refer to Chapter 13 for more information.

Third-Party Logistics and Fulfillment Centers

Exporting represents a significant opportunity for online small business retailers. Setting up an e-commerce site automatically puts you in front of a potential 2.4 billion online customers.[9] To service even a fraction of those customers, you've got to get up to speed on how to package and ship your products internationally.

A third-party logistics company (abbreviated 3PL) provides logistics services for part or all of your supply-chain-management functions. They can warehouse, pack, and ship your products to customers all over the world, for example. Some will even produce or procure goods for you. Many of these services can be scaled and customized to your needs.

Further, 3PLs allow you to leverage their industry expertise, achieve volume discounts, and realize other benefits (better carrier rates, for instance). To get up and running, many service providers require you to have a good technology program developer on board to install appropriate applications. Prepare accordingly.

Note Typically with a 3PL, you'll need to integrate your e-commerce platform closely with that of the 3PL's provider. Major carriers like UPS and FedEx, for example, offer tools or even application programming interfaces (APIs) that make it possible to calculate the landed cost and integrate shipping tools into your e-commerce platform. Consult with them on how to incorporate their APIs within your existing e-commerce platform.

Ask whether your provider can not only calculate the international shipping costs on transactions but handle the fulfillment part on B-to-C transactions as well. Decisions must be made on who will put your product in a box, label it, insert the appropriate commercial invoice (used as a customs declaration form), calculate shipping charges (including tariffs, duties, and taxes), and ensure the product arrives to a customer's final destination timely, economically, and safely. These are things a 3PL will do for you. It may be worth investigating one or more from the list we will look at to make the fulfillment part of e-commerce easier on yourself and your customers as well.

Third-Party Suppliers

Here is a short list of third-party suppliers (3PLs) who specialize in helping businesses ship internationally and deal with the customs, tariffs, and currency conversions worldwide. The whole point of using 3PLs is to enable you to reach customers globally and take on new customers by using existing technology systems—all without hiring extra employees.

1. *Pitney Bowes: Global Ecommerce*: (http://www.pb.com/ecommerce/). Pitney Bowes helps you extend your e-commerce all over the world by providing a seamless international checkout process (including the benefit of a landed price calculation on international shipments)—the last step in completing an online transaction and making a sale for your online retail environment.

2. *UPS: Order Management and Fulfillment*: (http://www.ups.com/content/us/en/resources/techsupport/alliances/application_order.html). With the help of UPS, you can select from a list of approved service providers who integrate UPS technology into their business applications and software solutions. Note: Using these companies might require the assistance of a technology program developer to get the application installed and up and running.

3. *Amazon Services: Fulfillment by Amazon*: (http://services.amazon.com/fulfillment-by-amazon/benefits.htm). With FBA, you can store your products in Amazon's fulfillment centers and have them picked, packed, and shipped by the company. The company also provides customer service for your products.

4. *Shipwire*: (http://www.shipwire.com/). With warehouses in the United States, Canada, the United Kingdom, and Hong Kong, Shipwire will work with your existing order-capture systems, including automating order submission, real-time shipping rates, and inventory status. Shipwire's warehouses process and ship orders typically the same day and are strategically located to reach customers worldwide within a few days. When the company contacts a customer, it determines the best carrier, service, and packaging to get your product to its destination efficiently, while allowing you to control your order, inventory, and supply chain operations across its warehouses.

5. *Bongo International*: (http://www.bongous.com/). Bongo was established to enable consumers worldwide to purchase and receive goods irrespective of their physical location or payment method. So if customers want to buy something online and the store doesn't accept their preferred international payment method, Bongo will. Membership is free. It focuses on enhancing your cross-border shopping experience and reducing the cost of international transportation. Not quite the supersize of UPS or Amazon but growing, Bongo International currently services ninety-five thousand international consumers and more than three thousand businesses globally.

6. *Fulfillrite*: (http://www.fulfillrite.com/). Fulfillrite's order fulfillment software directly integrates with all major e-commerce shopping carts, including but not limited to: Shopify, BigCommerce, Magento, 3DCart, eBay, Amazon, Paypal, and others. Similar to the other companies listed, upon receipt of your merchandise, Fulfillrite inspects and sorts it. It then enters your merchandise into its system, which you have access to via the web portal. It does the order picking and packing and ships to any international destination via a carrier of your choice: USPS, UPS, FedEx, or DHL Global (Fulfillrite's software is compatible with each of theirs).

7. *Ingram Micro*: (http://www.ingrammicro.com/). IM is a large wholesale distributor that primarily handles technology and is a global leader in IT supply chain, mobile device services, and logistics solutions. I am including it in the list just so you can get a glimpse of who the giants—Apple, Cisco, Hewlett-Packard, Wal-Mart, Amazon, IBM, Lenovo, Microsoft, Samsung, among others—use to distribute and market their technology and mobile products. IM also claims to work with companies of all sizes that can't afford to manage procurement and distribution.

8. *Speed Commerce*: (http://www.speedcommerce.com/). A recent partnership between Speed FC and Navarre, Speed Commerce, provides distribution, third-party logistics, supply chain management, and other related services for North American retailers and their suppliers. It does everything from distribution and sales, to supply chain management, to packaging services.

9. *Mercent:* (http://www.mercent.com/). The company designs e-commerce marketing software for retailers. It does this by providing compelling online e-commerce innovations and technology leadership. Limoges Jewelry, for example, increased its online revenues by 84 percent and reduced its acquisition costs by 10 percent by using Mercent's services.[10]

Tip Some people shy away from putting all their eggs in one basket. In the case of selling, distributing, and marketing your products worldwide, you might want to consider a master logistics provider that does it all. That way, you develop a strong relationship and achieve efficient distribution with fewer touch points (meaning less people handling your product), letting you focus on perfecting your sales and marketing methods.

Simple Methods to Improve Logistics and Boost Sales

There are a few other factors to consider before getting started with international carriers or 3PLs. Here are some steps you can take to improve your international e-commerce results:

1. *Comparison shop between carriers and the various carrier-shipping-fulfillment options.* Saving even pennies on each package you ship internationally can save you big bucks later on, and those savings can boost your bottom line. Use various online calculators (USPS, UPS, or FedEx, for instance) to get an idea of what it might cost to send your package to China as an example of the costs.

2. *Audit your shipping and fulfillments costs quarterly.* See if you are making or losing money. If you are losing money, switch carriers or take an entirely new approach toward the product you are exporting, the market you are entering, and the carrier you are using.

3. *Scrutinize the rates of different carriers to decide whether to opt for a flat-rate price on each package or go by weight or measurement (whichever is greater) on the calculation.*

Chapter 9 | Transport, Logistics, and Fulfillment Options

4. *To ship free or not to ship free? That is the key question.* Free shipping is a growing trend in e-commerce. The most popular offer is free shipping in exchange for a minimum order in dollars. Second to that is free shipping for a limited time only, such as three weeks prior to a Valentine's Day shipping deadline. I've always fallen for the free shipping offers, especially when I need a product and it's coming from overseas, showing that it does have a positive psychological influence on consumers, resulting in increased sales. If you offer free shipping, make sure you don't lose money on those sales!

■ **Tip** To quickly determine how easy or troublesome it might be to export to a particular market, go to the United States Postal Service's international Postage Price Calculator (http://ircalc.usps.gov/), click on the country you wish to export to, and select the type of package and weight (like "Package" and "Two pounds"). Then, click "Continue," select the next option based on your preferred delivery date, and click "Customs Forms" and "Other Service" to get an idea of what documentation is required. Make a note on any prohibitions and restrictions for that country. Bottom line: if you see anything that raises a red flag, whether messy customs restrictions or lengthy paperwork filing, cross the country off your list for doing business.

---

5. *Consider an international mail consolidator service.* As your shipping volume grows, you may wish to consider using this type of company to gather thousands of international mail packages from clients and deliver them directly to the postal system of each destination country. Depending on the services you use, an international consolidator can speed your package processing and provide good postal rate discounts. To find consolidators, conduct a search using the keywords "International mail consolidators." You will find dozens of companies that offer this service. Or a good listing of providers can be found on the "Shipping Consolidators" page of the USPS Web site at https://www.usps.com/business/shipping-consolidators.htm.

■ **Caution** No customers on your e-commerce site? You might ask individuals to buy from the countries you're targeting on your Web site on a test basis. Then, examine what could be preventing consumers from purchasing more from you online—and then carefully address all the reasons behind their reluctance. All things being equal, if you think you are doing everything right, only your customers can tell you how you are not meeting or exceeding their expectations.

Summary

You now have some guidelines telling you what transport and fulfillment methods are available to get your product to your customer and how to make a cost-effective choice. As you move on to put together a price quotation for your customer, including price per unit, total transport, and incidental charges, you'll see exactly how valuable working with a good global freight forwarder, logistics expert, or fulfillment company can be in making the sale and delivering the goods.

Notes

1. "Cisco Exec on Growth of Worldwide Ecommerce, Cultural Differences," Practical Ecommerce, June 10, 2011, http://www.practicalecommerce.com/articles/2841-Cisco-Exec-on-Growth-of-Worldwide-Ecommerce-Cultural-Differences.

2. Marc Levinson, *The Box: How the Shipping Container Made the World Smaller and the World Economy Bigger* (Princeton, NJ: Princeton University Press, 2006).

3. "The Role and Importance of International Shipping," International Maritime Organization, accessed October 31, 2013, http://www.imo.org/KnowledgeCentre/ShipsAndShippingFactsAndFigures/TheRoleandImportanceofInternationalShipping/Pages/TheRoleAndImportanceOfInternationalShipping.aspx.

4. "U.S. Containerized Exports Jump 5% in February," PIERS, *Data in Motion: the PIERS Industry Blog*, accessed October 27, 2013, http://pierstransportation.wordpress.com/2013/06/05/u-s-containerized-exports-jump-5-in-february/.

5. "The JOC Top 50 World Container Ports," *Journal of Commerce*, accessed October 31, 2013, http://www.joc.com/port-news/joc-top-50-world-container-ports_20130815.html.

6. "The Truck Driver Who Reinvented Shipping," Anthony J. Mayo and Nitin Nohria, Harvard Business School: Working Knowledge; the Thinking That Leads, accessed October 3, 2005, http://hbswk.hbs.edu/item/5026.html.

7. Levinson, *The Box*.
8. AES*Direct*, http://aesdirect.census.gov/.
9. "World Internet Usage and Population Statistics," Internet World Stats: Usage and Population Statistics, last modified June 30, 2012, http://www.internetworldstats.com/stats.htm.
10. "Case Studies," Mercent, accessed October 28, 2013, http://www.mercent.com/case_studies.

CHAPTER 10

Pricing and Preparing Quotations

A company's job is to find the market's acceptable price.

—J. Willard Marriott Jr., founder, Marriott International and Robert G. Cross, Robert G. Cross, chairman and chief executive of Aeronomics Inc.[1]

Pricing a product or service for the export market, determining its landed costs (the total cost of a product once it has arrived at your buyer's door, for example), and presenting the costs in quotation form are critical steps in the international sales operation. Price determines revenue. Presenting the pricing and providing the quotes for your goods or services in the right way are both crucial for a successful and ongoing export business. Prices must be high enough to generate and sustain a reasonable profit, yet low enough to penetrate a market, gain market share, attract customers, and be competitive in export markets.

In this chapter, I'll discuss several pricing strategies: how to establish an exporter's markup; how to develop export pricing (which differs from the preceding strategy); and how to work with a freight forwarder, logistics specialist, or fulfillment operation to arrive at good shipping rates that will please your customers. I will also show you how to use these figures to put together a pro forma invoice, a key document in every export transaction.

There are differences in pricing a product when you are a manufacturer's rep vs. when it's your own manufactured product. There is also a difference in pricing a product vs. a service. Be sure to distinguish between each of these pricing tactics as you read through the following pages.

Pricing for Product Exports

Let's look at the three areas of concern related to pricing for exporters.

Representing Exports for a Manufacturer: Product Markup

When you represent exports for a manufacturer, you must determine your breakeven points, where your exporter's commission on a product shipment covers your business operating costs. Theoretically, of course, if you have a customer, say Jane Doe Importing Wholesaler, willing to buy, you can price your product at almost any level, provided it doesn't exceed what the customer is willing to pay or what the market will bear. This assumes the manufacturer has granted you authorization to set any price. Just keep in mind that you don't want to alienate the customer or make it easy for your competitors to undercut you!

Typically, exporters take between a 10 and 15 percent markup on top of the cost the manufacturer charges them for the product. In other words, if your supplier charges you $1 per unit for his product, you might mark it up to anywhere from $1.10 to $1.15 per unit. That markup becomes your profit or commission. Consider the following criteria to determine just how high or low you can go on your markup. This also applies when you manufacture your own product for export, which I will cover later.

1. *Uniqueness*: If the product is a market "first," you can afford to charge a higher price.
2. *Quality*: Is the product's quality upscale? Or marginal? Price up or down accordingly.

3. *Your cost.* If the manufacturer has already priced the product high, keep your markup low. If a major manufacturer (which are those that achieve considerable economies of scale in production) is able to give you a low offering price, then you can afford to set your commission slightly higher. Be careful here, as this scenario can be deceptive. If your cost is low to begin with, it might mean that the product is a mass commodity rather than a specialty offering, and that the market is already flooded with similar "me-too" items. If so, you have to keep your profit margin very tight.

4. *Newness:* Is the product already established or is it new to market? Sometimes you can price higher when a product is new to market just because your customers need and want novel product offerings. But novelty also has its downsides. A new-to-market product doesn't have the brand recognition, image, and popularity that overseas customers tend to look for when they want a product with surefire consumer appeal.

5. *Customer contact:* Who's calling the shots, you or the customer? Did the customer ask you to find the product or did you approach the customer and offer it? This makes a difference. A customer who has asked you to source a product is usually more receptive to a slightly higher price because she really needs the item. Don't lose your head here, though; never, ever get greedy. Your customer knows a rip-off when she sees one.

6. *Product positioning:* Positioning your product in the best possible light determines the price at which you will be able to sell it. Use the product's pricing in the equivalent sector of the domestic market as a guide to your overseas profit margin. For example, if your price for a product is $1 and you are targeting the upscale specialty market overseas, the suggested retail price at a local upscale store could be $8.99, so you take a higher profit margin.

Caution Export and domestic pricing always differ due to a variety of factors. The difference in overseas market conditions, costs, volume, quoting formats, and currencies all affect what you should charge for your products or services in a foreign market.

7. *Direct (includes e-commerce) or indirect sale*: If you are selling directly to an end user, you can afford a higher profit margin. If your product is handled by a series of intermediaries—say, an export trading company, an importer, and a wholesaler—before it gets to the retailer and end user, remember that each of these middlemen will tack on his due percentage, and most likely without your consent, which can jack up the price substantially. If you price high at the beginning, your product will be priced right out of the market by the time it gets to the end user. Nobody wins.

8. *How desperate are you for income? Are you in a mood to see what you can get away with?* If this is the case, I won't stop you. But realize you may be making a big mistake from which you won't be able to recover—and thereby losing a customer altogether. You may really need income and feel you have nothing to lose, but don't forget the priorities of a successful exporter: the customer relationship comes first.

9. *Competition*: Price your products to stay in the global game. If you're up against unlimited competition, make sure you're offering comparable prices along with some extra form of value for your customers.

10. *Government policies*: Government policies can have both direct and indirect impact on pricing policies. Examples of factors that have a direct impact are taxes and tariffs. Examples of factors with an indirect impact are country deficits (spurring high interest rates) and currency fluctuations.

11. *Are you associated with an internationally known celebrity?* That makes a world of difference! No matter what you are offering, fans will buy your product at any price just because star power is attached. Stars whose meteoric success has allowed them to launch successful enterprises (with the help of enterprising people like you) include Jennifer Lopez with her perfume and clothing line sold through Kohl's, Jay Z with his Rocawear, and Jessica Alba with the Honest Co. The more popular your celeb is and the more difficult it is to get the product, the higher you can price it. Mainstream pop culture is the best marketing tool there is—look at Mickey Mouse and Andy Warhol! Consider yourself fortunate to be working with a celebrity, and go for the higher price!

How Pricing Works: Example Where I Represented the Exporting of a Chocolate Manufacturer

Here's an example of how I set pricing when representing a chocolate manufacturer in Chicago: I looked at my American supplier's pricing schedule and saw that a box of chocolates cost $3.00 wholesale (with a US retail price of $15.95 a box). I wanted to make a substantial profit right from the start.

First, I asked the supplier for a 25 percent discount off its standard domestic-price schedule based on a minimum order of a thousand boxes (with twelve units to a box). Hence, the supplier (manufacturer) could achieve economies of scale in production (large production runs that reduce per-unit costs) whenever it produced our overseas orders. It agreed to the price discount.

Next, I conducted market research to determine what the market would bear (including a thorough assessment of competition). Because there was nothing like our chocolates that existed in the market we were entering—Dubai—I decided to keep it clean and simple and price the product 10 percent lower than the standard domestic wholesale pricing or $2.70 per unit ($32.40 per case), even though we were actually getting a 25 percent discount from the supplier. That meant the price to the customer now included our 15 percent commission.

The price still could have been considered high, but the product had unique characteristics—the chocolate was of superb quality and would be available in an exotic flavor. Because I knew that most overseas consumers would love to try it, the packaging was beautifully done, and the retail price point was equally high here in the States, I was convinced that the product could be put into a luxury category. In addition, the product was ideally suited for special occasion celebrations and gift-giving seasons such as Christmas and Valentine's Day, or the equivalent in other parts of the world. All of these reasons assured me that upscale, affluent consumers overseas would be willing to buy such a product whatever it cost. The truth of the matter is that price is important, but it is not the only selling point in a deal.

I contacted a freight forwarder and asked how much it would cost to ship a container-load of boxed chocolates (about a thousand cases) overseas. I was given an estimate of $3,600 (a refrigerated container would be needed during summer months, making the transport price higher than usual), plus another hundred dollars or so for transaction costs. I figured in these transportation costs along with the cost per box to the customer and realized the landed cost of the chocolates was now up to $3.44 per box or $41.24 per case. I'll thoroughly cover how I arrived at this later on.

Then, I made an offer to my foreign customer on behalf of the manufacturer, and he agreed. I had a sale and was delighted that my research had paid off. Now, it was a matter of exceeding the customer's expectations in all respects and developing a great relationship that would grow into other opportunities to export to the same customer in the future.

Chapter 10 | Pricing and Preparing Quotations

Going It Alone: Establishing Product Pricing and Markup for Your Manufactured Product for Export

There's a big difference between pricing a product as an export representative and pricing your own manufactured product for export. When you represent a company for export, the company has already factored in all its direct and indirect costs related to the production of the product. You merely add on your commission in order to offset your operational costs and generate a profit. However, when you price a product that you manufacture for export, you must take into consideration all of the above plus factor in middlemen and apply the following accounting methods:

- Add in all the direct material, labor, and overhead costs involved in producing the goods. Isolate and allocate all the costs.

- Deduct all costs unrelated to an export order (marketing and legal, for example).

- Add in all of the out-of-pocket costs related to making the export sale happen (including but not limited to an export manager's salary and benefits, travel, legal, market research, promotional material, logistics fee, product modification, and translation costs).

- Set a slim margin (a minuscule percentage of the total costs) of error. Meaning, mistakes will happen when you are dealing in uncharted territory. Anticipate them by buffering your pricing to absorb fluctuations (such as higher shipping fees, currency fluctuations, fees for a payment method or early discount).

Caution Don't forget to factor fluctuations in currency into the price. If you plan to sell in currencies other than US dollars, although the exchange rate percentage may be small for converting to US dollars, it can add up over multiple shipments on a regular basis and erode profit margins.

- Make money. You are in the export business to grow and be profitable. Allow a reasonable markup and profit margin, but never lose sight of getting the best market penetration as fast as possible (revisit point number nine in the "Exports for a Manufacturer" section).

> **Tip** Many small business owners use what is called a cost-plus method of pricing. That's when you add up the total costs involved in producing a product, including all expenses related to getting export ready, and then add on a markup to cover an appropriate share of overhead costs plus a fair profit margin that will yield an adequate return on investment. Other business owners use penetration pricing, which is based on standard domestic pricing with a slight discount predicated on the anticipation of volume purchases. When doing penetration pricing, be sure to state an expiration date on your price schedule and indicate that prices are subject to change due to market conditions and the final pricing proposal. In either scenario, monitor results after the fact to ensure you make money.

A good international accountant is always helpful in determining the type of accounting data that should be used in planning and implementing a pricing strategy for the export activity of manufactured products. Your goal is to analyze and control costs to ensure you make a profit. The five key drivers in determining the best export price are: cost, demand (customers), distribution, competition, and government policies.

Test your price out on one of your customers (just as I did with the chocolates) with whom you have cultivated a strong relationship and to whom you've presented your product's positive sales attributes. See what reaction you get and then negotiate from there. If you priced the product with only a slim margin built in for yourself—so slim you cannot afford to go any lower—and your customer still balks at the price, consider renegotiating with your supplier. Oftentimes, if you explain that the only way to sell the product overseas is to price it more competitively, the supplier will agree to go back to the drawing board and see if it can rework the numbers. Don't attempt this too often though, because if you continue to have price problems the supplier will sooner or later catch on that you haven't properly checked out what the foreign market will bear.

Small business owner Caron Beesley, who also serves as the community moderator for the Small Business Administration, says, "Not charging enough is a common problem for small businesses simply because they often don't have the operational efficiencies of larger companies and frequently find that, whatever they sell, their costs are higher than they anticipated. Small businesses do have one advantage, though, and it's one that justifies charging a higher price—service!"[2] Keep this advice in mind as you price for export.

Complete Your Quotation with a Competitive Shipping Rate

Let's say you've given your product a markup of 15 cents on the $1 total cost per unit. By the time it lands at your customer's port, it costs her $1.25 per unit. How does that happen?

Just as in a domestic sale, you will be billing your customer for the costs of shipping when exporting your product. To finish your price quotation, you must first contact a freight forwarder, which will provide you with a competitive shipping rate. But before you contact the freight forwarder, collect the information in the sidebar and keep it right at your fingertips. If you don't have this information when you call, e-mail, or submit your inquiry online (a capability that most of them provide you), the company will require that you get it.

FOURTEEN QUESTIONS YOU WILL BE ASKED BY A FREIGHT FORWARDER

1. *What is your commodity? Is it perishable or nonperishable?*
2. *What is your product's commodity number?* You can look this up in the appropriate directory at your local international Small Business Administration office. A commodity number, generally known as an "HS/Schedule B product description," allows for easy classification by customs officials. It's important to be as specific as possible in determining your product classification, because transportation rates vary widely, even among products you would expect to fall under the same category. For example, there's a big difference between the transportation rates for computer hardware and computer software. If you are unable to determine the appropriate number, the freight forwarder will calculate an accurate shipping quote based on your product description.

   If your product is already a standard export but you are sending it to a new market, a freight forwarder will take your commodity number and assign an appropriate tariff number. That number will then be filed as the industry standard for all subsequent exports of that commodity to that location. Every time you export that product to that country, you must use the assigned tariff number to ensure the same rate.

3. *Are you shipping by air or by ocean?*
4. *How many cartons do you plan to ship?*
5. *What are the size of the cartons?* This needs to be assessed both in linear dimensions (height, length, width) and in cubic meters.

6. *What are the net and gross weights of the cartons in kilograms?* (The net weight is the weight of the product on its own; the gross weight adds the weight of the cartons to that of the product.)

7. *Do you plan to stack the cartons on pallets? If so, how many will be loaded on each pallet?* Your freight forwarder should be able to guesstimate how much weight and cubic space each pallet will take up and calculate the total weight and volume of the shipment accordingly.

8. *Do you have enough product to fill a container?* Full loads of cargo are generally known as "containers" (see Chapter 9) and average between twenty and forty-eight cubic feet. Once you have your total number of cases and total weight calculated, your freight forwarder should be able to tell you if you have enough product to fill a container. If you do, it's an advantage. Your product will be loaded into the container all by itself rather than being consolidated with other companies' products in order to fill the container, and a seal will be put on the door of the container. This means that nobody else will have access to your goods when they arrive at the port of destination, except your customer and his designated agent. This safety measure guards against potential theft, pilferage, and product tampering.

9. *From what location will the product be moved?* Usually, this is the manufacturer's factory door.

10. *To what port does your customer want the goods delivered?*

11. *Will your shipment require an export license?* (See Chapter 13 for a complete discussion of export licensing. To avoid shipping delays, it's best to make this determination as soon as you know what kind of product you'll be selling.)

12. *Are there any time constraints involved in getting the product to a customer?*

13. *Is insurance required for the shipping of your product, and, if so, who will be responsible for it?*

14. *Who will collect the payment on the transaction, and is there a preferred method?*

Having given the company all this information, you can expect a bit of a wait for its response. Generally, an efficient freight forwarder can get back to you with a quote within a few hours. If it's a large firm and a busy time, expect a callback or e-mail the next day. The forwarder should give you a very detailed analysis as to how it arrived at its rates. If there is anything you don't understand, stop and ask about it. Also, ask for a rate confirmation number so that when you call back, whether in a week or several months, the company will have a record of the quote and a way to access it. And don't forget to ask how long the rates are valid! After you've called a few forwarders, sit down and compare quotes.

Tip Many international shipping companies (UPS, for example) have a designated area on their site for calculating shipping costs and estimated delivery times to targeted countries. You will need to provide information about your shipment in required online fields, including destination, origin, shipment date and weight.

How Does the Freight Forwarder Arrive at a Rate?

Besides the physical logistics of your actual shipment, here are some extraneous factors that will affect how your freight forwarder calculates your shipping rate:

1. *The tariff on your product*: Unless the company files a new rate for your product and destination, as discussed in the second item of the sidebar, freight forwarders use rate books to determine the tariff.

2. *The amount of traffic to and from your destination point.* Competitive container port areas such as China and Singapore, for example, can create overcapacity situations in the container port sector, shipping delays, and higher prices on transportation.

3. *How the industry as a whole is performing*: One factor the freight forwarder might look at is whether demand is exceeding available transportation services or the other way around.

4. *Exchange rates*: These rates are a major factor in the transportation calculation. They will be reflected in your quote as the CAF, or currency adjustment factor. Let's say a freight forwarder quotes you a rate of $1,800 for shipping a twenty-foot container-load from a West Coast port in the United States to Tokyo and lists the CAF as 57 percent. That means you must add 57 percent onto the base rate to arrive at a total rate of U.S. $2,826.

Selecting the Best Freight Forwarder for Your Needs

Once you've got a few quotes, you'll need to compare more than the numbers to determine which freight forwarder offers the best value. Ask your customer which of the following should take priority:

1. Low-cost transportation
2. A timely delivery
3. Safe handling of product
4. Choice of transportation method
5. All of the above

Try to select a couple of forwarders that offer the last choice, all of the above, are always pleasant to talk with, and are financially solvent—and then stick with these companies through thick and thin. You do want to double-check the company's financial solvency, because if it goes out of business during the transit of one of your shipments, you are liable for the consequences. If, on the other hand, your customer needs a timely delivery to happen, then select the forwarder that specializes in speed, and so on.

Every time you have a customer who wants a quote, it pays to shop through your list, because you never know when the quality of service might change, the prices might go up, or the company might discontinue service to certain ports. Check and double-check on behalf of your customers. Always offer them the absolute best value you can find because it makes them want to keep coming back.

Chapter 10 | Pricing and Preparing Quotations

Reading Your Quotation

When your freight forwarder gives you a quote, the total charge will be broken down into line items, as shown in Figure 10-1:

Inland transport:	$_____
Ocean transport:	$_____
CAF ___ percent:	$_____
Documentation:	$_____
TOTAL:	$_____

Figure 10-1. Export quotation worksheet. *Inland transport* refers to the cost to move the product from a factory door to a port of exit within the same country. *Ocean transport* is the cost to move the product from the port of exit to the port of entry of the country of destination. *CAF* stands for currency adjustment factor, which is the going rate of exchange from one currency to another; for example, from the US dollar to the Chinese yuan. *Documentation* represents the freight forwarder's fee for handling all documentation associated with the shipment, including letters of credit.

Terms of Shipment

You should also familiarize yourself with the following terms of shipment, which are the ones that are the most commonly used. These are known as *Incoterms*, and according to the International Chamber of Commerce, "have become an essential part of the daily language of trade."[3] They have also been incorporated in contracts for the sale of goods worldwide. These terms of shipment will affect the final numbers on your export quotation as well as your financial responsibility for the shipment:

CIF

You are responsible for paying the cost, insurance, and freight (CIF) costs in advance to a named overseas port. You will collect these later, at the point when you invoice your customer. Normal practice is to insure a shipment for 110 percent of its CIF value. Let's say you are insuring a shipment to the

Far East (Japan, Korea, Taiwan) at a rate of $0.6175 per $100 (which includes war risk insurance and "special perils" coverage). The details are shown in Figure 10-2:

Invoice Value:	$ 12,000.00
Freight:	$ 1,200.00
Clearance/Handling:	$ 100.00
TOTAL:	$ 13,300.00
110% of TOTAL:	$ 14,630.00
INSURANCE:	$ 90.34
CIF TOTAL:	$ 14,720.34

Figure 10-2. Calculating CIF (cost, insurance, and freight) totals

Here's how you arrive at the CIF total: Add the invoice value (cost of the product), freight charges (typically includes fees for both inland/ocean shipping and CAF), and clearance/handling charges. Multiply this total by 110 percent for the cost of the insurance, and then divide by 100. Take the resulting figure and multiply it by $0.6175, which will result in your insurance charge of $90.34. Add this to your previous total of $14,630 for a CIF total of $14,720.34. It's good to know how this is done, but you won't have to concern yourself with this calculation or the actual issuance of the certificate if you use a freight forwarder. All you have to do is ask the freight forwarder to quote you insurance coverage at the 110 percent CIF rate.

CNF

The CNF refers to the cost and freight. The exporter is responsible for paying the freight costs to the named port of destination and collecting the charge from the customer later on.

Note An import duty is payable based on CIF prices, or what is considered the transaction value of invoice. For further clarification, check with the "Technical Information on Customs Valuation" page on the World Trade Organization's Web site (http://www.wto.org/english/tratop_e/cusval_e/cusval_info_e.htm)

FAS

FAS, or free alongside ship, refers to getting the goods shipside and ready to be loaded, all of the costs of which are the exporter's responsibility. The costs of loading the goods into transport vessels at the specified place and all other costs from that moment onward are the customer's responsibility.

FOB

The exporter must take care of all paperwork and/or expenses necessary to collect the goods from the supplier and place them on an international carrier. The buyer is responsible for all costs from the moment the goods are placed on board the vessel and onward, which is known as FOB, or free on board.

Ex-

Terms beginning with "ex," such as *ex-factory* or *ex-dock*, indicate that the price quoted to your customer applies only at the specified point of origin (either your own location, your supplier's factory, or a dock at the export point). This term means that you agree to place the goods at the disposal of the customer at the specified place within a fixed period of time. As the seller, you do not need to load the goods on any collecting vehicle. That is also the responsibility of the buyer.

In order to accommodate the ever-increasing use of the electronic data interchange (EDI), Incoterms have been revised to reflect new shipping methods, such as carrier paid to (CPT), carriage and insurance paid to (CIP), delivered at terminal (DAT), delivered at place (DAP), and delivered duty paid (DDP). Be sure to ask your freight forwarder how each of these terms of the transaction affect the ultimate price of the shipment as well as the logistics of shipping or contact the International Chamber of Commerce (ICC) for additional guidance.

Preparing the Cost Analysis and Pro Forma Invoice

Your next step is to add the itemized charges that appear on your invoice form, which becomes a pro forma invoice.

Your document will have all the familiar components of an ordinary domestic invoice: a description of the product, an itemized listing of charges, and sales terms. Let's say you want to get your customer a landed-price quote for a shipment of candy to her port of entry, in this case "CNF Tokyo."

If you have one hundred cases of candy, packed twelve units to a case, and each case is priced at $120, or $10 per unit, the total cost for the order would be $12,000. Figure 10-3 shows the invoice you would make up:

Pro Forma Invoice # _____	
Date: _____	
Selling price	$12,000 (FOB, with the origin being the factory door in the United States)
Inland transport	$ 700
Ocean transport	$ 1,500
Duty	$ 300
CAF	$ 1,250
Documentation	$ 125
TOTAL LANDED PRICE (or Total CNF Tokyo):	$ 15,875
We certify that Pro Forma Invoice No. _____ is true and correct	
The country of origin is _____	
This quote is valid for thirty days	

Figure 10-3. Pro forma invoice for a shipment of candy to Tokyo

The selling price is your cost to buy the product from the manufacturer plus your markup. Add to that figure the total shipping costs and divide that amount by the number of cases of candy. That gets you your landed price per case. Then, divide that figure by the number of units in a case. This will give you your landed price per unit.

So, if the total landed price for shipment were $15,875 (CNF Tokyo as shown above), and you divided this amount by one hundred cases of candy, you'd come up with $158.75 as the landed price per case. You'd then divide that price by the number of units in a case (twelve) to come up with $13.23 as the landed price per unit. Remember, the selling price is your cost to buy the product from the manufacturer plus your markup.

You have now finalized your price quotation and created a pro forma invoice. Don't forget to specify a precise time period during which your quote is valid (by including, "This quote expires on __/__/__," for example), and to add the freight forwarder's quote reference number.

Three additional critical steps on the pro forma invoice are: (1) Make a statement certifying that the pro forma invoice is true and correct, (2) make a statement that indicates the country of origin of the goods, and (3) mark your invoice clearly with the words "Pro forma invoice."

Once your customer approves the pro forma invoice, it will become your actual invoice for the order. The customer will also use the pro forma invoice to obtain any necessary funding (payment) or import licenses. Your customer should communicate acceptance (usually via fax or e-mail) in a short written sentence or two with a signature, as is done in the following: "We accept your pro forma invoice No. 1234 against our Purchase Order number ABCD." You will then respond: "We acknowledge and confirm your P.O. number ABCD against our pro forma invoice number 1234."

Tip Regardless of whether it has been requested or not, it is wise to prepare a pro forma invoice showing the cost of getting the product to the overseas buyer for any international quotation. Use the Incoterms correctly when quoting. You don't want to get stuck absorbing shipping costs only because you didn't understand how to use the sales terms correctly.

Pricing for Service Exports

Now, at this point, you might be saying, "That's all well and good, but I'm exporting services." Selling a service successfully requires even more people power than does product sales. Pricing a service, such as one that is professional, technical, financial, or franchise or insurance oriented, entails a somewhat-different approach because a service requires direct interaction with your customer, not just initially but for the duration of the service contract. And for some services, the quality of your interaction with your customer is exactly what they're paying for.

Whether pricing a product or a service for export, the fundamentals remain the same: you need to first conduct market research on the competition, the ease of entering a new market, the maturity of the industry, the uniqueness of the offering, and so forth.

But let's not get ahead of ourselves. Here's a look at the other factors that are important to consider concerning pricing a service export:

- You need to differentiate your service offering from existing offerings or convince a prospective customer to hire you to do something that's never been done before.

- Make sure you look at all costs associated with the service offering, including taxes, establishing a foreign branch office, sales visits, translation, IP protection, and so forth.

- Examine and factor in the amount of time that will be spent on the proposal (presales effort) and allocate your schedule accordingly.
- Pay close attention to cultural business practices specific to a country. Will you be pricing your service per hour, on a fixed-project basis, or in some other negotiated format that fits the protocol of the country's standards?
- Make sure to determine how you will account for after-sales nurturing and follow-up costs.
- You'll need to comply with applicable international standards. Learn the tax and legal implications for providing your service in an overseas market well in advance of submitting a proposal to a client.
- Make sure you factor in any promotional costs associated with supporting your services in the overseas market.
- Determine what the impact on your domestic business will be in terms of hiring additional staff, whether it be on the ground in the country in which you wish to conduct business or locally to support the new business.

Tip Set a benchmark price that reflects your brand and capabilities. Tuck away a slim margin that can be used later for negotiating purposes if need be (offering a new client a one-time courtesy discount, for example). Bear in mind you might be competing against more well-known and well-heeled competitors, but if your offering is unique, you've got as good a chance as anyone to land the business.

Pricing Model for a Service Export

I've said it before, but I'll say it again: consult with your international accountant to determine your best service export pricing strategy, especially one that favors healthy profits and minimal tax exposure.

Tip There are other pricing methods, such as variable cost pricing, skimming, and penetration (as touched upon earlier). The decision of which pricing model to use is largely based on the level of competition, innovation, market conditions, and available resources. Consult with your international accountant and also conduct a web search to learn more about each method.

Calculating "cost plus" pricing requires a complete understanding of your total costs (hence, the consultation with your accountant) for delivering your service into a target overseas market. To do that you must:

1. *Know all costs, margins, and expenses to get the service export out the door.* Don't forget to allocate for the after-sales service part of the contract.

2. *Realize you might not be competitive in all markets.* (Adjust your pricing accordingly, but if you find you can't be profitable, go someplace else where you can be).

3. *Align your service export price with its perceived benefits in the target market.* This holds true whether you are pricing a product or a service.

Once you establish the cost, add a margin (return on your investment) to cover profits and to reflect a price that is in line with your perceived market position (think along the lines of Apple providing a technology-export-service proposal vs. ABC Tech House doing so. Apple's pricing will be higher due to its prestige in the marketplace, and ABC Tech House's will be lower due to its unknown name and desire to get a foot in the door.) It is important that you have an understanding of the average margin in the export market for your industry and that you price your service offering competitively to guarantee two things—that someone will purchase the product or service you are offering and that you make money.

Just as on a product export, you need to finalize your pricing by preparing a pro forma invoice. You don't, however, have to concern yourself with Incoterms because you are not shipping products. The pro forma invoice will come in handy later when you discuss with your client how you will get paid (refer to Chapter 11).

Last Thoughts on Market Differences

Here are a few final thoughts on export pricing. Calculating a different price for each overseas market and segment of a market can be a seemingly daunting experience, but it might be necessary because:

- *Customers vary.* In Ireland, for example, you might be selling to distributors that sell to end users, while on your e-commerce site you sell directly to end users. In Dubai, you might sell to small independent retailers and a handful of big box retailers directly. Each of these examples calls for developing specially tailored pricing that meets the needs of the marketplace and provides profits for your business.

- *Markets vary.* Some countries have a five-step distribution method (where the product changes hands five times before an end user purchases it) and others might only have a door-to-door sales concept.

- *Competitors vary.* Tracking your competitors is not only prudent; it's beneficial for determining just how high or low you can set your pricing.

The bottom line is: you need to adapt and adjust.

In the export marketplace, you can never compete on price alone. While price is important, it is seldom the only factor in the buying decision. You need to compete on several different levels. The majority of customers worldwide take into account a combination of factors and look for the whole package before making a purchasing decision. Do your homework. Because the whole purpose of an export business is to gain new business, you need to have the winning combination in overlooked and unlikely market spaces and make money. Use pricing strategy as a spark to enhance export performance, and don't forget to charge what your products are worth.

Summary

You have learned how to coordinate a sale. You are now ready to enter the export business. From this point on, no additional changes should be made to the transaction by you or your customer until after the expiry date given on the pro forma invoice. Before you release the order for your product or the contract for your service, though, you and your customer must negotiate terms of payment. Read on for an overview of the most common—and the most secure—methods of arranging a payment for export goods and services as well as an array of export financing sources.

Notes

1. Peter Krass, *The Book of Management Wisdom.* New York: John Wiley & Sons, Inc., 2000.

2. "How to Price Your Small Business' Products and Services," Caron Beesley, SBA.gov, last modified November 28, 2012, http://www.sba.gov/community/blogs/how-price-your-small-business%E2%80%99-products-and-services.

3. "The Incoterms® Rules," International Chamber of Commerce: The World Business Organization, accessed October 28, 2013, http://www.iccwbo.org/products-and-services/trade-facilitation/incoterms-2010/the-incoterms-rules/.

CHAPTER 11

Getting Paid
Terms, Conditions, and Other Financing Options, Including Mobile Payments

> Ex-Im Bank approved $35.8 billion in total authorizations in FY 2012—an all-time Ex-Im record. This total includes more than $6.1 billion directly supporting small-business export sales—also an Ex-Im record. Ex-Im Bank's total authorizations are supporting an estimated $50 billion in U.S. export sales and approximately 255,000 American jobs in communities across the country.
>
> —PR Newswire[1]

The most important thing to negotiate before closing on an export sale is how payment will be made. In this chapter, I outline several strategies so that you can get paid in full and on time while minimizing risks. I also offer a brief overview of other nontraditional ways to finance an export transaction, should you find yourself unable to work out a standard method of payment.

Traditional Payment Methods

Let's talk about two types of customers. The first is the distributor, overseas agent, wholesaler, or retailer—the big-volume purchasers—who will use the more traditional payment methods I am going to talk about in this section. The other type of customer is your Everyday Joe—the overseas end user—who buys your product from an e-commerce site or mobile device or through an app, which I will explain in greater detail later.

Chapter 11 | Getting Paid

Let's start with the large-volume customer. To make a point fast, I want to share an experience I had when trying to establish a payment method with a new customer. It went like this.

In an early stage of my business, I had been communicating with a customer in Japan for several weeks. His company was large and established and had a solid reputation in the food industry. He was interested in our line of cookies and he placed a $21,000 order.

I responded to his inquiries with a pro forma invoice showing all the pertinent data. In addition, I stated that payment was to be made by a confirmed irrevocable letter of credit[2] (L/C) opened in favor of AB Cookie Kingdom Company (real name withheld for confidentiality reasons) through JP Morgan Chase. A few days later, the company gave the go-ahead to start producing the order. I assumed that it had accepted and approved our pro forma invoice and was about to open the L/C as requested.

A few more days went by.

I scheduled the production of the order. I faxed (that's how we communicated back then!) the company again with the production details and an inquiry as to when I would see a copy of the L/C.

No response. More days went by. Finally, I started to wonder about the customer. I sent another fax asking him exactly what was causing the delay on the L/C. The company finally replied that it had opened the L/C a week ago and that I should be receiving it any day. I phoned the bank and talked to a key contact in the international division. I asked that it keep a special lookout for an L/C coming in from Tokyo.

Still more days went by. The order was produced. The manufacturer invoiced me immediately. The balance was due in full thirty days from the invoice date.

My contact at the bank called me up and reported that he had received an L/C from AB Cookie Kingdom Company with the account number at the top. The bank couldn't understand a word of it, though. It was in Japanese. Note: This had happened to us more than once. We had a similar situation with a customer in Germany on a smaller transaction amount, so pay attention to the lesson we learned the hard way to ensure you don't make the same mistake!

I faxed my customer and asked that the company forward an English-language copy of the L/C so we could make sure we were complying with the terms and conditions.

The customer faxed us another copy of the L/C in Japanese. The inexplicable confusion persisted for several weeks. After we finally received the L/C in English, we found that a condition had been included in the text, stating that the shipper could not consolidate our product with other products to make up a full container-load. This left us with a wide-open payment risk, since shipping companies don't want to sail with a half-empty cargo hold, and our chances of meeting this condition were slim.

We faxed the customer again and asked him to amend the L/C (costing us money, I might add). The company responded by saying that we had instructed it on what to do and it had done that. We tried to tell the people there nicely that they had erred by including the clause prohibiting consolidated shipments.

More time went by. Our manufacturer was calling repeatedly and asking us when we were going to release the cargo. We didn't want to release it without secured payment from the customer.

The customer finally faxed again and requested that we ship "open account," whereby payment is not required until the goods are manufactured and delivered. By then, we were exhausted and desperate (a position you never want to put yourself in!) because we had produced goods that were sitting in a plant waiting to be released—and overwhelmed with frustration at having spent several weeks trying to accommodate our customer with a payment method when what was wanted all along was an open-account status.

We shipped open account. You should most emphatically *not* do that. Why? Many months later, and even then only with the help of the Embassy of the United States in Tokyo, we collected payment.

I learned a great deal from this transaction. Agree on the terms of payment in advance, and never ever sell on open account to a brand new customer. No ifs, ands, or buts. Just don't.

Red Flags

While reading the above account, you probably realized early on that I wasn't dealing with a customer. I was dealing with a noncustomer pretending to be a customer. This story is fortunately not typical, but it does highlight what can go wrong in setting up terms and conditions for an export sale. I caution you to beware of overseas contacts who:

- *Fall off the face of the earth for long periods of time.* A good customer communicates often and conscientiously. If a customer doesn't or can't communicate in an honest and responsible manner, he is not a customer.
- *Ignore instructions.* Get approval and acceptance of your terms and conditions in the form of a signature from a top executive—preferably the owner—of the company with which you are about to do business. If she's reputable, she'll be willing to be held accountable for the terms of the sale.

- *Force you to become lax on your terms and conditions.* A customer who pretends to be a special case, for some contrived and dubious reason, isn't. Don't fall for it.

- *Slip in new terms or information at the latest point in the negotiations without advance discussion.* This is, quite bluntly, the tactic of a con artist. Steer clear.

- *Make you feel desperate (as the Tokyo customer had done with us) or as if you have lost control of your own business.* Let this customer go with a clear conscience. It's better to find one good customer than a hundred bad ones.

These characteristics define what a customer should not be. But once you have found a good customer and have worked your way through the pro forma phase, you can arrange a form of payment that is satisfactory to both parties. In the following section, I will discuss the most common methods of export financing: payment in advance, payment by L/C, and the risky open account.

Choosing a Payment Method—Factors to Consider

Many circumstances and priorities will influence your choice of payment method. A lot will depend on how much you know about financing a sale and how willing your customer is to accept your terms and conditions. Other factors include:

- Your cash flow needs
- Your relationship with your customer
- The economic conditions in the country to which you are exporting
- Interest rates and currency adjustment factors
- The type of product
- Your customer's creditworthiness
- The terms your competitors are offering
- Your supplier's demands
- The urgency of the transaction and whether you are under time constraints

Exporting Essentials

Whatever terms of payment you negotiate, you must always (1) make sure they are understood by all parties and (2) have your customer sign a document that indicates acceptance, such as the pro forma invoice that I talked about earlier. This prevents some unpleasant surprises later on and reduces your shipment liability exposure.

Payment in Advance

Payment in advance is obviously the best of all payment methods since you can prevent possible collection problems and you have immediate use of the money. I use the advance payment method when I know absolutely nothing about the customer, when the speed of handling will make or break the sale, and when the transaction is less than $5,000. The only difficult part of this financing method is actually making it happen.

When your customer agrees to this arrangement, he accepts the full risk of the financial transfer. If he does accept it, ask him to make a wire transfer from his bank account to yours or issue a certified check made payable to you in US dollars, preferably sent by courier. It's reasonable to ask for half of the total sale in advance, with the balance to be paid thirty days from the bill-of-lading date. This reduces your customer's risk, thus helping to maintain goodwill. Make sure, though, that the advance amount covers your out-of-pocket costs.

■ **Note** Never accept cash for a high-value transaction. This poses a risk and could send a red flag to export regulatory officials.

■ **Tip** To get cash in advance, you must ask. Let's say a customer in Yugoslavia wants to import a thousand of your flash drives. So, you prepare a detailed pricing proposal showing all costs involved. Within the proposal you state in bold letters: "Method of Payment: Wire transfer in advance for full amount of order and payable in US dollars." Your customer wire transfers the full cost of the transaction plus your profits, paying a small wire transfer fee. In effect, you not only fronted the funding on the production of goods but you also built in a healthy profit margin to use for funding future growth.

Letters of Credit—Security with Flexibility

After payment in advance, securing payment with a letter of credit (L/C) is the next-best option. It's a more expensive and complicated arrangement, but it's worth it. An L/C is a commercial document issued by a bank at your customer's request in your favor and is based on the seller's instructions outlining desired terms and conditions. It guarantees you'll get paid, as long as the terms stated in it are fulfilled.

■ **Tip** To supplement this chapter (and expand your export resource data bank at the same time), I recommend that you contact a few banks, beginning with your own, and see if it will e-mail you its international banking directory at no charge. Nearly every large bank publishes one. It's usually a slim volume but as good as a fat encyclopedia for showing you every imaginable way to finance an export sale. Such a directory can be very useful for reference should your customer ask you a technical question about how her financing will work.

The Letter of Credit Process

There are four participants in an L/C transaction—two businesspeople and two banks:

1. *The buyer*: That's your customer. He opens the L/C.

2. *The opening bank*: The bank normally issues the L/C, so it is sometimes referred to as the "issuing bank." It assumes responsibility for the payment on behalf of the buyer. The opening bank can contact a corresponding bank near the seller in the United States to advise it on the opening of the L/C. If the L/C is confirmed, the US correspondent bank can confirm and pay on behalf of the buyer provided exact documents required for the L/C are provided and match up.

3. *The paying bank*: This is the bank under which the drafts or bills of exchange are drawn under the credit.

4. *The seller*: That's you—the global marketer, exporter, shipper, beneficiary—to whom the credit is issued.

To summarize the process: Once you and your customer agree on payment by L/C, it is the customer's responsibility to take your pro forma invoice to her bank or to complete the process of setting up the L/C online, with the invoice attached to the application, and opening the L/C in your favor. Once the opening bank has all the appropriate information from the customer, it advises you, the seller, that the L/C has been opened. Oftentimes this will be done by wire to the paying bank. Your bank then forwards that information to you. The L/C is final and subject to correction only for errors in transmission.

Although we live in an era when rapid data transmission by fax or e-mail has become the norm for business communications, some opening banks still prefer to wire advice of an opened L/C and then notify you by telephone (if you have a good international banking officer), e-mail, or snail mail, of its arrival. When you are expecting a an L/C to be opened in your favor, it's prudent to call your bank to notify it to be on the lookout for the L/C or to check the status of it. However the information gets into your hands, review it immediately by checking the terms and conditions against your pro forma invoice.

It is not unusual to find differences between the L/C and the pro forma invoice, such as incorrect product descriptions or reference numbers or an impossibly early shipment date. Once you have confirmed that your invoice is correct, you can try to preempt some of these errors by e-mailing the buyer what is called an L/C template (see http://www.key.com/pdf/sampleloc.pdf) to show him what the completed version should look like. You may find that he ignores it and opens the L/C in the standard format he uses. If that happens and you notice substantive discrepancies, bring them to your bank officer's attention at once. If you find that you cannot make adjustments to accommodate the customer, you must request an amendment to the L/C. This, unfortunately, costs money. Your bank officer can request that the opening bank contact your customer about the amendment or you can bypass the banks and contact your customer directly. Bypassing the bank will save your customer the charges for the amendment but doesn't always provide the safety you still need to maintain the security of the transaction.

If you do communicate directly with your customer, you will need him to acknowledge the discrepancy and state whether or not he will take action to modify the L/C. Buyers generally accomplish this by alerting their bank to the discrepancy when the documents are presented by the bank for approval and then formally waiving that discrepancy. If the customer cannot be relied upon to do this, you get stuck! So always consult with your banker before attempting any informal deals like this.

Accuracy in all details of your L/C is critically important. One of the most exasperating delays I've ever experienced was caused by a discrepancy our bank found between our company name and address on the L/C that I had just presented. It looked like this:

      GLOBAL TRADESOURCE LTD

      6807 N LAKEWOOD, UNIT LL

      CHICAGO, ILLINOIS 60626

      UNITED STATES OF AMERICA

On our commercial invoice, we had given our address as follows:

>Global TradeSource, Ltd.
>
>6807 N. Lakewood, Suite LL
>
>Chicago, IL 60626
>
>United States of America

Would you believe that, from the bank's standpoint, the differences in upper/lower letters, spacing and punctuation were sufficient to indicate a different beneficiary altogether? The bank said it could not present our documents unless we corrected the errors and made everything exactly the same as in the L/C. What choice did we have? We fixed it. We even went so far as to put everything in capitals the way the issuing bank had. Pay attention to the details so nothing will stand in the way of your getting paid!

This synopsis ought to give you some idea of the typical steps taken—and the typical delays—in the L/C process. Don't be surprised at what seems like an unreasonably long turnaround time.

Types of Letters of Credit

There are a number of different types of L/C; two are important enough to distinguish up-front and the others offer more payment flexibility.

Irrevocable Letter of Credit

An irrevocable L/C is a commercial document that the customer requests a bank to issue in your favor. Once issued, it cannot be modified without both parties' consent. In this case, "irrevocable" means that the bank must pay you even if your customer defaults, provided the documents presented are "clean." Clean documents are in complete compliance with the language of the L/C and are presented to the bank prior to the expiration date. It's the most secure method of payment and one that I suggest you use as often as possible. You can also request that the L/C be confirmed by any US office of the issuing bank prior to submission. This arrangement provides the greatest degree of protection because the bank must pay you even if your customer's bank defaults. If the L/C is unconfirmed, the US bank must wait until it receives funds from the foreign bank before it will credit your account.

Banks usually charge about one-eighth of 1 percent (based on the bank's policy and the relationship between the exporter and the bank) of the total transaction cost as a processing fee. Although many exporters complain about this expense, I am convinced that the payment security this document offers far outweighs the negligible fee.

Revocable Letter of Credit

A revocable L/C is a commercial document that your customer requests a bank to issue in your favor that can be modified without both parties' consent at any given point in time. Once this L/C has been issued, you have the following assurances as the beneficiary: the bank can assure you that, yes, your customer has arranged for the bank to pay you such an amount, and, yes, your customer is known, respected, and has been banking with the bank for decades. Unfortunately, you cannot rely on this type of L/C since the bank is under no obligation to cover it if your customer defaults. You may as well just run a credit check on the customer and ship using an open account. It's almost the same risk.

A letter of credit may be modified or restricted in a variety of ways. The most common arrangements are outlined briefly here. If you get stuck negotiating payment terms with your customer, check this section to see if you can find a mutually agreeable option. If you still can't resolve the matter, turn to your international banking advisor for guidance—that's what she's there for. Be creative and cooperative in investigating payment arrangements that will accommodate your customer, but always make sure *you* end up with a secure and timely payment.

Payment Timetables

You may extend varying payment terms within your L/C, ranging from a demand for payment on sight to an allowance of up to 180 days before payment is due. Let's look at each term.

Sight-Draft Payment

The time required to receive funds under an L/C drawing depends on the terms and the location of the paying bank. A sight draft is a payment instrument that requires your customer to pay the amount in full upon receipt of the documents—that is, "on sight"—before title to the goods can be transferred to him. A sight draft is not guaranteed by a bank, so it is vital to get payment before releasing cargo. This payment method is of obvious advantage to you.

Time-Draft Payment

If an L/C calls for a time draft, it is handled by a bank somewhat like a sight draft at the time payment is due; however, a time draft allows your customer some time, usually 30, 60, 90, or even up to 180 days, to pay the amount in full after title to the goods is transferred to her. Customers generally prefer this payment method, but obviously it can compromise your cash flow.

Banker's Acceptance

Once a time draft has been accepted by a bank, it becomes a "banker's acceptance." Since this acceptance is now the bank's liability, it holds payment in safekeeping until maturity and then pays you automatically. Banker's acceptances can also be used to obtain financing by selling the acceptance to the bank at a discount, although this practice is fairly rare.

Special Types and Uses of Letters of Credit

These are some specialized L/Cs that might gain you additional flexibility and security in financing your export transactions:

1. *Transferable L/Cs*: These L/Cs permit you to transfer your rights in part or in full to another party. They are typically used when the original beneficiary (you) acts as a middleman between the supplier of the merchandise and the buyer. The supplier is thus assured of payment for the goods even though it is not dealing directly with your customer. Keep in mind that no credit line is needed here since you are using your L/C as collateral. Once you transfer an L/C, there will be a nominal transaction fee involved.

2. *Assignment of proceeds*: This is very similar to a transferable L/C. The difference is that whether or not an L/C is issued in transferable form, you may request the paying bank to pay the proceeds guaranteed under the letter of credit to a third party. Again, no credit line is needed in this transaction, but you will be charged a nominal transaction fee. The assignment of proceeds, on the other hand, has no monetary value to the third-party assignee until the proceeds (the actual payment by the bank) become available. Therefore, if you neglect to ship merchandise as ordered or fail to submit proper documentation, no payment will be made to the assignee even if he can present the letter of assignment.

3. *Revolving L/Cs*: If you have a customer who intends to give you ongoing business, you may wish to open a revolving letter of credit. You can ask your banker for this, but you may not get it. Banks need to book the entire transaction amount, and for a revolving account, they have no idea what that amount will be. If you are fortunate to be extended this lenient credit arrangement, the amount of the L/C is automatically reinstated after a drawing of

funds or after a specified period of time. The purpose of a revolving L/C is to limit shipments of merchandise, and consequently drawings under the L/C, to limited quantities within a certain period of time. A revolving L/C has the effect of renewing the original set of payment terms and conditions so you don't have to renegotiate each time. Revolving letters of credit are set up differently depending on the particular requirements of each transaction, so always consult with your banker.

4. *Back-to-back* L/Cs: This setup is used fairly often by trading houses or middlemen that do not have the funds necessary to purchase the merchandise or the capital resources needed to obtain an unsecured loan from the bank. Its purpose is to extend indirectly the commitment of the issuing bank beyond the beneficiary to another party, usually the supplier of the merchandise. A back-to-back L/C is quite different from a transferable L/C or an assignment of proceeds in that it is an entirely separate transaction from the original or the master L/C. All parties involved must therefore rely on the successful completion of the original letter of credit. Since this is a more complex form of credit, a consultation with your banker is suggested.

5. *Standby L/Cs*: These serve as assurance that your customer will fulfill her obligations under a contract. In other words, you draw funds under the standby L/C only when your customer fails to meet his obligations. This type of L/C is generally used to repay money borrowed or advanced. It often works well to assure payment of invoices for sales made on open account.

Special Payment Structures

Even though I personally have never had occasion to use any of these special payment structures for an L/C, it is important to let you know that they're available. Consult your banker to find out how they might work for you and your customer.

- *"Red clause"*: Under a red-clause L/C, you are able to obtain advances against the credit in order to purchase and process merchandise. The red clause within the letter of credit outlines a specific payment arrangement over a specific period of time.

- *Installment payments*: Under an installment L/C, you can draw a portion of the credited amount by presenting a sight draft, accompanied by shipping documents and a promissory note for the full credited amount.

- *Progress payments*: A progress-payment L/C allows for you to draw funds against the L/C for amounts proportionate to the progress being made in the production of goods. Proof of progress can be in the form of an inspection certificate issued by you, your customer, or an independent party. This type of L/C is usually used to finance large, long-term projects, such as an economic and real estate development or sales of costly goods, such as large machinery. The balance of the credit becomes available to you once compliance with the terms of the L/C is complete.

- *Advance payments*: This arrangement for the L/C allows for the exporter to receive funds in advance that might be necessary to purchase or process merchandise for the buyer.

- *Deferred payments*: This arrangement calls for sight drafts specifying that the draft is payable at a later date.

- *Discounted payments*: This structure allows you to boost profits for your business with an L/C while satisfying your customer's payment preference. (I am elaborating on this method here because although it is rarely known or practiced, it can be an effective cash flow accelerator for your business.) You can elect to receive payment at sight provided the provisions of the letter of credit are met against an L/C to boost cash receivables and profits. However, this method hurts your customer's pocketbook because he has not, at this point, had a chance to sell the goods you just sold to him. As such, it can be a fairly big cash outlay for him. Alternatively, you can elect to receive a deferred payment (as previously noted), say after 180 days, to allow your buyer a grace period for payment. In that case, there's no boost to your profits or bank account until six months have passed, but your customer will be happy that you've given him more time.

    There is another option in the way of discounted payments that can benefit both the seller and buyer. In this arrangement, once the bank that opens the L/C has accepted the documents and drafts you present, it may discount the amount it owes you and pay you, the beneficiary of the L/C, in advance of the maturity date (a fixed or determinable future date) provided that you indicate that you want this to be done in the agreement. What that means is this: you can allow your customer 180 days after the sight of the original bill of lading to pay her bank, but you collect the money involved in the transaction immediately.

The interest rate on discounted payments for early payment varies from anywhere between 6 and 18 percent of the total transaction bill. It is your responsibility as the seller to absorb it, but it is generally based on the annual rate of interest on a loan, the risk of the country in which the bank opening the L/C is located, and the reputation of the bank. The end result is that you get cash fast from the export sale and your customer gets the 180 days she needs to pay.

- *Mixed drawings*: Sight and time drafts may be specified under the same L/C. For example, the L/C may call for payment of 50 percent at sight, 25 percent sixty days thereafter, and 25 percent ninety from then. The bank oversees and pays the procedural duties when they are due.

The Worst Method of Export Financing: Open Account

An open account transaction means that payment is not required until the goods are manufactured and delivered. This method of payment is fine if your customer is easily accessible. However, in the international business arena, where your customer can be fifteen thousand miles away, this method of payment cannot be used safely unless you are 100 percent certain that the buyer is creditworthy, and unless the country of destination is politically and economically stable. Otherwise, it's a huge risk to the seller (as I pointed out earlier with my Tokyo noncustomer). This is why I keep pushing for the L/C method. Or, at the very least, back up your open account terms with a standby L/C. You might also consider export-receivable insurance, which costs about the same as opening an L/C—about 1 percent of the transaction—but gives you the option of offering your customer open-account terms and retaining some protection. Your banker can assist you here.

But even the most compelling reasons for granting an open account are short-sighted at best. Many books on international sales propound the doctrine that export wannabes should always consider shipping on an open account basis, especially when you're first starting out and a major recognized company is interested in purchasing your products. For example, let's say an international conglomerate called Big Cheese LLC e-mails you a request for $25,000 worth of bicycle parts to be shipped immediately by air. How could a small shop like you, Little Cheese Export Enterprises, resist the chance to win an account like Big Cheese LLC? But we've all heard stories of what can happen to small, growing suppliers who deal with the big players. Conglomerates like our hypothetical Big Cheese LLC have been known to give high-volume business to small firms, enabling them to grow like mad. Then, virtually overnight, they switch vendors—and poof! Poor Little Cheese Export Enterprises bites the dust. It wouldn't be only the loss of the account that would do your company in but the delayed payment on the last order. In fact, some of my own worst payment experiences have been with huge companies that thought they were entitled to pay whenever their accounting department decided they should. I'd find myself waiting two months, three, six. Eventually they'd pay up, but was it worth it? Only if I had a good cash flow and a supplier that was willing to work with me. If you find yourself in circumstances in which you can afford to sweat out big-ticket deficits and you feel certain that somewhere down the line you'll get your money, then go ahead. But how many small-business owners—or beginning exporters—can comfortably operate this way? Take stock of your own situation and proceed accordingly.

If you find yourself in a position where none of these arrangements are possible and you cannot close a sale, you might explore a few of the following financing alternatives. Keep in mind that each industry has its own special government financing programs, so check with your industry associations at both the local and national level to see what they have to offer.

Noteworthy Export Noncash Payment Considerations

Consider the following additional ways to finance an export deal when other means are unavailable:

- *Countertrade:* In countertrade transactions, which involves trading in goods and services as opposed to money, cash does not change hands. Some business owners elect to use this payment method when there is a shortage of hard currency, surplus activity, lack of experience, or lack of credit. The benefits include but are not limited to: entering into difficult markets, increasing sales, overcoming credit problems, and gaining a competitive advantage. The downside is that it can be time-consuming and complex to negotiate.

- *Bartering (a type of countertrade)*: This involves a direct exchange between two parties of goods or services that have an equivalent value without using a cash transaction. In simple terms: it's a swap of one product for another product without the use of any money. The parties involved still must value the goods or services exchanged in the transaction as if they were cash. Doing so will be necessary for tax and customs purposes, so you need to be sure to comply with governmental requirements and accurately complete and file appropriate forms. Barter houses are often called on to assist companies of all sizes to convert what they have into what they need without any cash changing hands (conduct a web search to find ones that specialize in your industry and in a particular overseas market). Barter houses provide information and find potential buyers for goods received. They are particularly useful to the small exporter.

- *Consignment*: This involves an exporter (the seller) selling to a consignee (customer #1) but maintaining ownership of the goods and the consignee only taking possession of the goods in a foreign country. The consignee markets the goods and, when she makes a sale, the title transfers simultaneously from the exporter to customer #1 and customer #2 (the consignee's customer). It's only when the goods are sold—meaning that customer #2 pays customer #1, who in turn, pays the exporter—that the exporter gets paid. The exporter has the main role and is responsible for getting the product to the consignee. Consult with your international attorney to discuss the best terms and conditions for this type of contract arrangement for export sales.

Caution Transacting business in multiple currencies spanning several countries might be beneficial to a big operation interested in hedging against currency fluctuations, but for a small business, if not managed well, it can hurt the bottom line. It's best to negotiate terms in your own country's currency (US dollars, for example). This transfers the risk to the other party—the customer.

Regardless of payment method, it's important to try to keep the international payment process simple.

Export Financing Assistance

There are several federal agencies that offer financial assistance to exporters. These are just a few of the programs and types of assistance that are available to small businesses. Contact your bank to see if it is approved to underwrite any of these programs.

- *Small Business Investment Companies*: (http://www.sba.gov/content/sbic-program). These privately owned companies provide financing, equity capital, and long-term loans to small businesses.

- *International Trade Loan Program*: (http://www.sba.gov/content/international-trade-loan). This program offers loan financing of up to $5 million for fixed assets and working capital for small businesses in a position to either expand existing export markets or develop new markets. These loans are also available if your small business has been adversely affected by import competition and you can demonstrate that the loan proceeds will improve your global-competitive position.

- *Export Working Capital Program*: (http://www.sba.gov/content/export-working-capital-program). This program provides advances up to $5 million to fund export transactions. You can use the loan proceeds to finance suppliers, for work in process, or for production of export goods and services.

- *Export Express Loan Program*: (http://www.sba.gov/content/export-express-program). Considered the simplest export loan program, SBA Export Express offers financing up to $500,000, either as a term loan or a revolving line of credit. To qualify, you must have operated your business for at least twelve months (there are exceptions, so be sure to ask) and must demonstrate that the loan proceeds will be used to support export activity. You can use the loan proceeds to finance export orders, expand your production facility, purchase equipment, participate in overseas trade shows, or translate marketing material for foreign markets.

- *7(a) Regular Business Loan Program:* (http://www.sba.gov/category/navigation-structure/loans-grants/small-business-loans/sba-loan-programs/7a-loan-program): The Small Business Administration offers this long-term loan with a guarantee for small businesses that might not have been able to secure funding through normal lending channels.

- *Foreign Agricultural Service:* (http://www.fas.usda.gov/agx/financing/financing.asp. Run by the US Department of Agriculture, this service provides financial support to food exporters. Check with your state or regional department.

- *Overseas Private Investment Corporation:* (http://www.opic.gov/). OPIC educates small businesses about the benefits of expanding into developing markets and offers a number of products (political risk insurance, for example) and services to address their specific needs. OPIC's Small Business Center offers qualified small businesses with annual revenues less than $35 million the opportunity to utilize the organization's streamlined loan approval process.

- *Minority Business Development Agency:* (http://www.mbda.gov/). MBDA operates more than forty business centers throughout the United States. These organizations, in turn, provide business consulting, procurement matching, and financial assistance (relative to exporting) to minority-owned firms.

Tip Consult the *Trade Finance Guide: A Quick Reference for U.S. Exporters* (http://export.gov/TradeFinanceGuide/) on MBDA's site. It's very useful.

- *United States Trade and Development Agency:* (http://www.ustda.gov/). USTDA links US businesses to export opportunities by funding project planning activities, pilot projects, and reverse trade missions. USTDA is an independent US government foreign assistance agency that is funded by Congress.

Export-Import Bank of the United States

The Export-Import Bank of the United States (Ex-Im Bank; http://www.exim.gov/smallbusiness/) is responsible for assisting the export financing of US goods and services through a variety of loan guarantees and insurance programs. The goals of this agency are to offer superior service and to make a difference by providing exporters with needed support and providing taxpayers with enhanced value. The bank also assists exporters by serving as a liaison between US and foreign banks.

Ex-Im Bank's top five eligibility requirements for small business exporters to receive a loan are that they:

- Be located in the United States
- Have at least one year of operating history along with a positive net worth
- Have services that are performed by US-based employees
- Ship products from the United States to a foreign buyer
- Export products with more than 50 percent US-made content based on all direct and indirect costs

The following list describes just a few of the many programs and products offered by the Ex-Im Bank to exporters. Be sure to inquire further.

- *Working Capital Guarantee:* (http://www.exim.gov/smallbusiness/smallbusprod/Working-Capital-Guarantee.cfm). This is a 90 percent loan-backing guarantee offered to commercial lenders to facilitate small exporting businesses securing the crucial working capital they need to fund their export activities.
- *Global Credit Express:* (http://www.exim.gov/products/global-credit-express.cfm). This program delivers short-term working-capital loans directly to creditworthy small-business exporters. It adds liquidity to the US small-business export market by financing the business of exporting rather than specific export transactions.
- *Letter of Interest:* (http://www.exim.gov/tools/onlineservices/letterofinterest/). This letter states Ex-Im Bank's willingness to consider financing for an export transaction and serves to help small businesses secure financing and make the online application process fast, simple, affordable, and secure prior to export.

- *Export Credit Insurance*: (http://www.exim.gov/products/exportcreditinsurance/): This credit insurance can be purchased from Ex-Im Bank, either through an insurance broker or directly from the bank, to reduce foreign risk. It offers a variety of policies tailored to cover particular risks and situations; for example, the failure of an overseas customer to pay his credit obligation and competitive payment terms.

- *Small Business Insurance*: (http://www.exim.gov/products/exportcreditinsurance/smallbusiness-insurance/). This short-term insurance policy assumes 95 percent of the commercial risk and 100 percent of the political risk involved in extending credit to your overseas customer. Also available are the Umbrella Policy, the Short-Term Single Buyer Policy, and Medium-Term Insurance. Each policy has different requirements, so it is best to get the most updated information and determine how it applies to your export business.

- *Trade Credit Insurance*: (http://www.exim.gov/smallbusiness/moreinfo/Trade-Credit-Insurance.cfm). This policy "specifically covers payment for products or services that are delivered/rendered on open terms to approved buyers. The insurable loss events are insolvency/bankruptcy of the buyer or slow payment. A claim is filed when either of these events occur,"[3] says David Barrett, a sales agent for Euler Hermes North America, a leading provider of trade-related insurance solutions.

- *Working Capital Loans and Guarantees*: (http://www.exim.gov/smallbusiness/moreinfo/Working-Capital-Loans-and-Guarantees.cfm). These loans and guarantees of commercial financing are available to overseas buyers of US capital goods and related services. They offer a low interest rate, cover up to 85 percent of the export value, and generally give repayment terms of one year or more. In addition, they provide repayment protection to creditworthy buyers of US capital goods and related services for private-sector loans.

Since it is impossible to list all the programs offered by Ex-Im Bank, I suggest calling the regional export finance center closest to you (http://www.exim.gov/about/contact/index.cfm) or the Small Business Group (http://www.exim.gov/about/contact/small-business-group.cfm). Its purpose is to help expand local support to small businesses. Use it!

Chapter 11 | Getting Paid

> **Tip** Escrow services allow both exporters and importers to protect a transaction by placing funds in the hands of a trusted third party until a specified set of conditions is met. Shipments are tracked to ensure the seller shipped and the buyer received the merchandise. This can be a beneficial method of payment on international trade transactions. Escrow.com (https://www.escrow.com/why-escrowcom/security.aspx), for example, offers this type of service.

Online Payment Methods: E-Commerce and M-Commerce (Mobile Commerce)

We've already talked about payment options to use with large-volume customers; now let's look at the ones to use for Everyday Joe who only buys online. How will you collect money from him, especially if, for instance, he lives in Brazil? It depends. From this point on, proceed cautiously because no online payment—whether through a Web site, mobile device, or mobile app—will work effectively unless the country you're dealing with accepts it! It's vital to keep that at the top of your mind along with everything else you are about to read. It's also important to take consumers' online preferences into consideration before integrating a payment plan into your e-commerce and m-commerce platforms.

> **Note** By the time you read this, many banks will have launched a mobile payment service[4] that could potentially grow to rival those of credit card companies, especially if these payment methods receive financial institution backing. If these efforts are successful, it could challenge the business model for credit card companies such as Visa, American Express, and MasterCard, which rely on customers to use their branded credit cards for online payments. Watch closely for how this develops and how it might impact your business because the expanding digital payment arena, including wearable devices that make mobile payments, is just beginning to take off. We're living in fast-changing, ultra-tech-savvy times.

Credit, Debit, Global Prepaid Cards, and Third-Party Providers

The majority of online payment is done with credit or debit cards, and a high penetration of people use PayPal in conjunction with their own banks. That said, payment methods still can vary from country to country. How do you know which countries accept which payment method? You can find out by doing the following:

1. Check with your international banker.

2. Inquire with someone who lives in the country with which you desire to transact business.

3. Conduct an online search using the keywords "Preferred online payment methods, _____(country)." Your search entry might look like this: "Preferred online payment methods Norway." As of March 2012, the results would show that 62 percent of online buyers in Norway prefer to make credit card payment, 14 percent prefer using invoices, 8 percent prefer PayPal, 7 percent go with online bank payment, and 3 percent prefer cash on delivery.[5]

4. Check CyberSource's "Global Payment Options: Payment Methods in Select Countries" (https://www.cybersource.com/resources/collateral/Resource_Center/service_briefs/CYBS_Global_Payment_Services.pdf.

Credit Cards

Most US companies offer credit card payment options online because they offer the capability to conduct business throughout the world. Among the credit cards accepted are American Express, VISA, Mastercard, and Discover. All of these work for online transactions, provided the banking system within the country accepts them and they are secure. Many credit card companies charge anywhere from a 1.95 to 3.5 percent service fee on the total transaction price. If a country does not accept a particular credit card, find a comparable service used by the country to fill in the gaps. The greater the global reach for a card, the easier it will be on you for collecting payments.

In addition, several credit card companies now offer country-specific credit cards and other payment services, made possible by special payment features that collect "regional" global payments. These include Maestro offered by Mastercard for use in multiple countries; Dankort offered by Visa in Denmark; Visa's Carte Bleue used in France; Skrill, which facilitates global e-commerce; and debit cards for use in China, to name just a few.

Here is a list of the more popular and commonly used mobile payment methods used in this country:

- *MasterCard PayPass*: (https://www.paypass.com/). PayPass lets you accept everyday purchases quickly and safely through a MasterCard or Maestro-enabled card or device. Buyers can search worldwide for merchants—like you—who accept MasterCard PayPass. Note: Before implementing PayPass, check first with the card's bank to see which countries accept it payment method.

- *Visa payWave for Mobile*: (https://developer.visa.com/paywavemobile). This is a mobile payment system available for Visa issuers, mobile network operators, mobile device manufacturers, and third-party wallet providers looking to develop proprietary applications. According to Visa Developers, PayWave "enables Visa cardholders to simply wave their card or mobile device in front of a contactless payment terminal to make a payment."[6] Buyers can make payments, including credit, debit, and prepaid products for both online and offline contactless transactions.

- *Square*: (https://squareup.com). This online service allows you to start accepting credit cards in a heartbeat at 2.75 percent per swipe. Small businesses can opt to set up a monthly plan for $275 a month (as of this writing). Once you sign up, Square mails you a free Square card reader.

- *Clinkle*: (http://www.clinkle.com). This new mobile payment start-up has developed a practical way to replace credit cards with smart phones. The founders have been hush-hush about what their start-up even does. Word on the street is that Clinkle lets you do phone-to-phone payments via ultrasound exchanged on the phone. This is branded as "Aerolink." It's a work in progress and should be ready by the time you read this.[7]

- *PayAnywhere*: (http://www.payanywhere.com). This credit card reader and free app lets people pay anywhere using Visa, Mastercard, American Express, Discover, and debit cards. You can download it at the App Store, Google Play, and Blackberry App World. PayAnywhere was created by the multibillion-dollar credit-card-processing company North American Bancard, which has more than two decades of merchant-payment-processing experience.

The processing fees are competitive: 2.69 percent per swiped transaction; however, for a keyed-in transaction where you type the credit card number, the rate shifts to 3.49 percent plus a $0.19 transaction fee. There is no monthly fee, minimum required, or cancellation fee. PayAnywhere is compatible with iPhone, iPad, iPod touch, most Android phones or tablets, and Blackberry smart phones, and the company offers 24/7 live customer support through a toll-free number.

- *China UnionPay*: (http://en.unionpay.com/). The leading banking-card association in the world, with more than 3.2 billion issued cards, the company now gives Chinese shoppers with UnionPay cards the option to make online purchases at the Web sites of participating Discover Merchants. What that means is that UnionPay cardholders will have a safe and secure way to make purchases online around the world. In addition, China UnionPay provides access to Discover's services at all ATMs and electronic-payment merchants in Mainland China.

  And there's more. UnionPay recently partnered with PayPay to allow card members in China to use PayPal to shop online. That represents a phenomenal new opportunity for international retailers to sell to a large base of Chinese customers who, combined, hold 2.1 billion cards, according to a PayPal press release regarding the partnership.[8]

Debit Cards

Debit cards, where accepted, can be used instead of cash when making purchases. In some cases, they can be assigned exclusively for use on the Internet. According to FIS, a global provider of banking and payments technologies, "debit cards have surpassed credit cards as the most popular form of electronic payment (by transaction volume)."[9]

Caution The development of debit cards, unlike credit cards, has generally been country specific, resulting in a number of different systems around the world. Be sure to check what type of payment system a country uses or prefers to use before establishing an online payment method. You'll also want to consider the fees associated with every payment option.

Global Prepaid Cards

Inasmuch as U.S. banking credit cards are used widely, not all countries accept them. That is why global prepaid cards are increasingly important for global commerce and are quickly gaining popularity among the millennial generation (Generation Y). Global prepaid cards allow users to preload money and later make purchases and complete payments via American Express, Discover, MasterCard, and Visa cards, ATM networks, private networks, and the Internet. For travelers, prepaid cards are a more secure alternative to the once-popular traveler's checks or large sums of cash.

Take Western Union (WU), a global payment service provider, for example. WU announced in July 2013 that it would work with the Commercial Bank of Dubai (CBD) to create a cobranded prepaid payroll card in the United Arab Emirates.[10] Almost all banks offer global prepaid cards, such as the GoPayment Prepaid Visa Card offered by Intuit and the Global Cash Card offered by Visa and MasterCard.

O_2 mobile payment service, for example, works with VISA and MasterCard to provide UK consumers and businesses with specially tailored card payment options.[11] Another UK service provider, EE, has partnered with MasterCard to launch its first mobile payment system, Cash on Tap. The system lets UK consumers pay for goods and services using their mobile phone via an app, which acts as a digital wallet.[12] Watch for more of these country- and financial institution-specific developments in the future.

Payment-Processing Methods Offered by Third-Party Providers

We will look at the payment-processing methods offered by different third-party providers in this section. The companies' methods will guide you through the payment implementation process for e-commerce and m-commerce transactions. (Some are specific to e-commerce and others require a mobile app, so be sure to double check on what they can and can't do). Most charge a service fee ranging from zero to 2.9 percent, some tack on an additional per-transaction fee (thirty cents, for example), and others charge a monthly fee. Review their terms carefully.

Before you enter into an agreement with any company, find out which countries it services, the fees it charges on each transaction, how it handles disputes, what happens on charge-backs (the process where the cardholder's issuing bank requests a reversal of charges on behalf of the cardholder), what verification system it uses to minimize fraudulent activities, and how to terminate a plan, if need be.

There are many ways to get paid via third-party m-commerce and e-commerce companies. A few payment options offered by companies are given in the following list. There is also some information on the lesser-known payment options. Before making a decision, check reviews and chat rooms about these payment services to learn what users are saying.

- *ACH Payments:* (http://www.achpaymentsolutions.com/). ACH payments are electronic transfers made from one account to another. ACH processing allows you to use the Automated Clearing House (ACH) network to collect payments. Many large banks offer these payments. Bank of America Merrill Lynch is one.[13] PNC[14] and Chase[15] also offer them. Check with your bank.

- *Amazon Payments* (https://payments.amazon.com/): This service operates through your web browser, allowing other Amazon customers to e-mail you money and you to receive it using the accept-payment information in your Amazon.com account. On sales up to $2,999.99, fees range from 2.9 percent plus $0.30 per transaction or less. On transactions of $3,000.00–$9,999.99, fees drop to 2.5 percent plus $0.30 per transaction and so on. Volume discounts apply. Inquire.

    Through Amazon WebPay (https://payments.amazon.com/help/Personal-Accounts/WebPay-FAQ), also offered on this site, you can also send, receive, and request money from *other users* through the Web site. Even if someone does not have an Amazon account, you can still receive money from them provided they register with Amazon Payments to send payment. There is no charge to use the service. Payments are funded by using a credit card. Fees apply for minimum-transfer amounts (bank account withdrawals, for example).

    Using Amazon's payment method could be advantageous for people who have already had positive experiences with the company.

- *PayPal:* (http://www.paypal.com). PayPal allows you to set up a merchant account, through which you can make an online payment to or receive money from any person with an e-mail address. You can use it via the Internet, a mobile device, or in store. The company charges a 2.9 percent transaction fee on the total sale amount plus a $0.30 fee per transaction. The international charge is 3.9 percent transaction fee plus a fixed fee based on the currency received.[16] When you buy something, it is free of a service fee. Transferring money is free, too. PayPal's big advantage is its reach—it is in 193 markets and deals with twenty-five currencies around the world. To appreciate its scope: the company processes almost 8 million payments every day.[17]

- *Bill Me Later*: (https://www.billmelater.com/index.xhtml). A PayPal service, Bill Me Later offers buyers the option of buying now and paying later. It is available as a method of payment at many online stores, and once added to your PayPal account, it can be used almost everywhere PayPal is accepted. It's essentially a reusable credit line without the plastic. BML works well for larger-ticket items where providing financing for a certain period of time, such as six months, will enable a sale. Interest charges apply and accumulate at an APR of 19.99 percent starting from the date of purchase, a significant rate that is important to keep in mind when selling or buying using BML. PayPal tracks purchases and payments done with BML, and provides you an online statement showing all charges.

- *CyberSource*: (http://www.cybersource.com/). Offered by Visa, CyberSource is an online payment service that accepts many payment types preferred in local markets (including Bill Me Later and PayPal), transacts payments in more than 190 countries, and funds in twenty-one currencies. It can be integrated into most major commerce platforms with the help of a savvy tech programmer. In addition, it provides real-time tax calculation for sales originating worldwide so you can provide accurate totals for your customers at checkout. Costs (not listed on site) include set-up and implementation fees based on your specific billing requirements. A monthly usage fee will be charged based on either transaction or revenue volumes.

- *Samurai by FeeFighters*: (https://feefighters.com/samurai). Samurai is debuting as a gateway for online merchants to accept payments. Samurai claims, "No signup, 30 seconds, 19 lines of code" and you are up and running. Speed matters in the online world! According to Samurai, no credit card is needed for this service, which means they allow any business to send any transaction to any processor, with no lock in. Fees on a gateway and merchant account run 2.3 percent per transaction plus a $0.30 fee or $25.00 a month.

Samurai is a newcomer to the field of online payments. Its beauty is the "ability for transactions to be sent to multiple merchant accounts and [the company] will automatically send international and small ticket transactions to the cheapest processor."[18]

- *Dwolla*: (https://www.dwolla.com/). This payment network carries no percentage fees on transactions and charges $0.25 fee. The service is free for transactions of $10.00 or less. Dwolla allows any business to send, request, and accept money. The company's mission: "Allow anyone [or anything] connected to the internet to move money quickly, safely & at the lowest cost possible."[19] If this is true, it's worth a look.

- *Intuit Payment Network*: (https://ipn.intuit.com). From the makers of QuickBooks, Intuit Payment Network allows users to send and receive payments over the Internet. As the payer, it's free to send money and your financial information is never shared. The catch? The receiver's bank shells out $0.50 per transaction. One advantage of IPN is that QuickBook users can include a payment link on invoices so customers can pay conveniently online. The site also provides the option to add pay buttons with fixed or variable amounts on your existing web or e-commerce site. And since it is integrated with QuickBooks, if you are already a QuickBooks client, the ability to streamline your financial management system might make it worth considering. Check reviews online before signing up to gauge its effectiveness.

- *Google Wallet*: (http://www.google.com/wallet). "With the Google Wallet mobile app, you can make your phone your wallet." That's the claim Google makes about Google Wallet, a free digital wallet that securely stores credit cards, debit cards, offers, and more. With GW, your customers can buy in your store, online, and send money. Transactions are fast. There is no setup fee. Receiving money is always free. The fee for sending money using a credit or debit card is not prominently noted on Google's site, other than "There is a small transaction fee."

    According to Google, "You can use Google Wallet in stores, online, and to send money in the United States. Outside the United States, Google Wallet is available to purchase on Google Play in over 125 countries, and to purchase online in over 160 countries and territories."

Here's the catch: Google Wallet app is only available on select Android phones in some places. Google Wallet online can be used to make purchases on Google Play, "or across other Google properties, such as Google+, Google Offers, Google Drive, Chrome Web Store, and YouTube."[20]

■ **Note** Google Wallet could change dramatically when Google rolls it out to US Gmail users and non-Gmail users, so for current users, look for an invite in Gmail's new "Updates" tab if you already have a Gmail account. With the recent launch of Apple Pay, the challenge for any such service will be to take it global, country by country. Watch to see how adoption can be created outside of the US. Regardless, a wallet-less lifestyle is the way of the future.

- *Authorize.Net:* (http://www.authorize.net/). A CyberSource solution and a wholly owned subsidiary of Visa, Authorize.Net enables Internet merchants to authorize and accept online payments via credit card and e-check. The site manages the routing of transactions in a similar way to the traditional credit card swipe machine you find in brick-and-mortar stores. However, instead of using a phone line, it processes the charges over the Internet. Retail merchants can integrate Authorize.Net's payment service via a third-party POS (point-of-sale) payment solution. In addition, the site provides a free Authorize.Net Verified Merchant Seal that can be added to a merchant's Web site to establish trust and build consumer confidence.

  The site's fees run as follows: $99.00 for setup; $20.00 for monthly gateway; $0.10 per transaction fee; and $0.25 per batch (several transactions transmitted at once). Fees can vary according to prices set by Authorize.Net's resellers (the financial institutions that offer the site's payment services), who determine prices based on your type of business and transaction volume.

  Authorize.Net has been providing payment-gateway services since 1996, and as a wholly owned subsidiary of Visa, its reliable reputation makes the company a good choice, but at a price.

- *Stripe:* (https://stripe.com/). San Francisco-based Stripe makes it easy for developers, in specific, to accept credit cards on the web. The key differentiator? You don't need a merchant account or gateway to set up, but you do need a bank account. Stripe stores cards, subscriptions, and direct payouts to your bank account. The fees range from 2.9 percent per transaction plus a $0.30 per transaction fee. An interesting tidbit: the company is backed by PayPal founders Peter Thiel, Elon Musk, and Max Levchin. Most of the site's base is US and Canadian fans, but by the time you read this, that could change and the business could be taken all over the world. Study up.

- *Braintree:* (https://www.braintreepayments.com/). This company, founded in 2007, offers another way to accept payments online (including foreign currency) and on mobile apps. It provides a merchant account, a payment gateway, recurring billing, and credit card storage. Fees are 2.9 percent per transaction plus a $0.30 per transaction fee. There are no additional fees and no minimums. Due to legal and regulatory compliance reasons, Braintree does not work with everybody (door-to-door sales or negative response marketing, for example, are two things they don't do), so be sure to check on the site before making a decision. Braintree works with most of the leading e-commerce and billing platforms. Check to make sure yours is covered.

    At the bottom of their website, it states: "We'll be in more countries soon, get notified."

Caution Fraudulent activity is a pervasive issue when it comes to online payment activity. Be vigilant. Consult with your bank or credit card company to determine the best practice for preventing and managing online payment fraud.

- *Simply Commerce:* (https://www.simplify.com/commerce/). Owned by MasterCard, Simply Commerce (MSC) accepts e-commerce and mobile-commerce payments regardless of the payment brand (meaning, it doesn't just work with MasterCard) in a matter of minutes. It's developer friendly (provided you have a web developer on hand), in that it gives merchants, especially small businesses, the code instructions for accepting electronic payments. MSC serves as both a merchant account and payment gateway in a single, secure package deal. Fees range from 2.85 percent per transaction plus a $0.30 per transaction fee. There are no setup or monthly fees. MSC also works with most of the leading e-commerce (Magento, for example) and billing platforms (OpenCart, for example).

The biggest benefit to MSC is the MasterCard name, which projects security and reliability. Note: As discussed earlier MasterCard also has PayPass (http://www.mastercard.us/paypass.html), a payment method that lets you use your phone as your wallet to make everyday purchases without having to swipe the magnetic strip on your credit card or provide your signature.

Many third-party logistics and fulfillment suppliers (3PLs), discussed in Chapter 9, specialize in helping businesses ship internationally and collecting payment. Inquire.

Final note The information that I have shared in this chapter regarding online payment methods is just the tip of the iceberg. Watch for tremendous strides and breakthroughs in e-commerce and m-commerce payment methods for smart phones and tablets during the coming months—not years—which will bring new options to consumers worldwide.

Summary

Remember what I said earlier: The most important thing to negotiate before closing on an export sale is how payment will be made. Knowing that these solutions exist will allow you to fund, grow, and succeed in the export marketplace.

When you have wrapped up your export sale, either by finalizing secure payment terms or arranging a creative-financing package that satisfies both you and your customer, it's time to move your cargo. After a final review of everything you have put into place thus far, you're ready for the export wrap-up: booking, packing, marking, and insuring your shipment to make sure it arrives in the best condition for your customer and preparing export documentation. The following chapter will outline the most essential documents as well as the less common types you might be required to present. After a final review of terms of payment and documentation, your export goods will be on their way!

Notes

1. "Ex-Im Bank Authorizes $130 Million to Finance Export of U.S.-Manufactured Aircraft and Engines to Ethiopian Airlines," PR Newswire, Reuters, June 27, 2013, http://www.reuters.com/article/2013/06/27/ex-im-ethiopian-air-idUSnPNDC39945+1e0+PRN20130627.

2. An irrevocable letter of credit is a commercial document that your customer requests your bank to issue in your favor. Once issued, it cannot be modified without both parties' consent. "Irrevocable" means that the bank must pay you even if your customer defaults, provided the documents presented are "clean," meaning that they are in complete compliance with the language of the L/C and are presented to the bank prior to the expiration date. I discuss L/Cs in depth later in the chapter.

3. "International Trade Credit Insurance," Laurel Delaney, About.com: Import & Export, accessed October 30, 2013, http://importexport.about.com/od/Financing/a/International-Trade-Credit-Insurance.htm.

4. "Mobile Payments: Three Winning Strategies for Banks," SWIFT: White Paper, 2012, http://www.swift.com/resources/documents/SWIFT_white_paper_Mobile_Payments.pdf.

5. "Preferred Online Payment Methods in Norway 2012," eMarketer, TNS Gallup, Statista, 2013, http://www.statista.com/statistics/248360/preferred-online-payment-methods-among-online-buyers-in-norway/.

6. "Visa PayWave for Mobile," Visa Developers, accessed October 30, 2013, https://developer.visa.com/paywavemobile.

7. "There's Finally a Reason to Be Jealous of Clinkle's $25 Million Stanford Dropouts," Rebecca Greenfield, *Atlantic Wire*, July 2, 2013, http://www.theatlanticwire.com/technology/2013/07/what-is-clinkle/66792/.

8. "PayPal and China UnionPay Open the Global Marketplace to Chinese Consumers," PayPal, March 17, 2010, https://www.paypal-media.com/press-releases/20100317000566.1.

9. "Prepaid Cards," FIS, accessed October 30, 2013, http://www.fisglobal.com/products-card-prepaidcards.

10. "CBD, Western Union to Launch Prepaid Payroll Card in UAE," Staff, Emirates 24/7, July 24, 2013, http://www.emirates247.com/business/economy-finance/cbd-western-union-to-launch-prepaid-payroll-card-in-uae-2013-07-04-1.513215.

11. O_2, accessed October 30, 2013, http://www.o2.co.uk/business/products-and-services/mobile-and-tablets/mobile-payment-service.

12. "EE Cash on Tap Brings Contactless Payments to Mobiles," Expert Reviews, accessed October 30, 2013, http://www.expertreviews.co.uk/smartphones/1300867/ee-cash-on-tap-brings-contactless-payments-to-mobiles.

13. "Automated Clearning House (ACH)," Bank of America Merrill Lynch, accessed October 30, 2013, http://corp.bankofamerica.com/business/ci/landing/ach.

14. "Automated Clearing House," PNC, accessed November 3, 2013, https://www.pnc.com/webapp/unsec/ProductsAndService.do?siteArea=/pnccorp/PNC/Home/Corporate+and+Institutional/Treasury+Management/Collections+and+Deposits/Automated+Clearing+House+%28ACH%29.

15. "Chase ACH Payments," Chase, accessed October 30, 2013, https://www.chase.com/business-banking/online-banking/ach-payments.

16. "PayPal Fees For Purchases, Getting Paid and Personal Transfers," accessed November 3, 2013, https://www.paypal.com/us/webapps/mpp/paypal-fees.

17. "About PayPal," accessed November 3, 2013, https://www.paypal-media.com/about.

18. "FeeFighters Launches Payment Gateway Samurai," Leena Rao, TCTV, September 23, 2011, http://www.techcrunch.com/2011/09/23/feefighters-launches-payment-gateway-samurai/.

19. "Our Mission," Dwolla, accessed October 30, 2013, http://www.dwolla.com/about.

20. Google Wallet: Frequently Asked Questions, accessed October 30, 2013, http://www.google.com/wallet/faq.html.

CHAPTER 12

Booking, Marking, Labeling, and Insuring

Beware of little expenses. A small leak will sink a great ship.

—Benjamin Franklin

Many US companies lose more business in moving products overseas than in any other phase of the export process. In this chapter, I'll explain what the reason for this is and take you through the final steps of sending off your large-volume shipment. I'll also show you how to book your order with a global freight forwarder and how to pack, mark, and insure your cargo for a safe and timely delivery to your customer.

As I discussed in Chapter 9, an experienced global freight forwarder is worth its weight in gold because it will spare you the need to master all the complexities required to send off a shipment. Further, an experienced freight forwarder will let you work "on your export business" (thinking beyond what the day to day reality of your business calls you to do)[1] as opposed to working "in your business"—a classic line by Michael E. Gerber, who wrote *The E-Myth Revisited*.[2] In other words, you don't want to get buried in minutiae that someone else with experience can easily handle; instead, you can spend your time working on getting more export business. Too many details can make you crazy, so my intent here is not to overwhelm you. Rather, it's to provide you with the fundamentals of moving products overseas. After that, it's up to you to use the information as a guide while you work with transport experts to export your products.

A quick note: This section is not about the Everyday Joe who buys a single product online. In this chapter, I will treat big customers—those who buy from a couple of cases to thousands of cases at a time.

Ready? Let's move it!

Booking Your Order

Once you have a legitimate order and finalized terms of payment, it is time to call your freight forwarder and give it the go-ahead to book your shipment. The company should pull up your quote reference number and reconfirm the quote first. Once it books your shipment, it will give you a booking confirmation number. *Write it down* or track it somewhere safe (Evernote.com, for example), because if there's ever a problem later on, you will need to refer to that number constantly.

By now, after my warnings about the necessity of negotiating payment terms to minimize your risk, you're probably a bit nervous about sending off the shipment. What do you do if the payment terms you set up with your customer fall through at the last minute? You do have a means of escape, but it'll cost you. All the way up until it gets loaded onto the vessel, you can ask your forwarder to hold your shipment, but remember, you are liable for all freight costs even if the shipment never leaves port. If your cargo leaves port and you still don't have a guaranteed payment method from your customer, request that the cargo not be released to your customer when it arrives at the port of destination. Normally, it wouldn't be released anyway because your customer needs to produce certain documents in order to clear it—which he won't have received unless payment has been settled—but you never know. When in doubt, always take extra precautionary measures to reduce your risks.

■ **Caution** The scenario where a shipment leaves port and you still have not secured payment illustrates how an export can go wrong. Secure your payment term upfront to ensure you are not left holding the bag.

Let's say you have been assigned the booking number FAN 31063. (The booking number enables the steamship line or freight forwarder to keep track of your shipment from the point of origin to the final destination.) The freight forwarder then gives you sailing information that looks like this: "Dresden Express, V14E30; sailing out of Oakland on 8/19 with ETA Hamburg, Germany 9/20." The forwarder will also tell you the absolute latest you can have your goods ready at your factory door in time to meet the sailing date. You must prepare the necessary shipping documents before then. Pay careful attention to that date, because it's critical information, especially if you are shipping against a letter of credit (L/C) that has an unreasonable expiration date—in this case, September 20. If you miss that August 19 sailing date, you miss meeting one of the conditions of your L/C. When that happens, you lose your guarantee of payment from your customer! Naturally, you want to avoid this at all costs.

Tip You can find global sailing schedules at JOC Sailings (http://www.jocsailings.com/). There, you can filter search results by port locations, carrier, vessel type (break-bulk or container, for instance), departure and arrival dates, and so forth. I use it to do a fast check on transit times to port destinations worldwide. If I were to receive a client's order on July 19, as in the previous example, I would know that I have less than a month to produce goods in time to meet the sailing date out of Oakland. It works the same if a customer says she wants goods delivered to her port of entry by the middle of November. You can check the schedule to see when you need to get goods produced in time to meet the sailing date.

One of the first documents your freight forwarder needs is a Shipper's Export Declaration Form 7525-V (SED; http://aesdirect.census.gov). An SED is required anytime you use a freight forwarder or export directly using a steamship line or air carrier, the value of your shipment is greater than US$2,500 (or US$500 by mail), or the commodities require a license or license exemption (we'll discuss this in Chapter 13). This document specifies your product's commodity number, reaffirms what you have already communicated to the freight forwarder, and formally instructs the company to carry out the shipment. The freight forwarder will refer to the SED to verify that the ocean bill of lading is prepared exactly as your customer specified in the originally accepted pro forma invoice and to confirm the method of payment. The document also helps customs to keep track of exports and to monitor the type of license being used to cover each shipment. It is also used by the Census Bureau to compile statistics on US trade patterns. It must be prepared prior to shipment and presented to the carrier.

Whoever is handling your shipment will be able to provide the online link to the form and, in some cases, can even prepare the document on your behalf provided you authorize the company to do so with a power of attorney form (transport companies typically have this form template online for easy access). If the company does not provide it to you, the SED can be electronically filed at http://www.aesdirect.census.gov. Ask your freight forwarder or shipper how to prepare the form if you are unsure and the company will walk you through the process.

■ **Tip** When in doubt about anything, ask. Be fearless about getting answers. When you see a required field on the SED form, Port of Export code (where your shipment is leaving the country), for example, be sure to consult with your freight forwarder because this field can easily generate errors, penalties and delays in your export shipment if filed incorrectly. In fact, according to U.S. Customs Border Patrol (CBP), it is considered one of the top mistakes they issue penalties for!

Details, Details, Details: Preparing Goods for Overseas Shipment

Let's say you're an exporter specializing in handcrafted figurines and you're all set to move a carton of porcelain angels to your customer in Argentina. Piece of cake, right? Think again! Here are some of the logistics you will have to attend to before this shipment can get out the door:

1. How sturdy is the carton?
2. How secure is the seal that holds the carton together?
3. Is the inside packing strong enough to keep the porcelain undamaged if the box is thrown into a truck?
4. What is the weight of the carton?
5. Is your product a temperature-sensitive export (ice cream, chocolates, or fresh fruit, for example)?
6. What markings should you show on the outside of the carton?
7. Is it important that the package arrives at your customer's doorstep by a certain date?
8. Is any special documentation required to accompany the package?
9. Is it acceptable to leave the shipment outside your customer's factory door should he not be there when it arrives?

10. Do you require that your customer be notified one way or several different ways prior to delivery?

11. Do you require a confirmation of that delivery?

12. What about insurance? If the package gets lost or is damaged in transit, then what?

Caution I once had a client in Chicago who was shipping cookies to Japan in early September in a regular twenty-foot container. The weather is typically cool in Chicago around that time of year, but as it turned out, the temperature abruptly went up to 90°F the week the shipment was leaving. Although warned about the unsuitable weather conditions, the client decided to stay with the regular twenty-foot container to save money instead of using a refrigerated one. When the cookies arrived in Japan, they were a mushy mess due to the unusual heat during transit. It took us weeks to figure out how to correct the situation, a tricky issue since the client had also elected not to insure the shipment. Needless to say, we did come up with a solution, but not without experiencing a lot of stress, needless aggravation, and delays. This illustrates two more examples of what can go wrong on an export shipment—those being the wrong choice on the mode of transport and a bad decision on insurance coverage!

Fortunately, not all products will be as much of a headache as porcelain figurines can be. But every export shipment calls for appropriate attention to the packing and shipping process so that your customers will receive their goods in perfect order. You need to pack your goods carefully so that they will survive the trip undamaged and mark your packages liberally with all the information necessary to ensure proper handling and tracking. You also need to envision the route step by step, from the time it leaves the factory door to the time it gets to your customer, and provide for all contingencies.

Carton Markings for Export

To pack your product effectively for export, you must provide complete, appropriate, and accurate package markings. There are several considerations that govern your shipment marking. First, you must make sure that whatever markings you put on the outside of a carton can easily be read by anyone, anywhere in the world. Second, you must meet shipping regulations and ensure the proper handling of your goods. Finally, you must know when it is appropriate to mark the outside of your cartons with what is truly in the inside—there are times when that's the last thing you should do. Your customer should be your best advisor as to how to mark your cartons for export, but if she seems ill informed or cannot be reached for consultation, the following guidelines ought to cover most situations.

If you are shipping a container-load or more, simple identification of your cargo should be enough, but take extra precaution so that reading your package is easy on the cargo handlers. Pretend the lights are out and your flashlight is dead—and you have to read your cartons. If you were in a gloomy warehouse trying to identify the contents of a stack of cartons, what would you hope for? That whoever prepared the cartons for shipment would have given some thought to making sure their goods could be identified even in the worst-case scenario and marked them accordingly. Mark your cartons with big, bold letters that can be read even at a distance and in poor light. Think about moisture; think about dust; think about accidental grease splattering all over your cartons. Use waterproof markers or waterproof labeling with durable adhesive. The more aggressive and durable your markings, the better your chances of avoiding misunderstandings and delays in shipping.

If you are shipping a smaller quantity of goods, such as a single carton or several cartons to be placed on a pallet, you also need to provide much more detailed identification on the outside of the carton, including the following:

1. *A shipping address label*: Your consignee's (customer's) name, address, and key contact person, and preferably also a telephone number, e-mail address, and fax number should be placed on your shipping label, along with the customer purchase or order number.

2. *A return address label*: Your company name, address, key contact person, and communications numbers (telephone, fax, and/or e-mail) should be placed on each carton, so that if a problem arises en route you can be notified immediately.

3. *The country of origin*: Your return address label should show your country in which you do business, which may not be the actual origin or place where the goods are manufactured. Check with your customer, transport company, or local consulate to see how the country of origin should be represented on the carton. This marking supports all your documentation and streamlines processing at the port of destination.

4. *A description of the contents*: What's included in the package should be marked on the outside—unless you're shipping a product in high demand. If you're shipping a low-price product that you consider a commodity item—canned peas, for example—you might think it's all right to mark the outside of your carton "Canned Peas," right? Not always! If the demand for the product in the importing country is phenomenal and the country can't keep up with it locally, you could be asking for theft or hijacking. Talk to your customer about substituting a different product identification on your carton to make your goods less tempting. For example, if Malaysian consumers love peas and hate green beans, you and your customer can agree ahead of time that, for purposes of your shipment, "Canned Green Beans" means "Canned Peas." This practice, sometimes referred to as blind marking, is simple but effective. However, you and your customer must change your code names every so often or else you'll attract the notice of the smarter and more organized thieves who keep track of what is moving in and out of the ports. More obvious high-value products, such as cameras, computers, or televisions, can also be shipped under blind markings. In all other cases, of course, it's best to mark the outside of your carton with exactly what's inside. That minimizes confusion for customs, your customers, and intermediary handlers at every stage of the shipment.

5. *Markings that are in English*: Unless notified otherwise, everything you write on the outside of your package should be in English. Your customer or your transportation company should be able to tell you whether it is required to provide any carton markings in the language of the importing country as well. If such markings are required, call up a local translator and have the necessary language rendered appropriately. Better yet, contact the country's local consulate to help you—they are always eager to facilitate trade, and it may even provide the service at no charge. But be sure to get your translation approved by your customer. You don't want to be too eager to finish up the labeling chore, only to find that your translation is inaccurate, ambiguous, or even offensive! Note: Foreign law might dictate the need for a translation in the foreign country's language, especially if the item is a hazardous substance. Be sure to check.

6. *Phrases and symbols for immediate identification of packages needing special handling*: There are numerous standard international phrases that signal the need for careful handling of hazardous or breakable products, such as "This side up," "Fragile—Handle with care," "Flammable," and "Keep dry." The International Organization for Standardization (ISO) provides a set of graphical symbols to help overcome language and other barriers (refer to "The International Language of ISO Graphical Symbols," http://www.iso.org/iso/graphical-symbols_booklet.pdf). In addition, they offer a shipping container handling symbol report (refer to "Shipping Container Marketing Specification," http://lineagepower.com/docs/ContainerMarking.pdf).[3] Be sure to also find out which international symbols apply to your product. When in doubt, label your cartons with both words and standard symbols.

7. *An identification of the number of cartons you are shipping*: This should be written on each carton. For example, number each of the respective cartons "One of three," "Two of three," and "Three of three." This ensures that all of the cartons in your shipment will arrive—together—at the port of destination.

8. *A marking on all sides of the package*: If possible, have your cartons marked on five sides—that is, on all four sides and the top. If your plant or transport company cannot do all sides, have markings placed on at least two of them—the long and short ends. But, again, the ideal strategy is to mark five sides. That way, no matter how your cartons are positioned, they can easily be read from any direction. Also, don't forget to remove any old markings. You do not want to create confusion for the receiver of your package.

9. *Weight and measurement markings*: Make sure that your container is marked with the net and gross weight and measurements (dimensions) on the outside and in the appropriate system of measurement, which is generally accepted to be metric.

Caution A lot can go wrong on a shipment when you are in a hurry, because the focus generally tends to be on the quality of the product and how excited the customer will be when he receives it. There's more to getting an export shipment from Point A to Point B. To minimize risks, always take your time and do your homework to avoid awkward surprises that can cause delays, nonpayment, or a customer refusal.

Insure, Insure, Insure!

Insurance is as vital to your product delivery plans as safe vehicles and good sturdy cartons. When you ship important cargo many miles away and it is completely out of your control, you do not want to take any chances on your vessel foundering in a massive midocean storm or your airline simply losing track of your cargo altogether. If situations like these occur, you must be compensated for your cargo's value.

Insurance coverage for export shipments is traditionally provided either through your airline or freight forwarder or by an insurance company specializing in ocean and air cargo. There are three types of coverage commonly provided for export shipments: perils, broad-named perils, and all-risks. Since most transport companies offer an all-risks plan and few, if any, shippers are likely to want to skimp on coverage, I will concentrate on this type of coverage here.

An all-risks policy covers all physical loss or damage incurred by any external occurrence, excluding loss or damage caused by an extenuating circumstance such as war, riots, strikes, or civil disobedience. This type of policy generally costs between 1 and 2 percent of the declared value of your shipment. Coverage varies according to your product type and your destination point—you can get coverage for a portside-to-portside shipment or from the factory door to the customer's door, for example—so be sure to ask your policy provider which type best suits your needs and those of your customer. Keep in mind, though, that no insurance coverage protects you against your customer refusing your cargo or against her failure to secure a required import license delaying shipment clearance, so plan accordingly.

Here are four points to consider when securing air or marine insurance:

1. *Get enough coverage.* Talk to your transportation company about what amount of insurance coverage you will need should your cargo get lost or destroyed. Many people ask for coverage of 110 percent of their transaction value, including freight costs and the insurance. The extra 10 percent is to compensate for your lost time, profits, and any legal or other expenses you might incur from the ordeal. You do not want to find out later (insurance claims typically take anywhere from one to six months to settle) that you are only covered for 20 percent of your transaction value!

2. *Decide who will secure the insurance.* How much control do you want as the exporter (seller) should something go wrong with your shipment? Your terms of sale usually determine this. Your liability ends at the point at which the title to the goods changes from seller to buyer. If you are guaranteed payment for your shipment regardless of its condition upon arrival, you might be more easygoing about letting your customer handle insurance. In addition, if you are shipping open account, I recommend that you not only secure the insurance yourself but also do so through a US company to see that any claims will be settled expeditiously. Don't forget: Your customer is usually the first to discover damage or loss of cargo. He must take all reasonable measures to minimize the loss or damage and to keep the merchandise as evidence for claim settlement.

3. *Decide who pays for it.* Sometimes your customers will request the insurance and offer to pay for it, and sometimes they won't. How you and your customer assign financial responsibility for insurance depends on the cost of the coverage and how the expense will affect each party's bottom line. Negotiate the point to achieve a win-win situation.

4. *Leave a paper trail.* No matter who arranges and pays for the insurance, there are specific documents you must be prepared to present in the event of filing a claim. These include a letter of claim along with a copy of the bill of lading covering the shipment; a copy of an insurance certificate (prepared by your transport company or if you purchased insurance through an independent carrier, by you); and a survey report issued by a claim agent, plus an invoice showing the amount of damage or loss. Timeliness is of the essence—do not miss filing deadlines.

One export shipment that doesn't reach your customer's door is one too many! You could sustain severe financial loss as a consequence; maybe even the collapse of your enterprise. So, protect your business, your cargo, and your customer's interests before releasing merchandise by securing the appropriate insurance coverage.

Summary

At this stage, you will be able to sit back and congratulate yourself because your export goods are on their way! But don't get too comfortable. Within a week, you'll need to prepare all necessary export documentation to ensure that you get paid and that your customer receives the cargo without undue delay. In the next chapter, I will cover the most essential documents as well as the less common ones you might be required to present. In addition, I will talk about the two types of export licenses, when a license is required, and how to procure it. After a final review of terms of payment and documentation, your export transaction will be complete.

Notes

1. "The Book, The Brand, The Business | Working On It™," accessed November 3, 2013, http://www.michael-egerbercompanies.com/1311-the-book-the-brand-the-business-working-on-it/.

2. Michael E. Gerber, *The E-Myth Revisited: Why Most Small Businesses Don't Work and What to Do About It* (New York: Collins Business, 2005).

3. "ISO International Packaging Symbols," accessed November 3, 2013, http://www.gobookee.org/iso-international-packaging-symbols/.

CHAPTER 13

Documentation, Export Licensing, and Other Procedures

One day there will be no borders, no boundaries, no flags, and no countries and the only passport will be the heart.

—Attributed to Mexican-American musician Carlos Santana

In these past several chapters, I've walked you through the somewhat-complex process of getting your export shipment together with the help of your global freight forwarder. In this chapter, I'll go over another set of painstaking but critical details—the preparation of shipping documentation to coincide with your transport and payment methods. I will also address the often anxiety-producing (but needlessly so!) issue of the exporter's licensing responsibilities. Finally, I will provide a checklist for a final inspection of your documentation to make sure everything's letter perfect.

Export Documentation

The first step in preparing export documentation is to carefully list the shipping arrangements you have just made for your customer. You want your export sale to be a complete success, and this is a critical phase. The documentation for an export follows the same pattern as that for a domestic sale. When you sell your widgets to your customers across town, you invoice them, right? That's where you start with your overseas customers as well. Where your local customer sometimes has special requirements for the order, such as a packing list or specified outside markings on each case shipped, your export transaction will have special documentation requirements, too. These will vary according to the country of destination and the type of goods shipped.

If you've selected a freight forwarder that has a history of shipping your type of product, the company should be right on the ball about the current documentation requirements and also offer you the option to process most if not all documentation online. Take the initiative, though, and ask a lot of questions. Use the company's expertise to your advantage.

Nine times out of ten, you will need the following basic documents to complete an export sale:

1. A commercial invoice
2. A packing list
3. A certificate of origin (where applicable)
4. Three original ocean or air bills of lading and copies of them
5. A payment instrument

Other important documents required for some destinations and some commodities:

- A quality-inspection certificate
- A consular invoice
- An import or export license
- An insurance certificate
- Dock and warehouse receipts
- A health inspection certificate
- An IATA (International Air Transport Association) shipper's certificate for restricted or dangerous products

I will review each document thoroughly so you will feel comfortable preparing it. Be aware, too, that there are software programs available that will execute your export documents online efficiently—Unz & Co. offers one (http://www.unzco.com/software/unzexpdoc.htm). As your business grows, you might consider installing one of these programs. Most freight forwarders provide these documents online as well. Whenever you need to review a document to see what it looks like, just conduct an online search to pull one up.

> **Tip** The exports I talk about in this chapter are all ongoing, but that won't always be the case. If you have temporary exports, say if you are exhibiting at a trade show (look back at Chapter 7) in a foreign market and need to send cases of product samples for display, you might consider getting a Carnet. A Carnet is an international customs and export document that is used to clear customs without the need to pay any duties and taxes on merchandise that will be used for trade shows and sales solicitations to prospects. You can learn more at Boomerang Carnets: http://www.atacarnet.com/.

Commercial Invoice

A commercial invoice (for an example, see http://www.unzco.com/forms/commercialinvoices.htm) usually describes what you are exporting and references important transaction numbers. Your invoice must be prepared exactly as you and your customer agreed upon in your pro forma invoice. If both of you agreed on a change in the sale terms later on, record that change on your invoice. In addition, always include the following information, even if it isn't asked for:

1. The customer-reference purchase order number for the pro forma invoice
2. The method of payment, including any and all reference numbers pertaining to it
3. The shipping terms from your price quotation (for example, cost and freight (CNF) Tokyo, free alongside ship (FAS) Seattle, free on board (FOB) New York)
4. The currency in which the transaction will be made (US dollars, Japanese yen, French francs, etc.)
5. The bill of lading number
6. The container number, if shipped by container
7. The ports of exit and entry
8. Marine or air transit instructions: the name of vessel or aircraft, voyage or airway bill number, date of departure, and date of arrival at destination

Packing List

A packing list (for an example, see http://www.unzco.com/forms/packing_envelopes.htm#packinglist) is used to inform transportation companies about what they are moving as well as to allow the customer and others involved in the transaction to check what has been shipped against the pro forma invoice. It's a good safeguard against shipping incorrect cargo! To prepare your packing list, delete all the prices on the invoice and double-check to see that the number of cases; weight (net, gross, metric); and measurements appear on the invoice. Then rename the document "Packing list," and write it in big, bold letters, and you're all set. Your freight forwarder, bank, and customer should indicate how many copies they will need and where each copy will need to be attached (outside of each shipping container in a waterproof envelope, for one) and distributed to the appropriate parties to the transaction (along with your other original documents in line with the terms and condition of the sale), some weeks in advance of when the shipment takes place. I always make three to four extra copies for my file just in case.

Certificate of Origin

Not all export shipments require a separate certificate of origin (for an example, see http://www.unzco.com/forms/certoforigin.htm#General). Often, merely stating the country of origin on your commercial invoice is sufficient. When a certificate is required, it's usually because the country to which you are exporting allows some preferential treatment for shipments like yours, such as a lower duty rate under a trade agreement with the United States, which must be detailed in a separate document. (For example, Mexico, Israel, and Canada have preferential arrangements with the United States if a shipment is intended to be duty-free.) The certificate also protects customers from unknowingly bringing in goods from countries with which trade is prohibited by embargoes, cartels, or other political or economic factors.

Composing the document is utterly simple. Just type up your own sample form for the certificate claiming that your goods are of a certain origin. It would look like this:

> We hereby certify that the goods reflected in our Invoice No. _____ dated _____ were produced and manufactured in the United States of America on _____, 20__.
>
> XYZ Export Co.
>
> _____
>
> Ms. Betsy MacDonald, President

Bear in mind that there are two components to determining the country of origin: (1) the goods must be shipped from that country, and (2) a substantial percentage¹ of the value of the product must be added in that country.

Your customer might request that you have this document certified by your local Chamber of Commerce. To have this done, send the Chamber your prepared certificate along with a letter requesting the certification and three copies of your commercial invoice. The Chamber will take the statement that you provide, retype it verbatim on Chamber letterhead and certify it with notary seal and signature. Most Chambers charge a flat fee ranging from $15 to $25 for this certification. Be sure to read the fine lines of your customer's terms and conditions to determine whether or not you need to have this done. Turnaround time can be as short as twenty-four hours, but you may want to call in advance if you are setting up a shipment in a hurry.

NAFTA Certificate of Origin

Check with your carrier to find out if your product qualifies for a reduction or elimination of duty under the North American Free Trade Agreement (NAFTA). For information regarding eligibility, contact your local US Customs and Border Protection (CBP) office (http://www.cbp.gov/). If it qualifies, the NAFTA Certificate of Origin form (for an example, see http://www.unzco.com/forms/certoforigin.htm#CBP434) should be used to receive the benefits of reduced duty, which will be passed along to your customer. Sample forms can be found at the CBP site (http://www.cbp.gov/xp/cgov/trade/trade_programs/international_agreements/free_trade/nafta/resources/nafta_forms_lp.xml).

■ **Tip** Transactions valued less than $2,500 do not require the NAFTA Certificate of Origin, but you will still be required to make a statement on your commercial invoice to the effect of: "I certify that the goods referenced in this invoice comply with the origin requirements specified for these goods in the North American Free Trade Agreement, and that further processing or assembly outside the territories of the parties has not occurred subsequent to processing or assembly in the NAFTA region." If you do regular shipments of the same group of commodities to the same destination over the course of the year, you can ask your freight forwarder or transport specialist if you can complete a blanket NAFTA Certificate of Origin so as not to have to complete the form for each and every shipment. My theory is, whenever you find something is a royal pain in the #%@, ask how to simplify the process!

Bills of Lading

Depending upon how fast you want to get cargo to your customer and how much she is willing to spend, you will either ship by ocean or by air. Accordingly, there are two types of bills of lading, the ocean bill of lading (for an example, see http://www.unzco.com/forms/ocean.htm) and the airway bill (see http://www.ups.com/aircargo/using/services/supplies/airwaybill.html).

An ocean bill of lading serves both as a receipt for the cargo and as a contract for transportation between you, the exporter, and the carrier. It also symbolizes ownership; accordingly, if it is in negotiable form, it can be bought, sold, or traded while the goods are in transit.

When you use air freight, an airway bill is issued in lieu of a bill of lading. It serves as a through bill of lading, which covers domestic and international flights moving cargo to a specific destination. Your air transportation carrier will advise you of the house airway bill number (shipper's document of receipt) and the master airway bill number (freight forwarder's document of receipt) assigned to your shipment. You must be sure to communicate these to your customer along with other transportation details. Airway bills of lading serve functions similar to those of ocean bills, but they are only issued in nonnegotiable form. This means that you and your bank have less protection because you lose title to the goods once shipment commences. Be sure to refer back to Chapter 9 if you are shipping hazardous goods. Special forms are required.

I will describe ocean bills of lading in further detail because ocean freight is the most economical—and therefore the most frequently used—method of export shipment. To have one made up, you must prepare and submit a Shipper's Letter of Instructions form to your freight forwarder so that it can issue it accurately. This form indicates if the transaction is being made against a letter of credit (L/C), whether insurance is required, where to send documents, and so forth. Once you've finalized terms of payment with your customer, you need to furnish these facts to your freight forwarder. Most bills of lading are issued with three originals and several copies.

There are numerous different types of ocean bills of lading, but you will find that the following are the most commonly used:

- *Straight (nonnegotiable):* This type of bill of lading provides for delivery to the person whose name appears on it. It must be marked "Nonnegotiable." Only the person named can claim the goods upon arrival. A straight bill of lading is usually used for goods shipped on an open-account payment basis in cases where the exporter is not concerned about the importer receiving the goods without payment.

- *Shipper's order (negotiable):* This type of bill is used when you want to impose conditions on the delivery of the goods, such as requiring an acceptance of a draft. This type works well when payment has been secured by a L/C because you can make sure that the terms of the letter of credit are met before the goods are released.

- *Clean:* This type of bill is issued when the shipment is received in good order. If there is any damage or a shortage of product is found, a clean bill of lading will not be issued.

- *Onboard:* This type is issued when the cargo has been placed aboard the named vessel. It is signed and certified by the master of the vessel. For a L/C transaction, an onboard bill of lading is required in order for you, the exporter, to get paid.

Most of my customers ask for a shipper's order bill of lading, which authorizes their bank to take title of the goods should they default on payment. The bank does not release title of the goods to the buyer until payment is received. The bank will also not release these funds to you, the exporter, until all conditions of the sale have been fulfilled at your end.

Payment Instruments

As I discussed in Chapter 11, getting paid is an essential part of the export transaction. Numerous criteria are applied by businesses when determining which payment instrument to offer as a term of sale. A payment instrument in this case refers to documentary collections such as a sight or time draft, which is widely used in international trade. A documentary collection is the collection by a bank of funds due from a buyer against the delivery of specific documents relating to an export sale. The seller (exporter) sends a draft or other demand for payment with the related shipping documents to the buyer's bank. Compared to open account sales, the documentary collection offers more security to the seller (exporter), but less than a letter of credit.

Other Important Documents

Over the years, I have found that the following documents have also been required from time to time. This is not a complete listing, but it will give you an idea of what to expect in the way of special documentation requirements. Note: I am providing a more comprehensive approach to the Import and Export License section to resolve any potential confusion or questions you might have on this topic.

Quality-Inspection Certificate

When shipping high-value products or when you are dealing with a very conscientious customer, an inspection certificate might be requested. An inspection certificate provides proof that what you are shipping is, in fact, what the customer ordered and is also of good quality. If a customer requests this document, agree to it—but see that he covers the administrative and inspection fees. Also, ask him to recommend an independent inspection agency to perform the review at your end. If he doesn't have one, ask your export resource bank for a suitable contact.

Tip I once had a customer in Tokyo who asked to have an inspection of his goods done prior to their leaving the factory in Chicago. He requested that his close friend, living in Chicago, conduct the inspection. When the goods were ready for dispatch, my customer's friend arrived at the plant and opened a few cartons here and there to ensure that we were not shipping inferior merchandise. Then, she eyeballed all the cartons to see that they were marked on the outside in the way her friend had requested. Finding everything in order, she signed the inspection certificate and copies we had prepared in advance. In this case, the inspection didn't cost the customer a cent, everything was certified as A-OK, and we were all happy!

Consular Invoices

A few countries still require consular invoices, which are special forms that must be legalized by a consulate of the country to which you are exporting. This procedure prevents under- or overpricing and also helps the consulates pull in a little extra revenue.

Import and Export Licenses

Recently, I received an e-mail from a woman who works at a small manufacturing company. She explained that her company had recently exhibited at a jewelry show in the United States and a German man had expressed interest in a product at her booth. He had said he would buy ten thousand of her pierced-earring backings if she could ship to the port of Hamburg within sixty days. He had a big fair coming up and knew he could preview the holders to his customers and garner much interest.

She was thinking through the details but was very apprehensive about getting involved in exporting because people had told her that it's hard to get an exporting license. "What is this 'license'?" she asked. I could tell by her message that this single issue was worrying her more than any other aspect of the export transaction requirements I've covered thus far. And, to tell you the truth, I didn't have an answer for her, so I said I would check with the Export Administration Regulations (EAR) and get back to her.

We all fear the unknown, and government bureaucracy is especially scary. Most of us don't want to add more phases to a business process, like exporting, that's already complex enough—especially ones that might slow the project down indefinitely. But don't let an obstacle like this cause you to give up on a good overseas lead! You can find your way around export licensing with less trouble than you think. Let me show you how. As for the woman with the pierced-earring backing holders, it turns out she did not need a license.

First of all, don't worry—just because you have to apply for a license does not mean that there is a possibility that your application will be automatically denied and you'll be barred from exporting your shipment. The licensing process is undertaken for specific governmental purposes, primarily to monitor outbound shipping traffic. There are two types of export licenses: a general license (GL) and a validated license (VL). A general export license is a standing permission given by the government to export a certain category of products. Individual exporters do not need to apply for one. A validated export license, on the other hand, is assigned to a specific exporter for a specific product, either for a designated period of time or for a single transaction. Exporters should know that failure to comply with the regulations surrounding either type of license carries both civil and criminal penalties, so pay close attention.

Determining Which License You Need—General or Validated

The Bureau of Export Administration (BXA) maintains the *Export Administration Regulations* (EAR), which includes the "Commerce Control List" (CCL). The CCL includes items such as software, commodities, and technology, which are subject to the export licensing authority of the BXA. Once you know what you are exporting and where it is going, you can consult these materials to determine which export license you need and find out whether any restrictions apply.

Chapter 13 | Documentation, Export Licensing, and Other Procedures

Note The "Export Administration Regulations" page on the US Bureau of Industry and Security Web site includes downloadable files on everything mentioned in this section—from the "Table of Contents" for the EAR, to the "Index," to the "Commerce Control List," to "License Exceptions." Bookmark it for future reference: http://www.bis.doc.gov/index.php/regulations/export-administration-regulations-ear.

Some sections of the EAR (http://www.bis.doc.gov/index.php/regulations/export-administration-regulations-ear) to check out include:

1. *Part 732, Table of Contents:* "Steps for Using the Ear," is a step-by-step guide to general license obligations.

2. *Parts 738 and 774:* "Commerce Control List Overview and the Country Chart," Part 738, and the "Commerce Control List," Part 774, will tell you which country group your export destination falls into. Don't let the numbers and abbreviations scare you. Once you're looking at the EAR, getting to the right section isn't terribly difficult.

3. *Supplement No. 1 to Part 738:* This supplement to the country chart offers comprehensive instructions on using the chart along with a detailed example. If your country of destination is not listed here, you do not need a validated license unless your commodity meets one of the technical exceptions noted within the export commodity control number (ECCN; an item that may be subject to a short supply control, for example).

4. *Part 774, in reference to the country destinations that require a validated license:* In addition to listing your country grouping, the "Commerce Control List" in Part 774 also lists country export destinations that require a license. If your product is on the list, an "X" appears next to the country you intend to export to. The next step in the export process is to apply for an appropriate license electronically through the Simplified Network Application Process Redesign (SNAP-R). Everything you want to know about SNAP-R can be found at http://www.bis.doc.gov/snap/ and https://snapr.bis.doc.gov/snapr/docs/snaprFAQ.htm. Before applying for a license, check with your customer on what documentation is required.

5. *Part 748*: The "Application Classification Advisory and License," featured in this part, allows you to find the ECCN assigned to your type of product yourself if the Department of Commerce can't help you. For items subject to the EAR but not listed on the CCL, the proper classification is EAR99. This number, which appears at the end of each category in the CCL, is a "melting pot" classification for items not specified under any CCL entry.

You can also contact the Office of Exporter Services at your local department of commerce (DOC) by phone or e-mail to go over these steps. If it can't help you, do the research on your own and then visit one of the DOC counselors to confirm your findings. Check with your international attorney on specific export transactions because the EAR is complicated; the index to the "Commerce Control List" alone is seventy-five pages.

A brief alert: Various requirements of the EAR depend upon your knowledge of the end use, end user, ultimate destination, or other details of the export transaction. If you can discuss your transaction in good conscience with DOC counselors and with complete confidence, then there should not be any cause for an agency intervention. But if you cannot explain whom you are selling your product to, why the customer is buying it in the first place, or what she will do with it once it is purchased, you've got a problem. If this is the case, you should refrain from pursuing the transaction, advise the BXA, and wait. The BXA is there to help you, not hurt you. Its role is to prevent exports and reexports that go against the national security and foreign policy interests of the United States. It is good to consider it our duty as citizens to work in partnership with the agency to maintain the highest standards of protection for our country.

Caution To comply with export law, map out an export-compliance strategy. This is vital. But keep it simple and easy to understand because you don't want to accidentally end up exporting a product that will be used for other wrongful purposes later on. US export controls help protect our country by keeping products and technologies away from countries of concern, persons who might use the products against us, or terrorists. Violations of this nature can result in both criminal and administrative penalties. Assigning one person to track the complete export process carefully and always address the how, what, when, where, why, and originating party of every export is a start to meeting US exporting regulations and keeping our country safe. For more information, visit the US Bureau of Industry and Security (http://www.bis.doc.gov/seminarsandtraining/seminardescription.htm).

Must You Obtain the Import License for the Destination Country, Too?

Obtaining an import license is not your responsibility. It is your customer's. If you have secured payment with him, for example, with an Irrevocable Letter of Credit, it is up to your customer to take the appropriate measures to determine whether he needs an import license. If he does need a license and neglects to apply for it, and you ship against the L/C, you are still entitled to payment because you took care of things at your end. The customer, however, will not be able to clear the product at the port of entry until he clears up the licensing problem. If he fails to get an import license and you ship on open account, you may not get paid until weeks or months later. That said, it is a good idea to find out from your customer if an import license is needed, even though it is not your responsibility to arrange it. Whether or not the license is needed, be sure to secure payment.

Other Port-of-Destination Requirements

It's important to be aware of the standards and regulations of the importing country. Ideally, your customer will be knowledgeable about possible barriers to entry, but it helps to be aware of shipping restrictions and documentation requirements yourself. For example, if you are exporting food, medical, or electrical goods, your customer may not be able to import these items until she conducts an inspection to see that the goods meet local standards. Most developed nations have organizations comparable to the US Food & Drug Administration that monitor product safety. So, before your customer imports so much as a cheese sandwich, she will have to check with the organization that is equivalent to the FDA in his country to make sure the product can be imported. Once you've made sure that there is no reason why your product should be barred from entry, you may be ready to ship.

Shipping Under a General License

If you've checked the EAR and confirmed with your department of commerce that you do *not* need a validated license (VL), you can proceed with your shipment under a general license without having to apply for a formal license. The good news is that the majority of products exported are covered by a general license. You should still check to see, however, if your shipment requires an SED, which, as mentioned earlier, helps US customs to monitor shipment licensing.

Shipping Under a Validated License

On the other hand, you might have found out that the country you want to export to requires a VL for your product. Usually, the following types of products are subject to export controls and will require a VL:

1. Goods that pose potential harm to your own country's security
2. Goods that cause a shortage of supply in your own country
3. Goods that affect your country's foreign policy

As the exporter, you must prepare a Form BXA-622P, "Application for Export License," and submit it to the BXA. Be very, very careful in preparing your submission. Be sure to include any technical or supportive documentation necessary for your product presentation. *Whatever you do, do not ship your goods without first getting a validated license and number.* If you do, you risk severe civil and criminal penalties.

To ensure a smooth license application process, avoid these common pitfalls:

1. Leaving out important information on the application
2. Failing to sign the application
3. Handwriting instead of typing the application
4. Leaving information out of your product description in Section 9b. Be specific and include all appropriate supporting materials
5. Leaving information out of your end-use description in Section 12

The review process to obtain a VL generally takes about two weeks, unless it has to be reviewed by the Department of Defense. Then, it can take longer. If, for example, you are shipping military equipment or other goods with a military application, you have to go all the way to Congress for approval. Depending on the nature and volume of the product to be shipped and the political stability of the country of destination, it can take months before you get the appropriate licenses and authorization. I recommend these guidelines: If your transaction is significant (i.e., it carries a large value in US dollars or requires some secrecy or confidentiality) and is destined for a newly industrialized country or one with which the United States does not have well-developed political or commercial ties, apply for your license several months in advance of production in order to ensure a timely delivery to your customer. Keep in mind that an export of this type is a rarity, especially for a newcomer in the industry.

Once your product is approved and a license number assigned, the license will be mailed to you. This number must be used when you prepare your SED, as previously covered. An SED must accompany all shipments under a VL—no ifs, ands, or buts about it.

Treat the VL as you would a document you are preparing for the IRS. Keep accurate records of all shipments you make against a VL and retain it for at least five years. For further record-keeping measures, refer to Section 787.13 of the EAR.

I recommend that you inquire with your international attorney, your local DOC, and your local Export Assistance Center for further ins and outs of licensing and also to get some hands-on experience in using the reference materials discussed here.

Tip There are license exemptions or exceptions that authorize you to export or reexport items subject to the EAR (see Section 508/Part 740), under stated conditions, where they would otherwise require a license. Check with the Bureau of Industry and Security at the U.S. Department of Commerce at http://www.bis.doc.gov/index.php/564-federal-register-notices-2011-beta-copy.

Insurance Certificate

If the customer requests that you provide insurance, then you must issue an insurance certificate evidencing the type and amount of coverage for the cargo being shipped (refer to Chapter 12). Be aware, though, that some countries prohibit insurance coverage issued in the United States, so check in advance with your freight forwarder before making any insurance commitment to your customer. The forwarder will quote you insurance coverage at the 110 percent CIF (cost of goods, insurance, and freight) value and prepare the certificate for you. The company probably knows that the certificate should be made in negotiable form and must be endorsed before it is submitted to the bank.

Dock and Warehouse Receipts

The dock receipt is issued once the export product has been moved by the domestic carrier to a port of exit and left with the next responsible carrier, which will then take it from the port of exit to the overseas destination. The receipt proves that a transfer has been made from one carrier to another. The warehouse receipt lists the goods received for storage at a warehouse.

Health Inspection Certificate

It is important to know about the destination country's health and sanitary regulations that pertain to the product you are about to export. The best way to find out about these regulations is to contact officials in the Office of Food Safety and Technical Services (OFSTS) at the Foreign Agricultural Service (FAS) located in Washington, DC. This office is largely responsible for overseeing manufacturing, production, and shipping practices that affect food safety, such as food additives, product standards, and packaging.

If you are exporting an agricultural product, you might need a Phytosanitary Certificate detailing inspection. This certificate is issued by the US Department of Agriculture (USDA) to satisfy import regulations for foreign countries. It indicates that a US shipment has been inspected and is free from toxic plant and pest diseases. In addition to the Phytosanitary Certificate, the USDA issues the Export Certificate for Processed Plant Products and the Certificate of Quality and Condition. If a processed plant product cannot be given a Phytosanitary Certificate but has been denied entry to one or more countries for lack of a health certification, an Export Certificate can be issued. Some products in this category are bulk nuts that are salted, roasted, or vacuum packed (in or out of their shells); soy-fortified products; and meal extracted from seeds by solvent. The Certificate of Quality and Condition is offered by the USDA's Processed Products Branch following official inspection and grading of canned, frozen, and dehydrated fruits and vegetables and related products. This certificate is available on a fee basis and can be tailored to meet your specific export needs.

International Air Transport Association (IATA) Shipper's Certificate

An IATA shipper's certificate for restricted or dangerous products is required for all dangerous goods shipments transported by air carriers and air-freight forwarders (http://www.unzco.com/forms/interndangergooddec.htm#IATAdec). The exporter (shipper) is responsible for accurately completing the information on the form per the instructions of IATA (http://www.unzco.com/forms/instructions/DG_IATA.pdf) and ensuring that all requirements have been met through IATA's Dangerous Goods Regulations (http://www.iata.org/publications/dgr/Pages/index.aspx). Compliance measures include, but are not limited to packaging (shipping carton is adequate, for example), marking (the product exported is identified correctly), and required information related to the product exported.

Get It Right the First Time, So That It Is the Only Time

Even a minor documentation problem can cost you and your customer time and trouble. Once, a very upset Greek customer faxed me about a documentation problem on a shipment he had just received. He complained that I should have prepared the commercial invoice to match up exactly with the pro forma—yes, I know I've just been lecturing you on the importance of doing that, but back then I didn't realize just how important it really was. My customer told me that the local customs officials would not allow clearance of the goods because of that particular discrepancy. Although I was a little confused by the extra data they wanted included on the commercial invoice, I reissued it within minutes, not just in one new version but in three, just in case the first one didn't suit the people at customs. As it turned out, all three of them worked, so they settled on the one that best suited their needs and cleared their shipment.

Fortunately for me, that mistake was easily resolved. In fact, to this day—twenty years later—the customer still brings up this story because he never had a supplier go to such great lengths to get it right the second time! Now, my guiding principle is to go to great lengths to get it right the first time so that it is the only time. It should be yours, too.

Tip Most transport companies can alert you to documentation problems and take care of them on your behalf. The only thing that might be required is your approval on a reissuance of a document and perhaps a signature (online or offline).

Summary

Hopefully this chapter has alleviated any concerns you might have relative to what is essential when preparing shipping documentation to coincide with your transport and payment methods. You're well on your way to becoming a successful exporter.

I have emphasized again and again that the world of international business is driven by relationships. If you want to succeed in building your own network of relationships, you may need to rethink the way you do business and make a comprehensive commitment to customer service. Much of your success will have to do with communicating regularly, following up to ensure satisfaction, following through on promises, and becoming a valued participant in your customer's business and professional growth.

And that's it! It's been a whirlwind tour of exporting, but I have given you just what you need to succeed. Start the export journey to growth and prosperity for your business. Remember, it's never too late. If I can create an exporting company, so can you. *Go for it!*

And One More Thing . . .

I want to leave you with an invitation to join the Export Guide Group (MOOD), a massive open online dialog that I established on LinkedIn. It's where you will find me and everyone else, like you, who has read this book and has a relentless desire to keep learning and growing. There, we connect and answer questions, process new ideas, and exchange best practices in exporting. I liken this practice to a radical export revolution. Come join the conversation: http://tinyurl.com/kpgbdwf. See you there!

Note

1. See http://www.ftc.gov/os/1997/12/epsmadeusa.htm#e16

Index

A
Ad valorem duties, 35
Air cargo containers, 127
Air cargo pallets, 127
Air transport, 127
    air cargo containers, 127
    air cargo pallets, 127
    IATA, 127
All-risks policy, 203
Amazon services, 137
Architectural, construction, and engineering services, 73

B
Back-of-the-napkin export business plan, 18
Binational societies, councils and trade associations, 54, 98
Bongo International, 138
Booking, 195
    legitimate order, 196
    letter of credit (L/C), 197
    SED, 197–198
    steamship line, 197
Boost sales improvement methods, 139
Born-global companies, 11
Break-bulk shipments, 130
    crates, 131
    pallets, 131
    slipsheets, 131
Bulk-hatch containers, 133
Bulk loading, 131
Bureau of Economic Analysis (BEA), 54
Bureau of Export Administration (BXA), 215
Business intelligence companies, 52, 94
BusinessUSA, 50

C
Carton markings, 199
    description, 201
    gloomy warehouse, 200
    identification of number, 202
    in English, 201
    phrases and symbols, 202
    return address label, 200
    shipping address label, 200
    sides, 202
    weight and measurement, 202
Commerce Control List (CCL), 215
Commercial, professional, technical and business services, 73
Community moderator, 149
Competitive analysis (market and customer), 24
Competitive shipping rate
    best freight forwarder, 153
    cartons, 150
    CIF, 154–155
    CNF, 155
    commodity number, 150

Competitive shipping rate (cont.)
  containers, 151
  domestic sale, 150
  ex-factory, 156
  export quotation worksheet, 154
  FAS, 156
  FOB, 156
  freight forwarder, 152
  pro forma invoice, 157
  terms of shipment, 154
Compound/mixed duties, 36
Container alliance, 132
Container loading, 132
Corporate, legal, financial and logistical considerations, 27–28
Cost, insurance and freight (CIF), 154
Country riskline report, 86
Credit cards
  China UnionPay, 185
  Clinkle, 184
  Mastercard PayPass, 184
  PayAnywhere, 184
  Square, 184
  Visa payWave for Mobile, 184
Cross-border customers
  definition, 84
  distributor/importing wholesaler, 84
    characteristics, 85
    distributors, 86
    questions, 86
  e-commerce, 90
  overseas agent/representative (importer), 88
  overseas end user, 89
  overseas retailers, 88
  trading company, 89–90

D

Datamyne, 95
Debit cards, 185
Department of Commerce (DOC), 47
DHL, logistic experts, 135
Direct exporting
  advantages, 102
  disadvantages, 102

E

eAtlas of Global Development, 53
E-commerce, 90
Economical transport package
  motorbridge service, 130
  NVOCCs, 129
  shipping lines, 129
  start-to-finish transport, 129
Education and training services, 73
Electronic export information (EEI), 135
Entertainment and media, 73
Environmental services, 73
Euromonitor International, 53
Exchange rates, 153
Export
  awaits, 1
  born-global companies, 11
  definition, 2
  foreign (overseas) markets, 5
  global mindset
    assessment, 8
    local business model, 10
    self-awareness, 8
  Internet, 1
  local marketing service, 4
  overview, 1
  product and service
    export process, 6
    people power drives, 7
  product business, 2
  social networks, 2
Export Administration Regulations (EAR), 215
Export Assistance Centers (EACs), 47
Export business plan
  development, 15
  express and experience, 26
  market conditions, 17
  overview, 13–14
  pointers for development, 17
  purposes for, 14
  types
    back-of-the-napkin, 18
    components, 18
    LEBP, 23
    traditional business plan, 19

Export documentation, 207
- bills of lading, 212
  - clean, 213
  - onboard, 213
  - shipper's order (negotiable), 213
  - straight (nonnegotiable), 213
- certificate of origin, 210–211
- commercial invoice, 209
- consular invoices, 214
- destinations and commodities, 208
- dock and warehouse receipts, 220
- export sale, 208
- health inspection certificate, 221
- IATA, 221
- import and export licenses, 215
  - general license, 218
  - general/validated, 215
  - GL and VL, 215
  - import license, 218
  - port-of-destination requirements, 218
  - validated license, 219
- insurance certificate, 220
- minor documentation, 222
- NAFTA, 211
- packing list, 210
- payment instruments, 213–214
- quality-inspection certificate, 214

Export dream team (EDT), 25
- accountant, 29
- banker and logistics expert, 29
- business bank account, 33
- IC-DISC, 36
- lawyer, 28
- legal considerations
  - intellectual property, 31
  - labor laws, contracts and agreements, 32
  - online environment, 31
- start small, 29
- tax benefits for multinational business, 34
- trade and customs duties, 35

Export-Import Bank (US), 50

Export management companies (EMCs), 88, 103

Export market data
- additional instant resources, 55
- binational societies, councils and trade associations, 54
- Bureau of Economic Analysis, 54
- business intelligence companies, 52
- colleges and universities, 51
- Doing Business site, 53
- eAtlas of global development, 53
- Euromonitor International, 53
- export practitioner, 52
- federal exports
  - additional resources, 51
  - Export-Import Bank (US), 50
  - FAS, 51
- foreign trade, 52
- International Trade Statistics Yearbook, 54
- physical locations, 46
  - DOC, 47
  - SBA, 46
  - US commercial service, 48
- US and World Population Clock, 53
- web sites (trade statistics)
  - BusinessUSA, 50
  - market research index, 49
  - TradeStats express, 49
  - United States International Trade Commission, 50
  - USA Trade Online, 49
  - USEmbassy.gov, 50
  - WTO, 50
- World Bank Atlas method, 53
- World Factbook, 53

Export practitioner, 52

F

FedEx small business center, 135

Financial services, 73

Financing assistance
- export express loan program, 178
- export-import bank, united states, 180
  - capital guarantee, 180
  - capital loans and guarantees, 181
  - export credit insurance, 181
  - global credit express, 180
  - letter of interest, 180
  - requirements, 180

Index

Financing assistance (cont.)
    short-term insurance policy, 181
    trade credit insurance, 181
  export working capital program, 178
  foreign agricultural service, 179
  international trade loan program, 178
  MBDA, 179
  OPIC, 179
  regular business loan program, 179
  small business investment companies, 178
  USTDA, 179

Finding cross-border customers, 83
  binational societies, councils and trade associations, 98
  business intelligence companies, 94
  customer contacts, 90
  Gold Key Matching Service (see Gold Key Matching Service (GKMS))
  government-sponsored trade mission, 97
  IBP, 94
  IPS, 94
  platinum key service, 94
  snag customers worldwide (see Snag customers worldwide)
  tap local clients, 98
  trade leads database, 94
  US Export Assistance Centers, 93

Finding cross-border customers. See Cross-border customers)

Flat-rack containers, 133

Foreign Agricultural Service (FAS), 51

Foreign trade, 52

Foreign trade zones (FTZs), 36

Free alongside ship(FAS), 156

Freight forwarders, international transportation, 135

Fulfillment part, 136

Fulfillrite, 138

G

Garment containers, 133

Global freight forwarder, 134

Global strategic alliance (GSA), 110
  advantageous alliances, 111
  advantages, 112
  autonomy and independence, 115
  business/geographic market, 110
  consideration, 115–116
  cost of, 111
  disadvantages, 113–114
  negotiations, 114
  small business, 111

Gloomy warehouse, 200

Gold Key Matching Service (GKMS)
  benefits, 92
  help us, 92
  in India, 93

Government-Sponsored Trade Mission, 97

H

Hand loading, 131

Healthcare, 74

High-cube containers, 133

Huntington Bank, 70

I

In-country factors, 107

Indirect exporting, 103
  advantages, 105
  conference/trade, 104
  disadvantages, 105
  EMC, 103
  export trading company, 104
  freight forwarders, 104
  international division, 104
  local trade association, 104
  small business assistance center, 104

Ingram Micro, 138

Insurance, 203
  definition, 203
  insurance coverage, 203
    all-risks policy, 203
    types, 203
  marine insurance, 203
    discover damage or loss of cargo, 204
    financial responsibility, 204
    insurance coverage, 203
    paper trail, 204

Index | 229

Interest-charge domestic international sales corporation (IC-DISC), 36
International Air Transport Association (IATA), 127, 221
International Buyer Program (IBP), 94
International Company Profile (ICP), 87
International franchising
    benefits, 118
    definition, 117
    examples of, 118
    get started, 119
    resources, 119
International Partner Search (IPS), 94
International Trade Statistics Yearbook, 54
Internet Corporation for Assigned Names and Numbers (ICANN), 31

J, K

Joint venture, 116
Journal of Commerce (JOC), 95

L

Laurel export business plan (LEBP)
    company description, 23
    competitive analysis (market and customer), 24
    executive summary, 23
    financials (export budget), 25
    future development, 25
    information technology plan, 25
    introduction, 23
    logistics plan, 25
    management structure, 25
    marketing and sales plan, 24
    operations plan, 24
    strategic leadership, 23
    strategy implementation, 25
    target export market, 24
Letter of credit (L/C), 164, 197
    buyer, businesspeople, 168–169
    commercial invoice, 170
    fax/e-mail, 169
    opening bank, 168
    paying bank, 168
    pro forma invoice process, 168–169
    securing payment, 168
    seller, business people, 168
    special payment structures
        advance payments, 174
        deferred payments, 174
        discounted payments, 174
        installment payments, 174
        mixed drawings, 175
        progress payments, 174
        red clause, 173
    timetables
        banker's acceptance, 172
        sight-draft payment, 171
        time-draft payment, 171
    types
        assignment of proceeds, 172
        back-to-back setup, 173
        irrevocable, 170
        revocable, 171
        revolving, 172
        standby, 173
        transferable, 172
Licensing, 121
Logistics. *See* Third-party logistics company (3PL)
Logistics improvement methods, 139

M

Marine insurance
    discover damage/loss of cargo, 204
    financial responsibility, 204
    insurance coverage, 203
    paper trail, 204
Market research
    action plan creation, 55
    customers, 40
    foreign maket, 39
    market conditions, 43
    market research, 40
    pleasure, profit, competitive advantage/challenge, 41
    segmentation, 42
Market research. Export market data
Market Research Index, 49
Mercent, 139

Index

Methods of exporting, 102
    collaborative sales, 109
        global strategic alliance (see
            Global strategic alliance (GSA))
        joint venture, 116
        partnership, 110
    direct exporting (see Direct exporting)
    factors, 101
    foreign office/acquiring, 120
    in-country factors, 107
    indirect exporting (see Indirect
        exporting)
    international franchising
        benefits, 118
        definition, 117
        examples of, 118
        get started, 119
        resources, 119
    licensing, 121
    questions, 106
Million Dollar Database (MDDI), 87
Minority Business Development
    Agency(MBDA), 179

N

Non-vessel-operating common carriers,
    and shipper's (NVOCCS)
    associations, 129
North American Free Trade Agreement
    (NAFTA), 211

O

Ocean transport, 128
Online environment
    domain name protection, 31
    ICANN, 31
Open-top containers, 133
Overseas marketplace, 59
    account cultural sensitivities, 61
    bilingual label, 64
    CE mark, 63
    Chinese consumers, 60
    competition, 65
    cultural environment affects, 66
    cultural significance, 64
    customers, 62
    electrical products, 65
    export country's expectations, 62
    extend current product
        applications, 65
    foreign market's local language, 61
    handle warranties, guarantees,
        consignment sales and
        service calls overseas, 65
    local product regulations, 66
    overall packaging and
        labeling design, 62
    packaging and product, 59
    packaging material, 64
    physical environment affects, 66
    picture tells, 64
    purchases online, 63
    standardized products and services, 60
    weights and measurements, 63
Overseas Private Investment
    Corporation(OPIC), 179

P

Payment methods, 163
    advance payment, 167
    big-ticket deficits, 176
    E-commerce and M-commerce, 182
        credit cards (see Credit cards)
        debit cards, 185
        global prepaid cards, 186
        online payment, 183
        third-party providers
            (see Third-Party providers)
    e-commerce site/mobile
        device, 163
    factors, 166
    financing assistance (see Financing
        assistance)
    international conglomerate, 175
    L/C (see Letter of credit (L/C))
    noncash payment
        considerations, 176
        bartering, 177
        consignment, 177
        countertrade, 176
    open account transaction, 175
    red flags, 165

Index

Phrases and symbols, 202
PIERS, 95
Pitney Bowes, 137
Platinum Key Service (PKS), 94
Pricing, 143
    market, 161
        customers vary, 161
        product exports (see Product exports)
        service exports, 158
            fundamentals, 158
            pricing model, 159
Product exports
    accounting methods, 148
    chocolate manufacturer, 147
    community moderator, 149
    establishment, 148
    key drivers, 149
    manufacturering company, 144
        celebrity, 146
        competition, 146
        cost, 145
        customer contact, 145
        direct/indirect sale, 146
        government policies, 146
        newness, 145
        product positioning, 145
        quality, 144
        uniqueness, 144
Product vs. service (difference), 71

Q

Quotations, 143
    competitive shipping rate, 150
        best freight forwarder, 153
        cartons, 150
        CIF, 154–155
        CNF, 155
        commodity number, 150
        containers, 151
        domestic sale, 150
        ex-factory, 156
        export quotation worksheet, 154
        FAS, 156
        FOB, 156
        freight forwarder, 152
        pro forma invoice, 157
        terms of shipment, 154

R

Refrigerated containers, 133
Retail and wholesale trade, 74

S

Service Corps of Retired Executives (SCORE), 47
Service export
    architectural, construction, and engineering services, 73
    commercial, professional, technical and business services, 73
    demand worldwide, 73
    destination volume, 75
    education and training services, 73
    entertainment and media, 73
    environmental services, 73
    financial services, 73
    healthcare, 74
    Huntington Bank, 70
    Internet markets, 80
    launch service
        acquisition, joint venture, partnership/franchise, 78
        approach foreign companies, 78
        existing domestic clients, 78
        seek representatives/agents, 79
        target market, 79
        virtual consultant (teleconsultant), 79
        working relationships, 78
    overcoming market barriers, 76
        cultural differences, 77
        economics, 77
        government, 76
        local practice and custom, 77
    overview, 69
    people power drives, 72
    product-export business, 75
    product vs. service (difference), 71
    retail and wholesale trade, 74
    supply chain and distribution, 74
    telecommunications and information services, 74
    transportation, shipping, distribution and logistic services, 74

Index

Service export (*cont.*)
  travel and tourism, 74
  wildflower-nursery business, 79
Service exports
  fundamentals, 158
  pricing model, 159
Shipment Overseas, 198
Shipper's Export Declaration(SED), 197
Shipping address label, 200
Shipping lines, 129
  conference lines, 129
  independent lines, 129
Shipwire, 137
Small Business Administration (SBA), 46
Snag customers worldwide, 96
  domestic (local) trade shows, 96
  international trade shows, 97
Special payment structures
  advance payments, 174
  deferred payments, 174
  discounted payments, 174
  installment payments, 174
  mixed drawings, 175
  progress payments, 174
  red clause, 173
Speed Commerce, 138
Steamship line, 197
Supply chain and distribution, 74

T

Tariff, 127
Telecommunications and information services, 74
Third-party logistics company (3PL), 136
Third-Party providers
  ACH payments, 187
  Amazon WebPay, 187
  Authorize.Net, 190
  Bill Me Later, 188
  Braintree, 191
  CyberSource, 188
  Dwolla, 189

FeeFighters, 188
Google Wallet mobile app, 189
Intuit Payment Network, 189
MSC, 191–192
PayPal, 187
Stripe, 190
Third-party suppliers (3PLs), 136
  Amazon services, 137
  Bongo International, 138
  Fulfillrite, 138
  Ingram Micro, 138
  Mercent, 139
  Pitney Bowes, 137
  Shipwire, 137
  Speed Commerce, 138
  UPS, 137
Timetables
  banker's acceptance, 172
  sight-draft payment, 171
  time-draft payment, 171
TNT, logistic experts, 135
Trade and customs duties, 35
Trade Leads Database (TLD), 94
TradeStats express, 49
Traditional Export Business Plan, 19
Transportation, shipping, distribution, and logistic services, 74
Travel and tourism, 74
Types
  assignment of proceeds, 172
  back-to-back setup, 173
  irrevocable, 170
  revocable, 171
  revolving, 172
  standby, 173
  transferable, 172

U

United States International Trade Commission, 50
United States Trade and Development Agency (USTDA), 179
Unit loading, 131

UPS, 137
UPS global trade, 135
USA Trade Online, 49
US commercial service
    (USCS), 48
USEmbassy.gov, 50
US Export Assistance Centers (EAC), 93

V

Vented containers, 133

W, X, Y, Z

Wildflower-nursery business, 79
World Bank Atlas Method, 53
World Trade Organization (WTO), 50

Get the eBook for only $10!

Now you can take the weightless companion with you anywhere, anytime. Your purchase of this book entitles you to 3 electronic versions for only $10.

This Apress title will prove so indispensible that you'll want to carry it with you everywhere, which is why we are offering the eBook in 3 formats for only $10 if you have already purchased the print book.

Convenient and fully searchable, the PDF version enables you to easily find and copy code—or perform examples by quickly toggling between instructions and applications. The MOBI format is ideal for your Kindle, while the ePUB can be utilized on a variety of mobile devices.

Go to www.apress.com/promo/tendollars to purchase your companion eBook.

All Apress eBooks are subject to copyright. All rights are reserved by the Publisher, whether the whole or part of the material is concerned, specifically the rights of translation, reprinting, reuse of illustrations, recitation, broadcasting, reproduction on microfilms or in any other physical way, and transmission or information storage and retrieval, electronic adaptation, computer software, or by similar or dissimilar methodology now known or hereafter developed. Exempted from this legal reservation are brief excerpts in connection with reviews or scholarly analysis or material supplied specifically for the purpose of being entered and executed on a computer system, for exclusive use by the purchaser of the work. Duplication of this publication or parts thereof is permitted only under the provisions of the Copyright Law of the Publisher's location, in its current version, and permission for use must always be obtained from Springer. Permissions for use may be obtained through RightsLink at the Copyright Clearance Center. Violations are liable to prosecution under the respective Copyright Law.

Other Apress Business Titles You Will Find Useful

Tax Strategies for the Small Business Owner
Fox
978-1-4302-4842-2

Plan Your Own Estate
Wheatley-Liss
978-1-4302-4494-3

Getting a Business Loan
Kiisel
978-1-4302-4998-6

Design Thinking for Entrepreneurs and Small Businesses
Ingle
978-1-4302-6181-0

Improving Profit
Cleland
978-1-4302-6307-4

Unite the Tribes, 2nd Edition
Duncan
978-1-4302-5872-8

Sales Hunting
Monty
978-1-4302-6770-6

Common Sense
Tanner
978-1-4302-4152-2

When to Hire—or Not Hire—a Consultant
Orr/Orr
978-1-4302-4734-0

Available at www.apress.com

GPSR Compliance

The European Union's (EU) General Product Safety Regulation (GPSR) is a set of rules that requires consumer products to be safe and our obligations to ensure this.

If you have any concerns about our products, you can contact us on

ProductSafety@springernature.com

In case Publisher is established outside the EU, the EU authorized representative is:

Springer Nature Customer Service Center GmbH
Europaplatz 3
69115 Heidelberg, Germany

www.ingramcontent.com/pod-product-compliance
Lightning Source LLC
LaVergne TN
LVHW040735250326
834688LV00031B/303